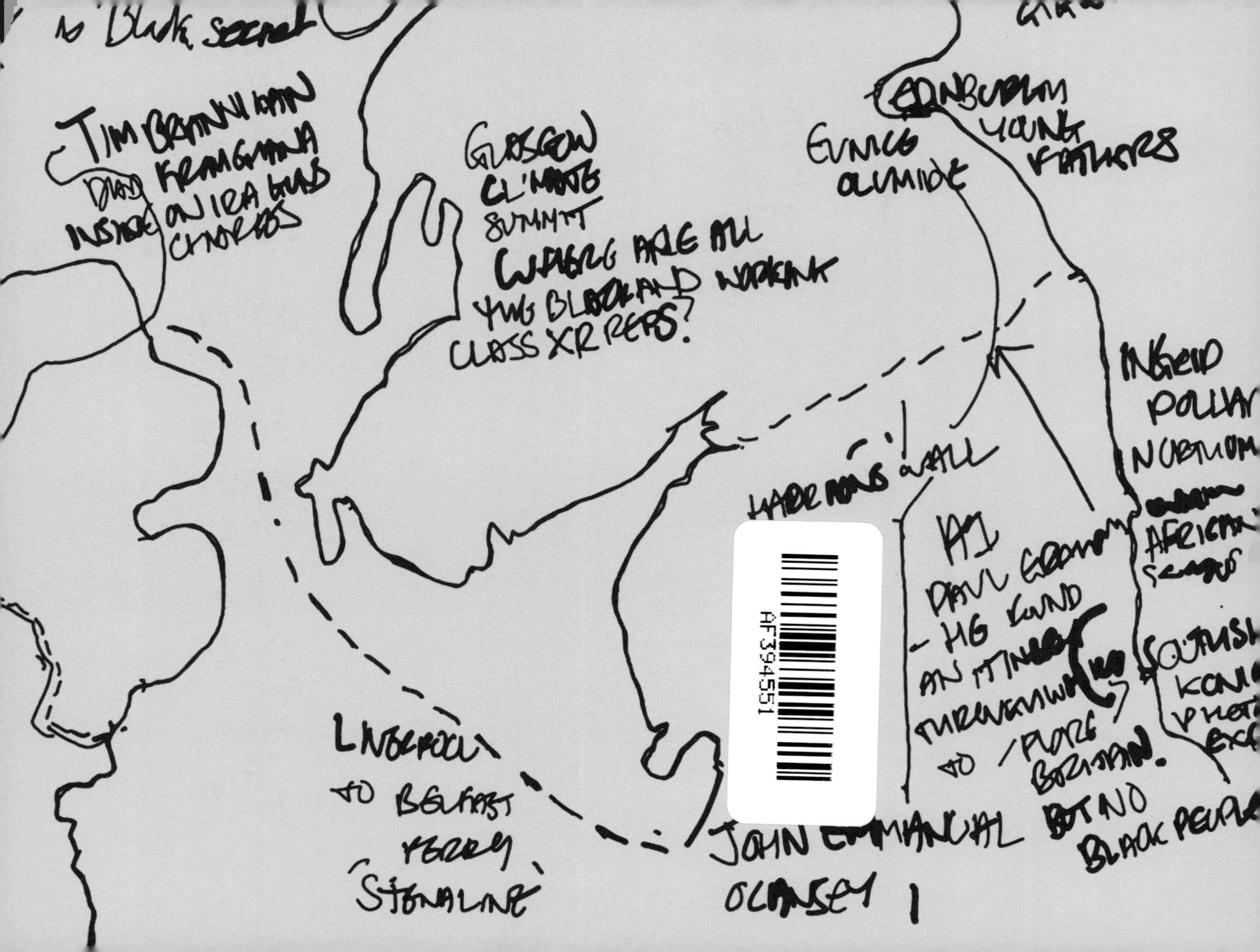

to 'Black Secret'
TIM BRANNIGAN
Glasgow Climate Summit
CLIMBERS ARE ALL YNG BLOOD AND WORKING CLASS XR REPS?
EUNICE OLUMIDE
EDINBURGH YOUNG FATHERS
INGRID POLLARD NORTHUM
AFRICAN SLUMS
HADRIAN'S WALL
PAUL GILROY
AN ITINERARY
BUT NO BLACK PEOPLE
SCOTTISH
LIVERPOOL TO BELFAST FERRY 'STENALINE'
JOHN EMMANUEL ODYSSEY 1
AF394551

Home Is Not A Place

Photos by Johny Pitts
Words by Roger Robinson

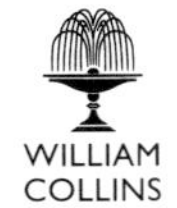

WILLIAM
COLLINS

Hiss

First a hiss
like the air in trees,
or the pull of waves
in nighttime seas.

Radio static
of dials between stations,
or steaming wands
of coffee machines.

To think I could live here,
a young Black man like me,
that upon this coast
I could live so free,

but as I walk this town
I hear rather than see
the sibilance of discontent
that aims its whispers at me.

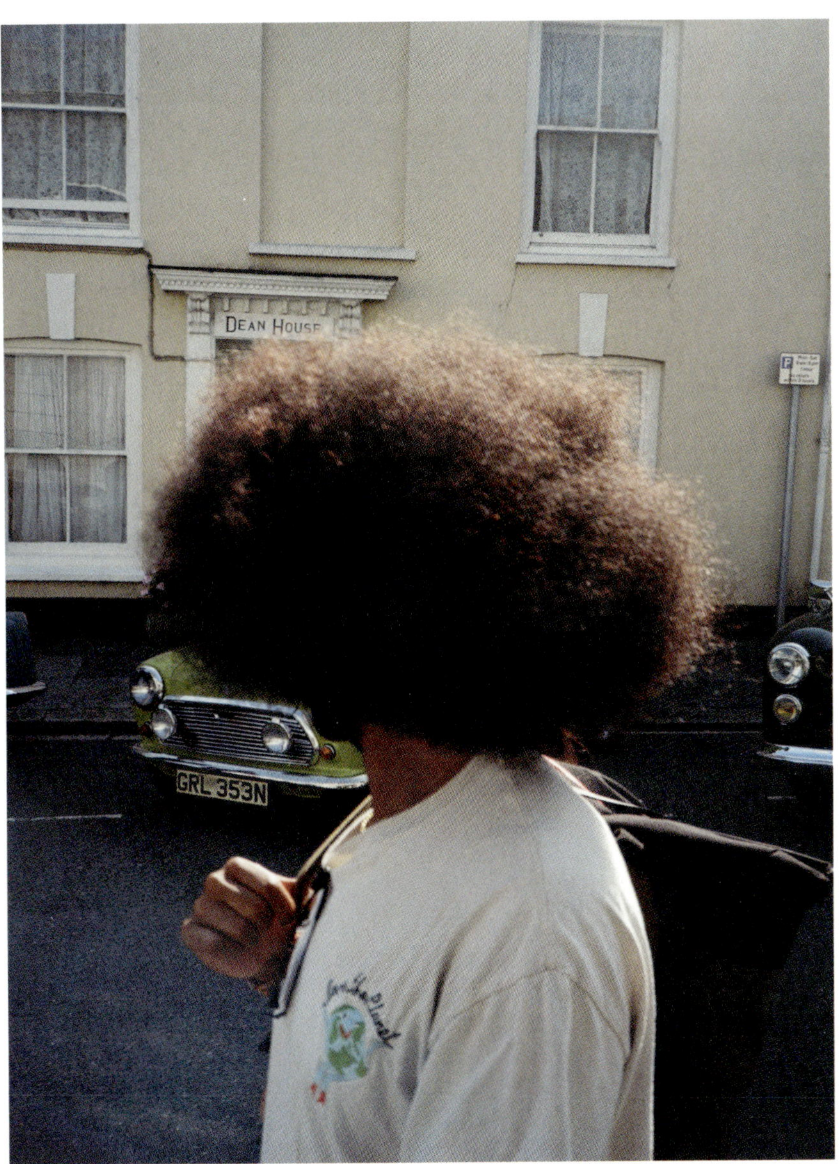

DEAN HOUSE
GRL 353N

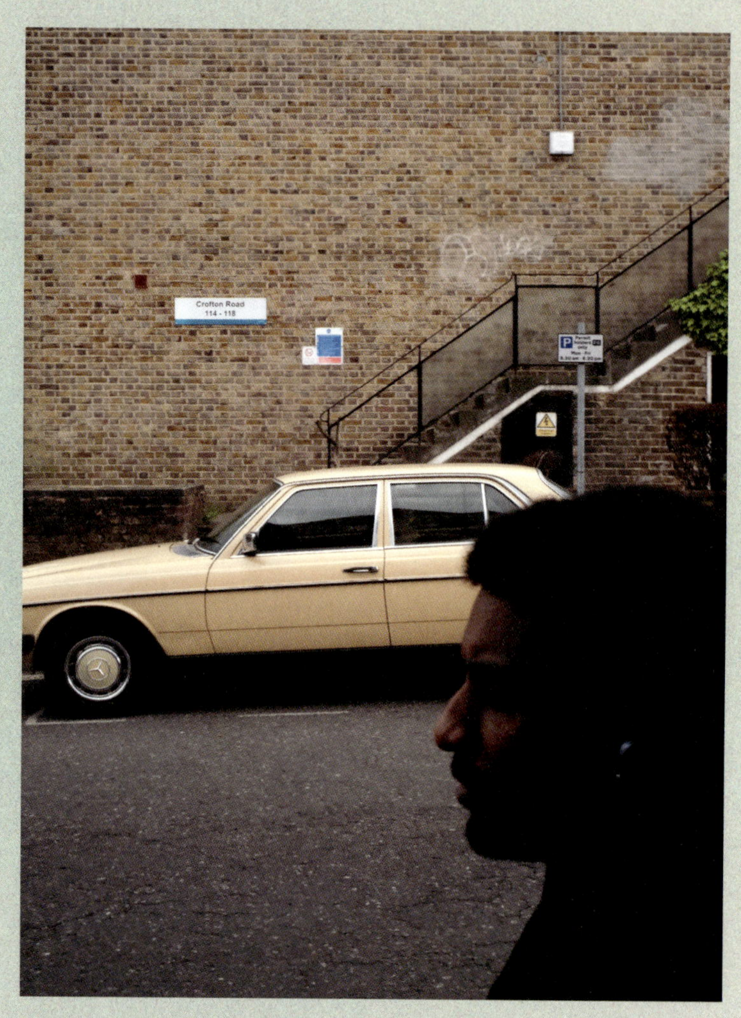
Crofton Road
114 - 118

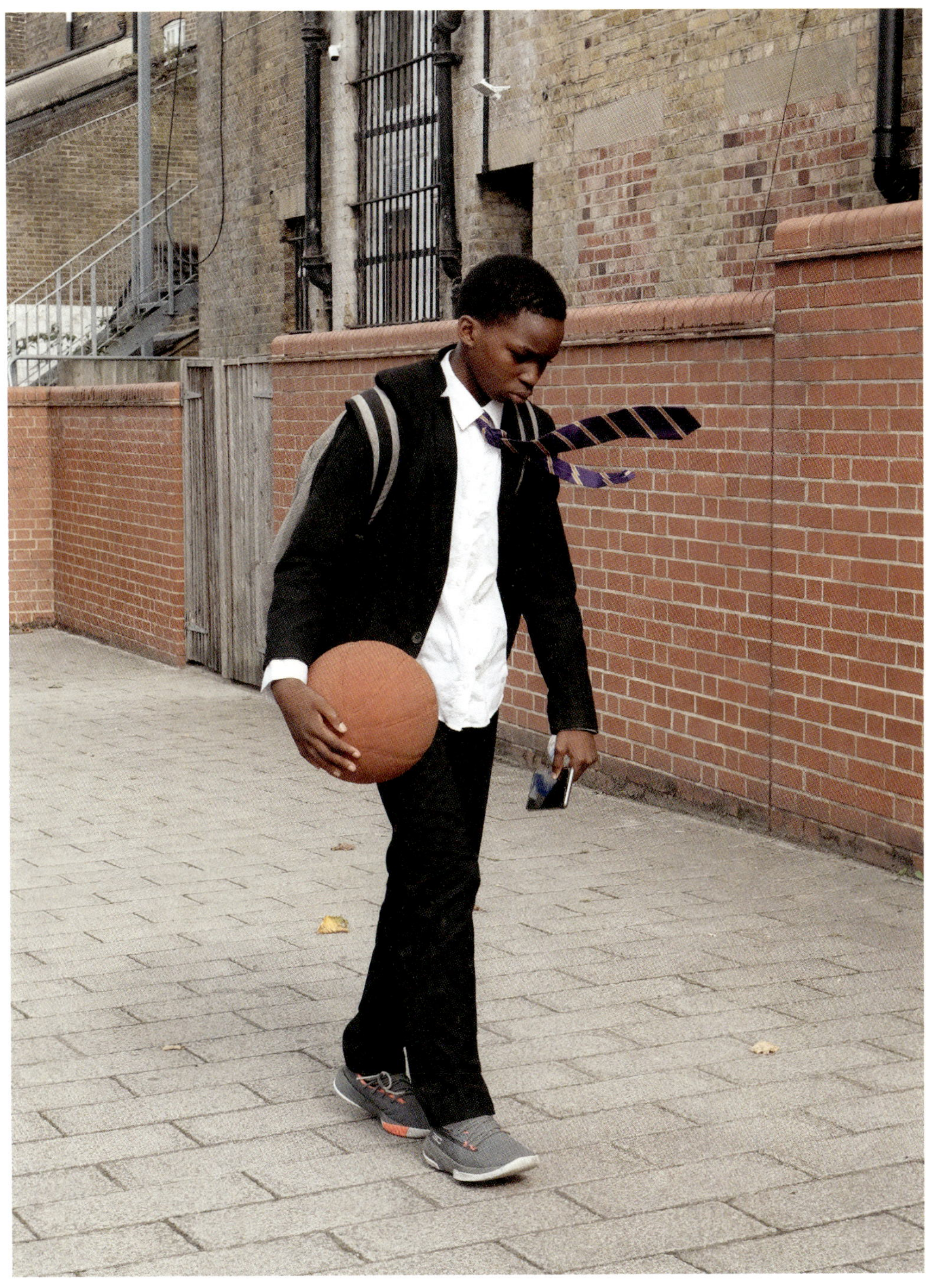

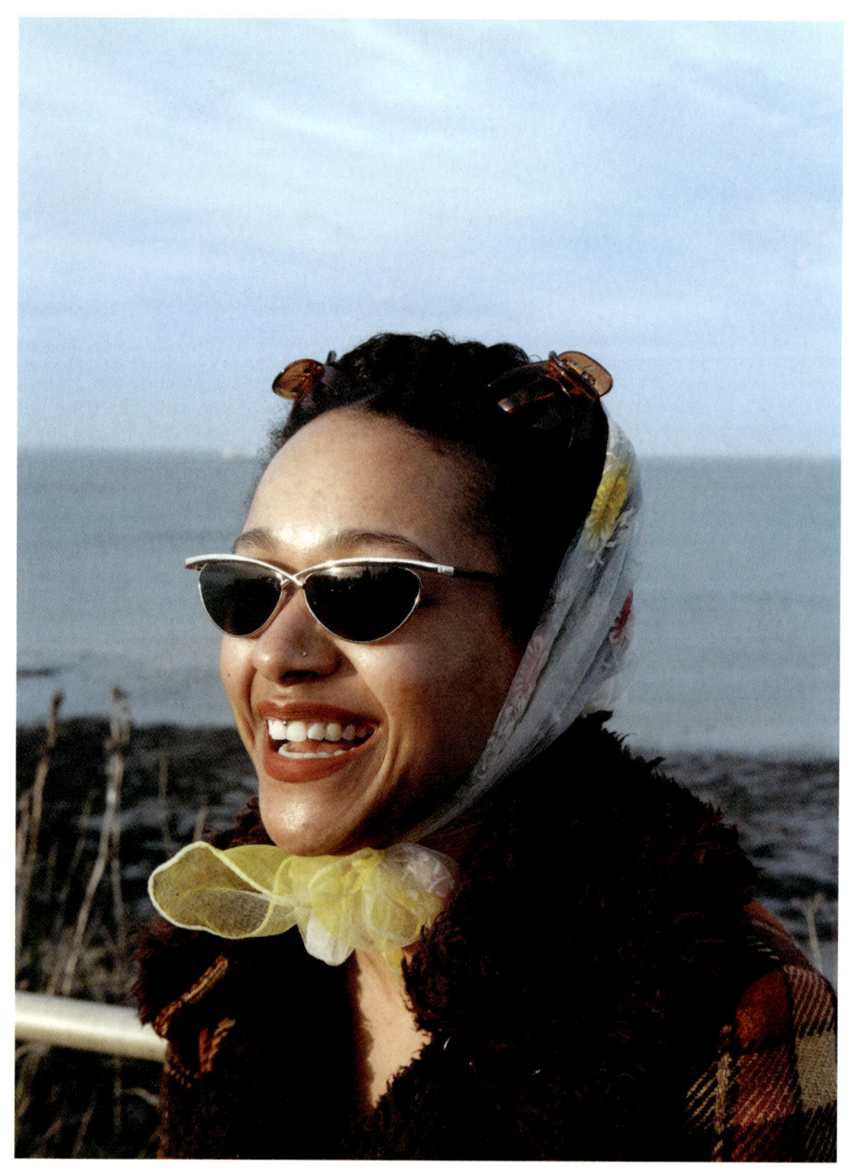

The Quality of Light

A Saint Lucian and a Nigerian are talking
about the quality of light, in art and writing.
Whether you describe the specific
light of where you're from or the certain light
of where you live. Whether you can describe
the quality of light and/or occupy that light
at the same time. Perhaps it has something
to do with skin, whether it remembers the sun's
slanted rays as a bronze burnish or a rose blotch.
Or maybe you prefer the marine light
from the salted roar of waves or the bluegreen
light of a pond's still algae, what is lived
and what is visited, whether the frosted light
of winter evens your skin to porcelain
or dries it to ash. Maybe it's about who
you're writing for and what you're reading,
where you've lived and where you've been
and what light does to the skin you're in.

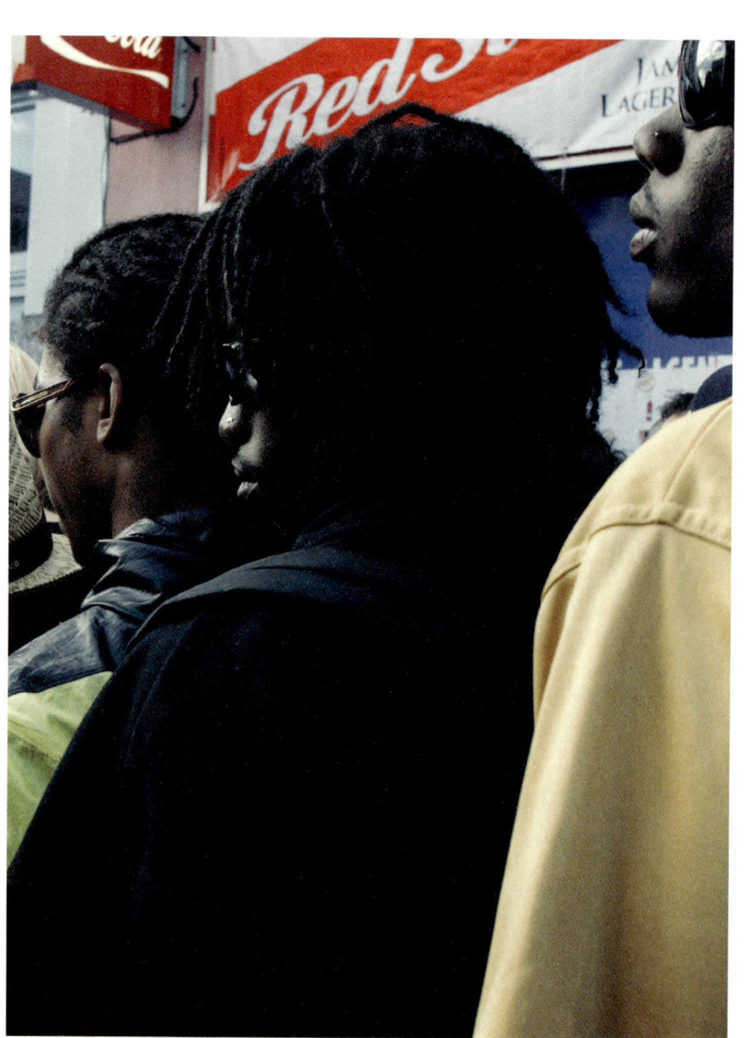
Red
JAM
LAGER

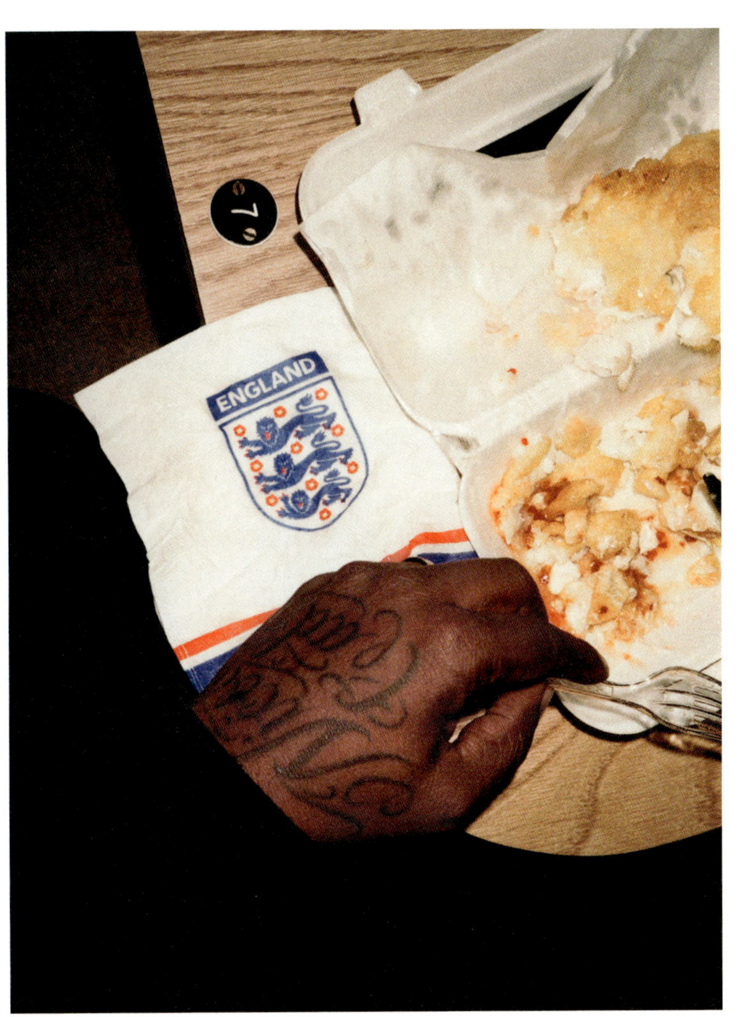

Taxidermy

We have all seen the hunting trophies
set against shields, the wavy pointed horns
of blackbuck or impala or the magnificent
branched antlers of the red deer stag.

I have seen candy red, blue and yellow
birds crowded in museum-glass dioramas.
I have seen a family dog or rabbit,
skin and fur mounted on a mold for eternity.

But when a slaver so loved his servant slave
Fanny that he removed her hand for taxidermy
and it became a cherished heirloom passing
from generation to generation to generation –

the dark skin of her hand with its pink
nails with crescent-moon cuticles on her thumbs
hanging from the picture rail above the dining-room fire,
it's knuckles knobbly and blackened,

while they ate their wild pheasant and wine,
from family to family; children growing old
knowing the Black slave hand they thought
they loved; in this act of preserved mutilation

how the children in their pinafores and frilly bonnets
who never knew her played with her hand;
how her hand remained a slave in the way
it remained captured in service against her will –

I have never wished so hard that her long
lean fingers could make a firm balled fist,
perfectly clenched, with the veins in her hand
bulging, overlooking their bland pea soup starter.

Franny Joseph's death is presumed to have been in the early 1800s.
Her preserved severed hand was only buried in 1997.

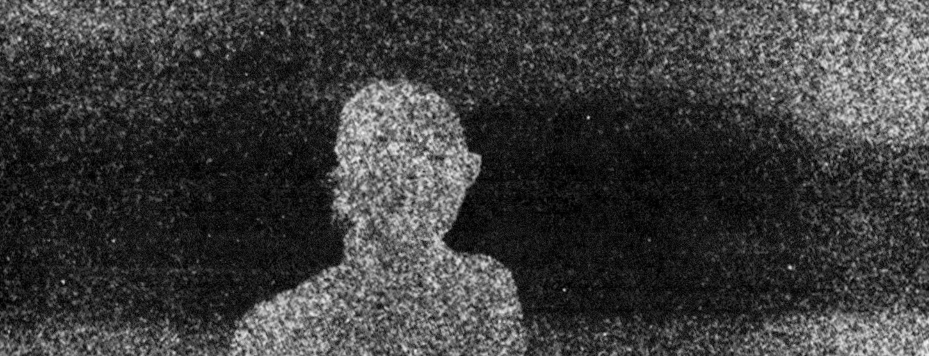

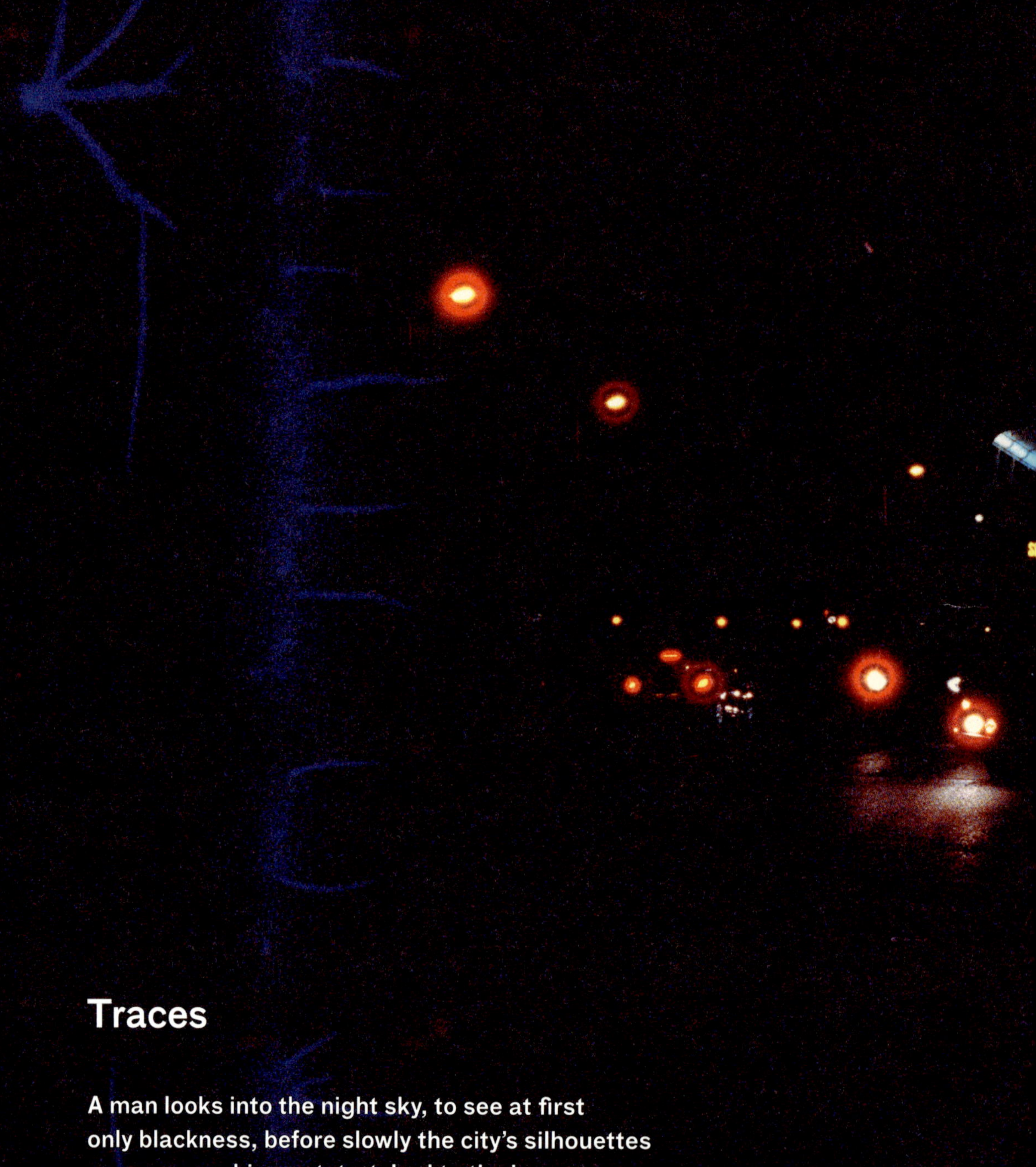

Traces

A man looks into the night sky, to see at first
only blackness, before slowly the city's silhouettes
emerge, reaching outstretched to the heavens.
Night clouds swirl like milk, parting to reveal
the neutral light of a bone moon, on a man
whose hurt is a roaming, sleepless thing.

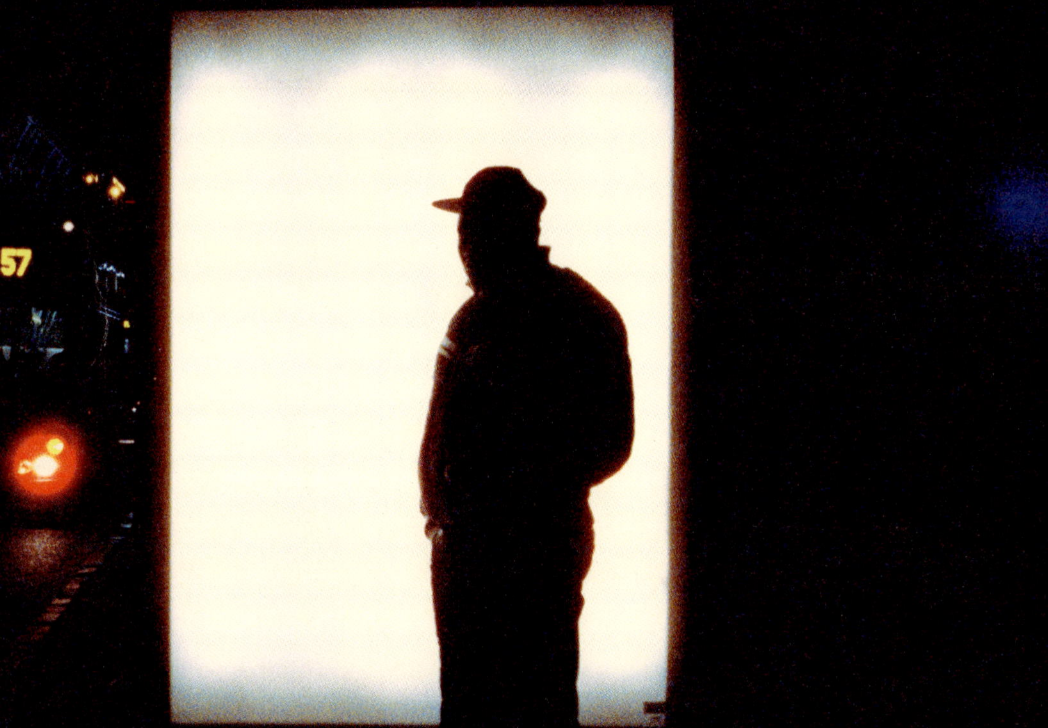

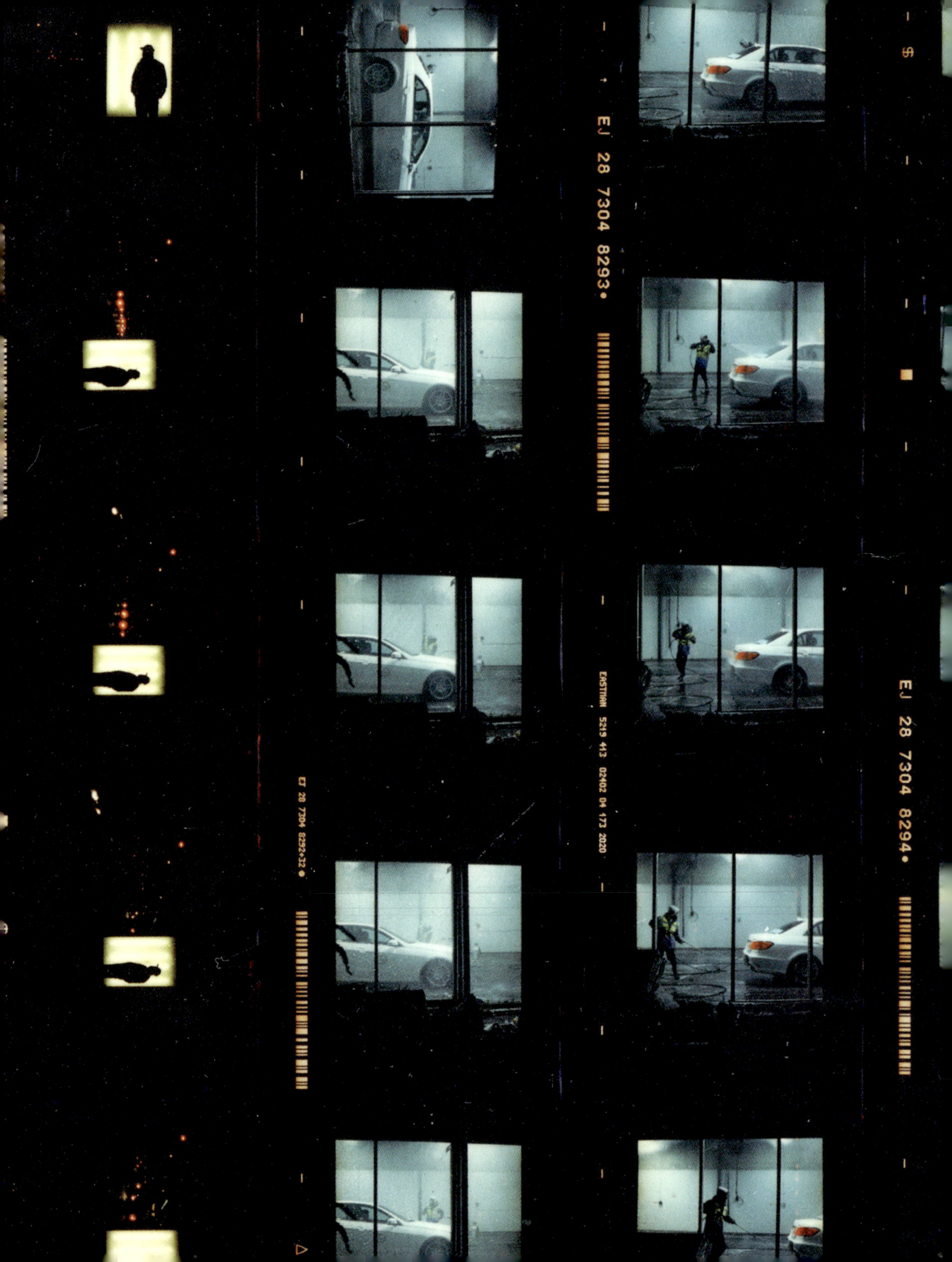
EJ 28 7304 8293•
EJ 28 7304 8294•

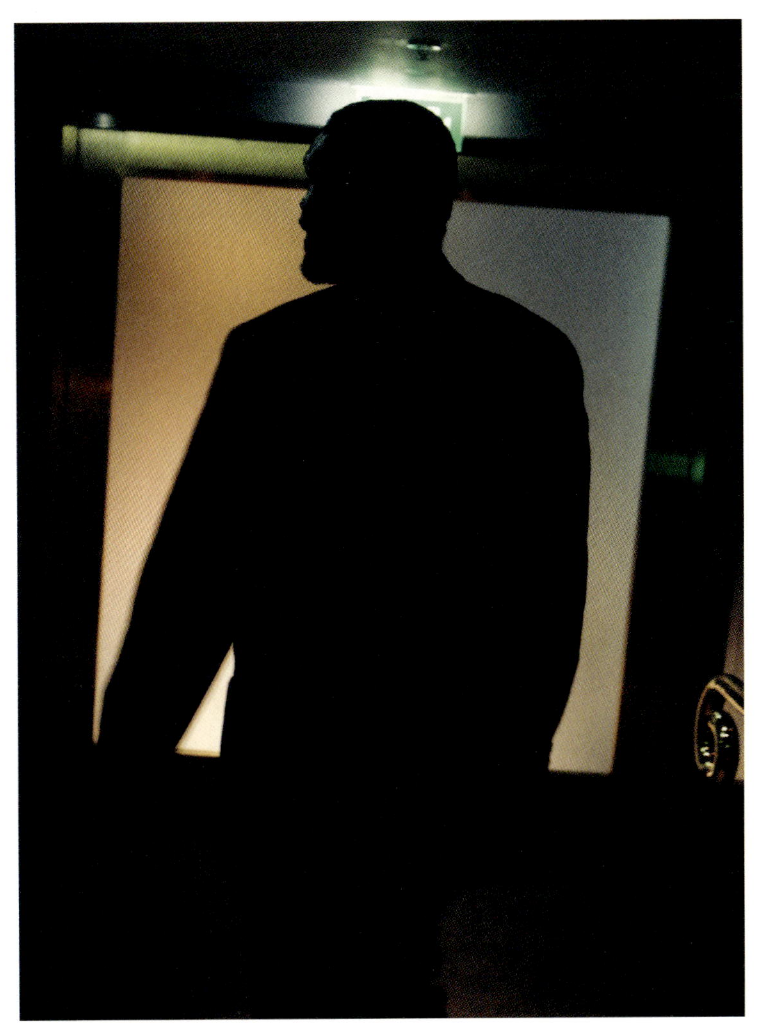

Guy Fawkes Night

My child is frightened of firework bangs,
a fragile fear in his wide, teary eyes.
I help with his coat to walk into night
towards the bursts of light and bombs of sound.
For in each father's life, he'll guide his son
past their crying to view dark skies with awe.

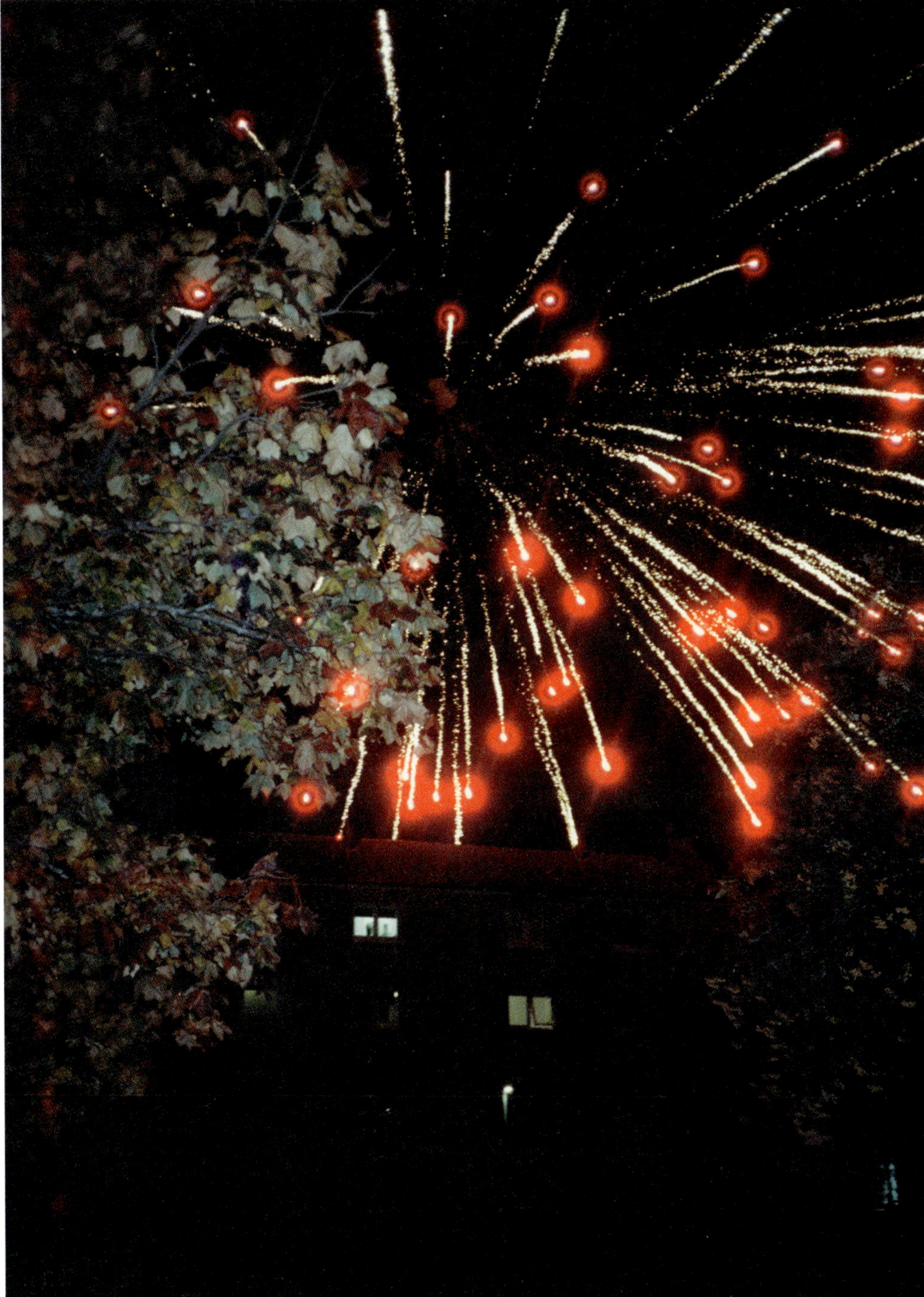

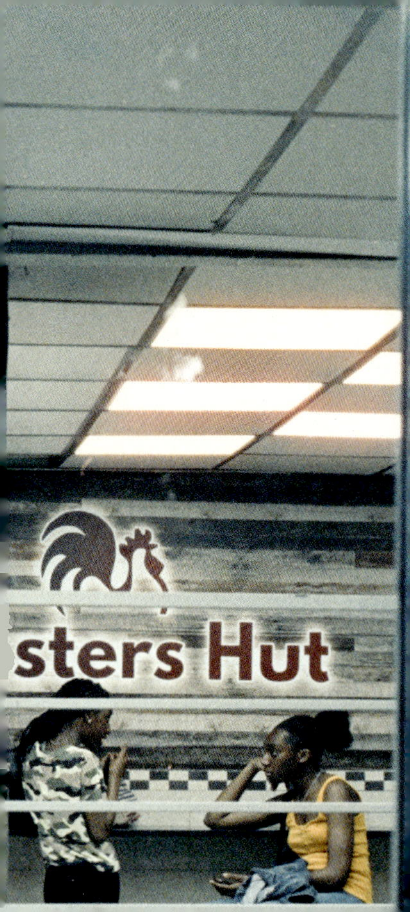
sters Hut

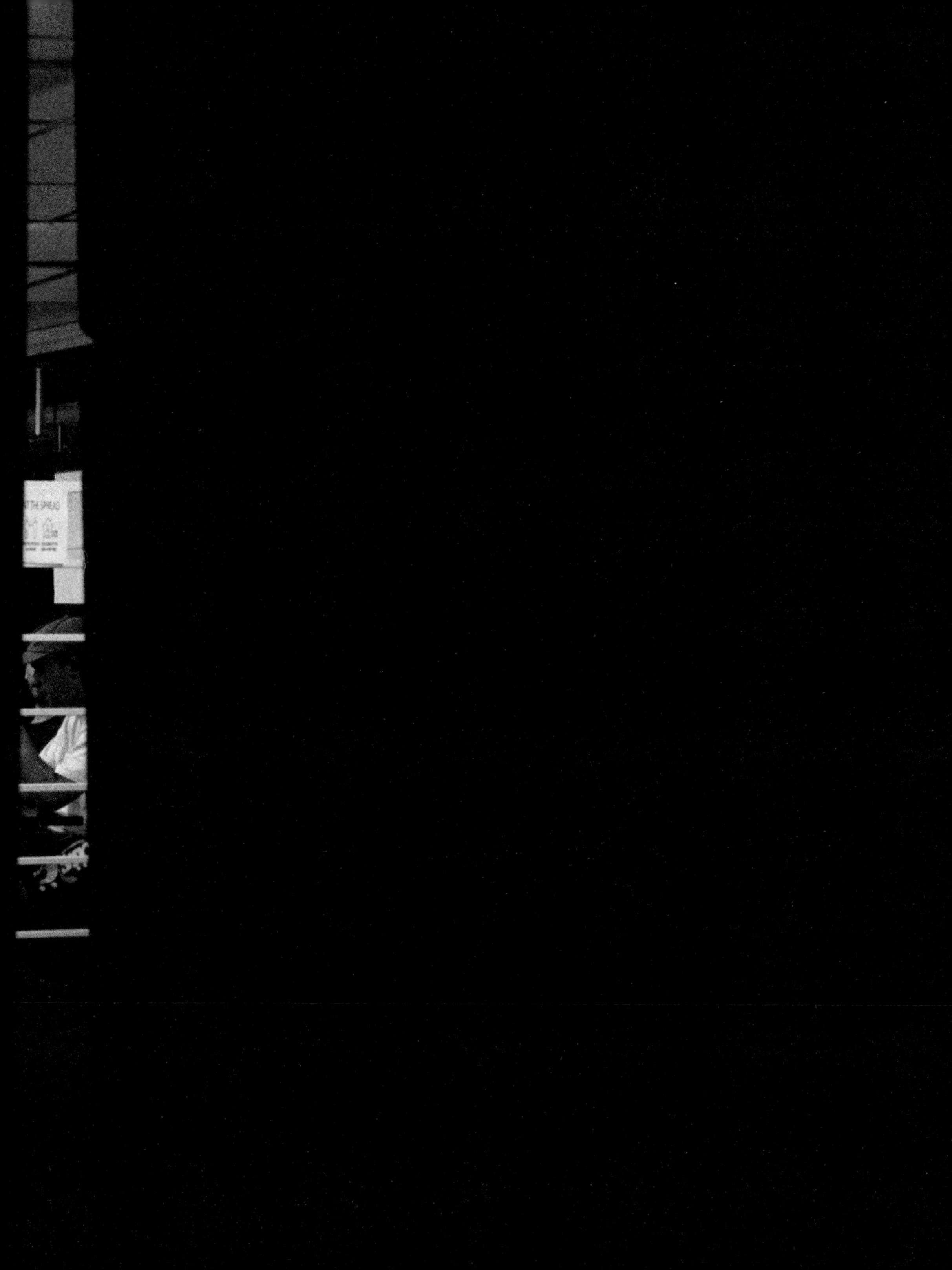

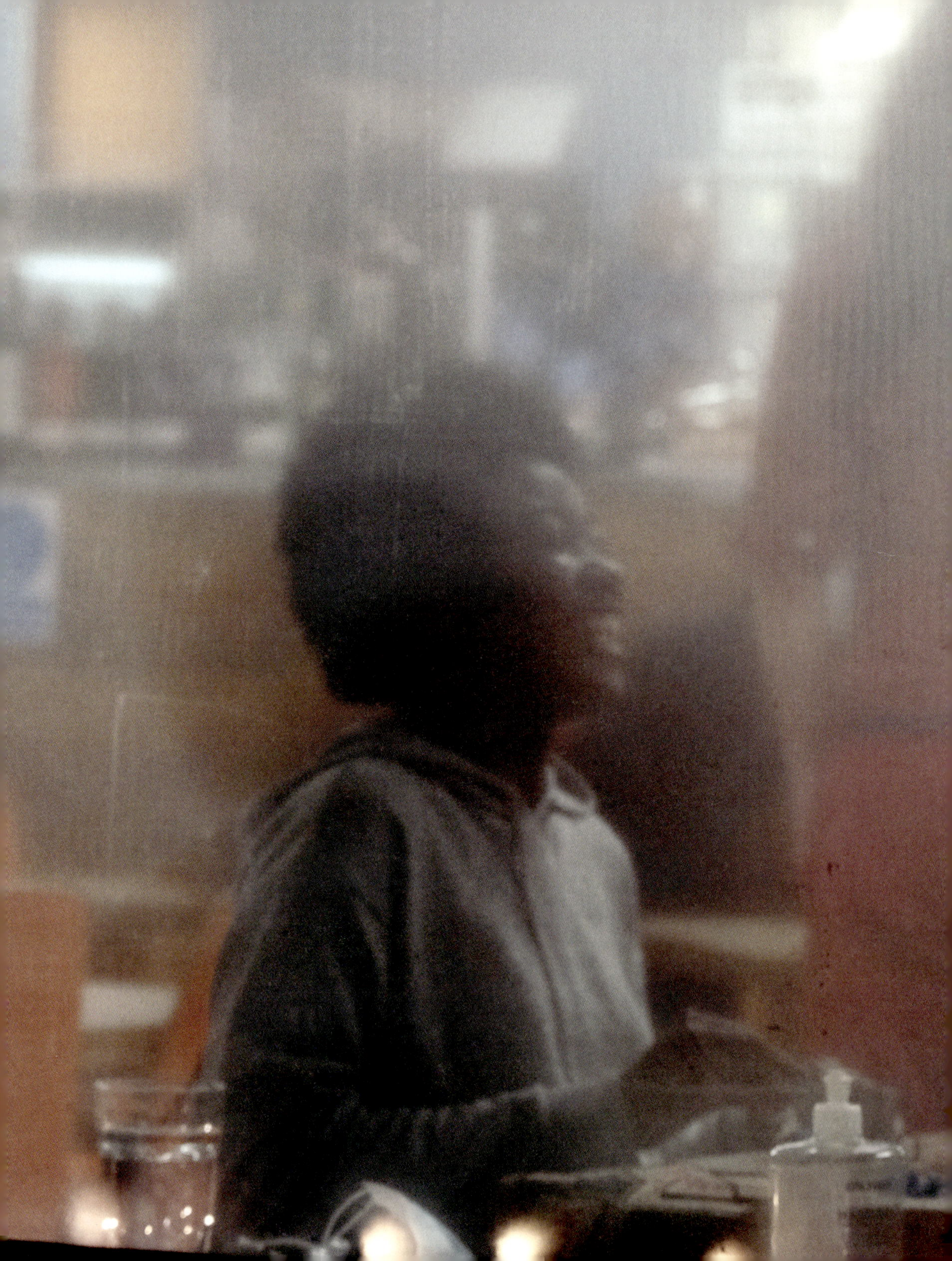

Halos

The lamplights are softened into halos
floating below a tracing-paper moon.

The puddles are illuminated, while main roads
and side streets are fog haunted.

Perhaps this is the work of smudged light –
to soften the world and expand our story,

or maybe to dull the world into a new story
from each yellowed window, the day's survival.

And from each day's survival the drift
into dreams, a reset, a hazy forgetting,

much like this town bathed this night
in fog, and then morning becoming anew.

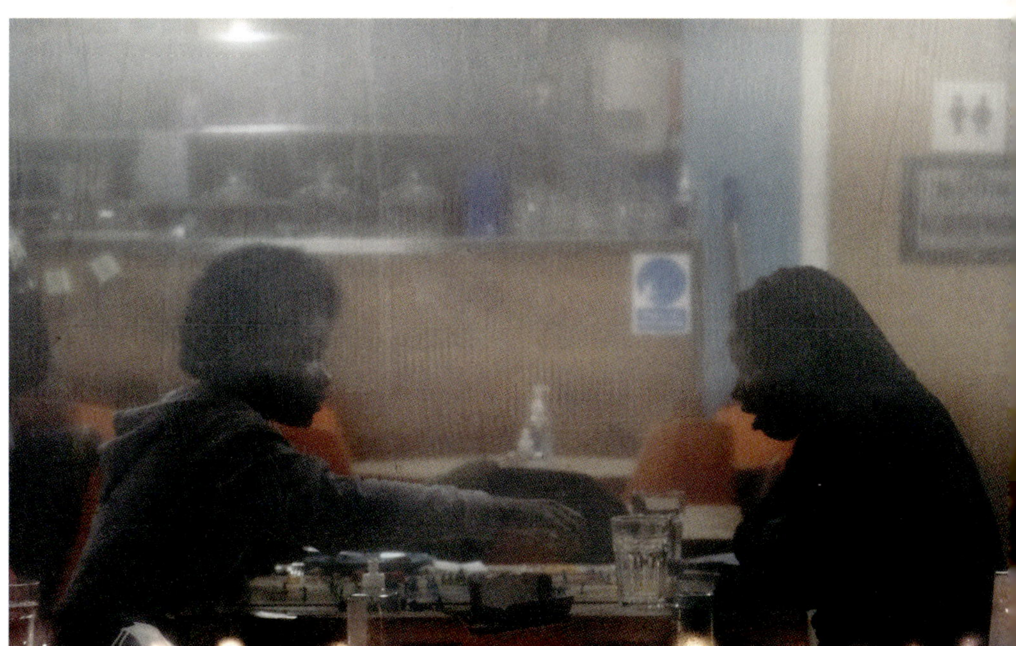

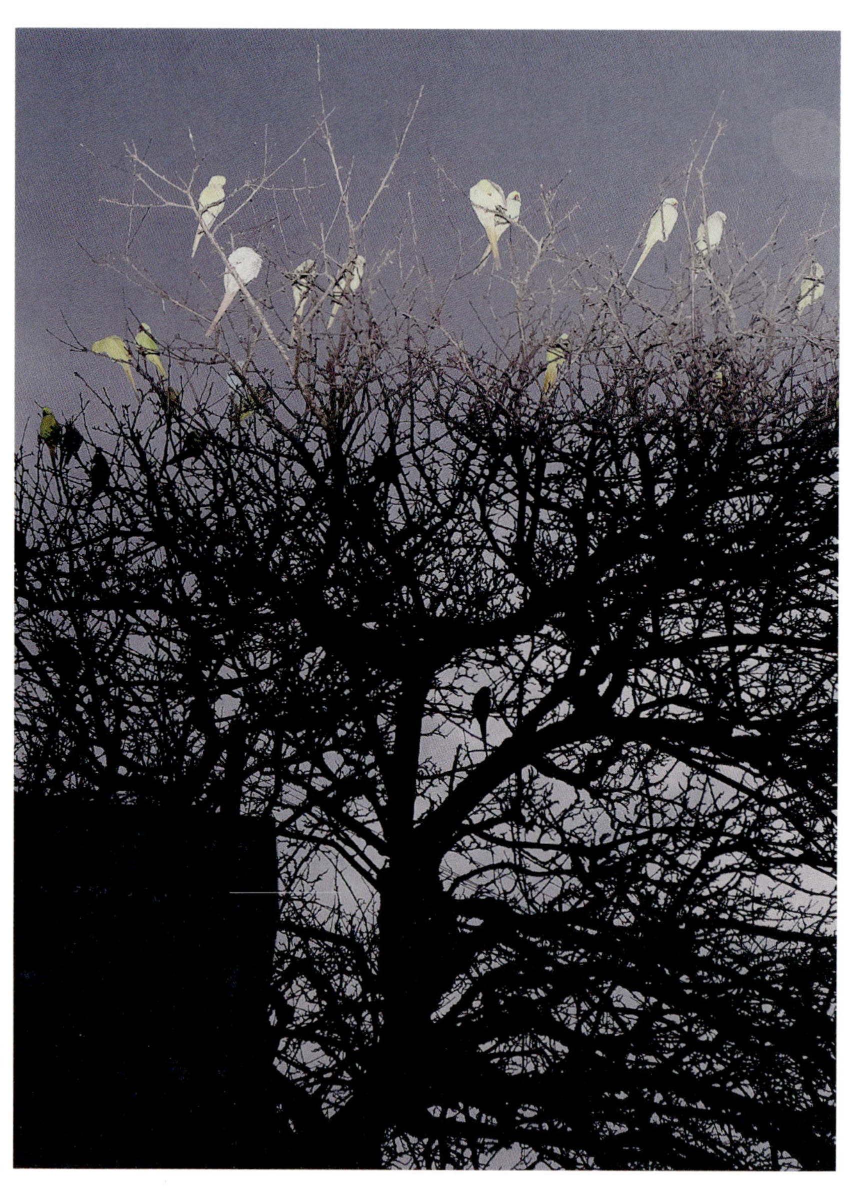

Twenty Parakeets

Not the common caw of the crow, not
ripened fruit, not blossoming
flower nor flames.

Not an imagined tropical film set
nor festive Christmas lights.

But twenty parakeets at home in a tree
outside a Dover car park, as content
as in any mango tree in Curaçao.

Ignoring the calls of being illegal
immigrants and the murmurs
that they may be a danger to local birds,

they seem assured in their fellowship
enough to sing their calypso
and look down on the city's streets
as people march by carrying orange
supermarket bags, watching the streaks
of red brake-lights from passing cars
and children pointing at them shouting
Look, look at the birdies, Mum, look at them
dressed in their bright yellow anoraks.

Carnival Posse 2018

I done told Janine to stop
handing out her number
to these crusty boys outside
of McDonald's when they
won't even buy her a small fries.

And I don't know why we're always
waiting around for Lynette
because it takes so long just
to do her hair and yet
her hair always looks like the most
f'ed-up part of her outfit.

And Yasmin was coming out
to Carnival in her brand-new Huaraches
and we told her not to because they will
get destroyed. She ignored us.
By the first day the shoes looked
100 years old. Jokes, my days.

And Suzette always insists on thinking
some guy been trying to check her which
they wasn't and if they was she wouldn't
even know what to do as she is the only
girl in our crew with absolutely no bants.

Anyway these are my girls
and I got big love for my crew
and we come to dance but don't think you
can slide up behind us because we
ain't having it.

We came out together and we're heading
home together and if you're fighting one
of us you're fighting us all. Trust.

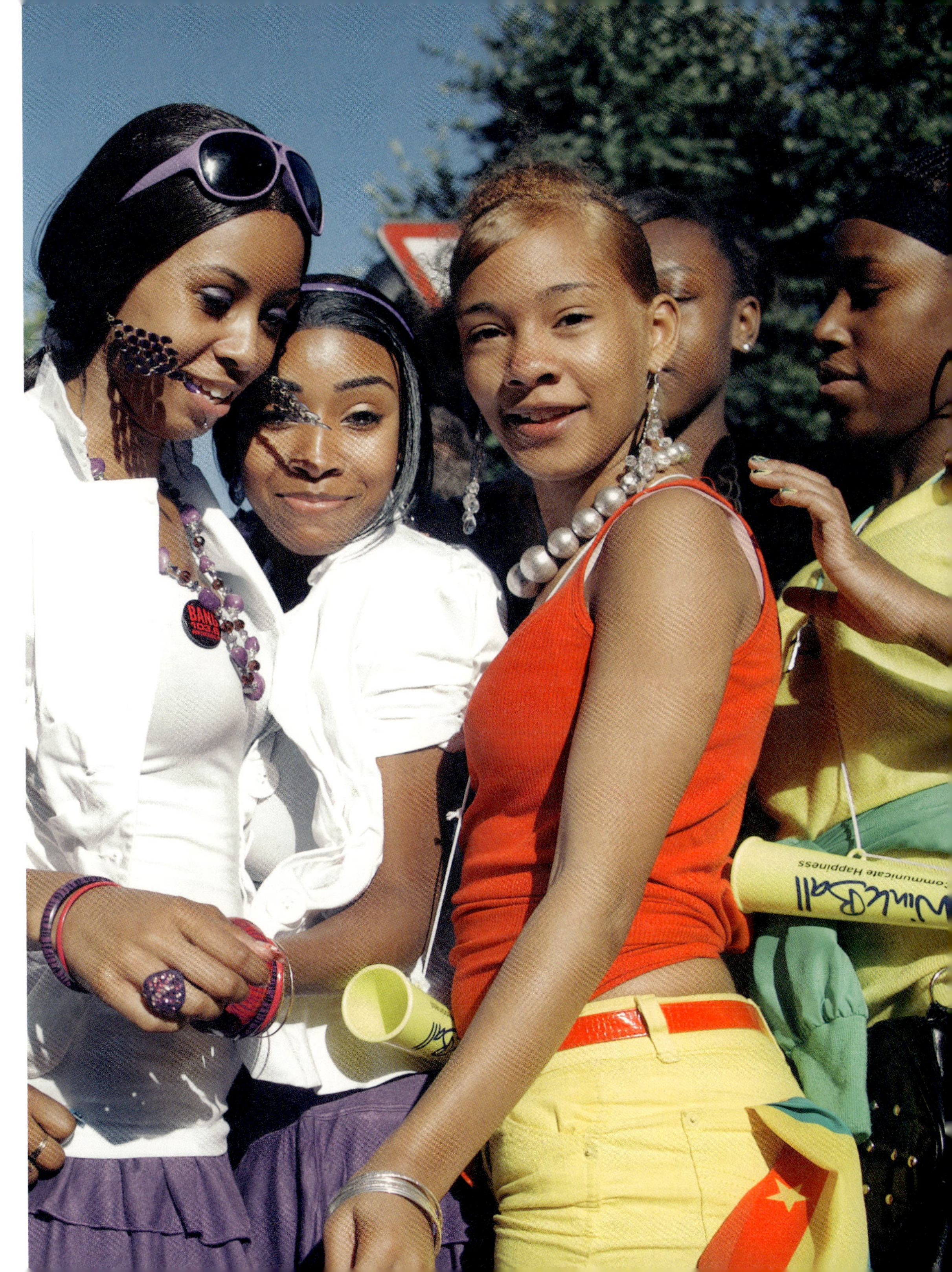

BANG
103.6
Winik Ball
:ommunicate Happiness

Janet Kay Singing 'Silly Games'
Live on *Top of the Pops* in 1979

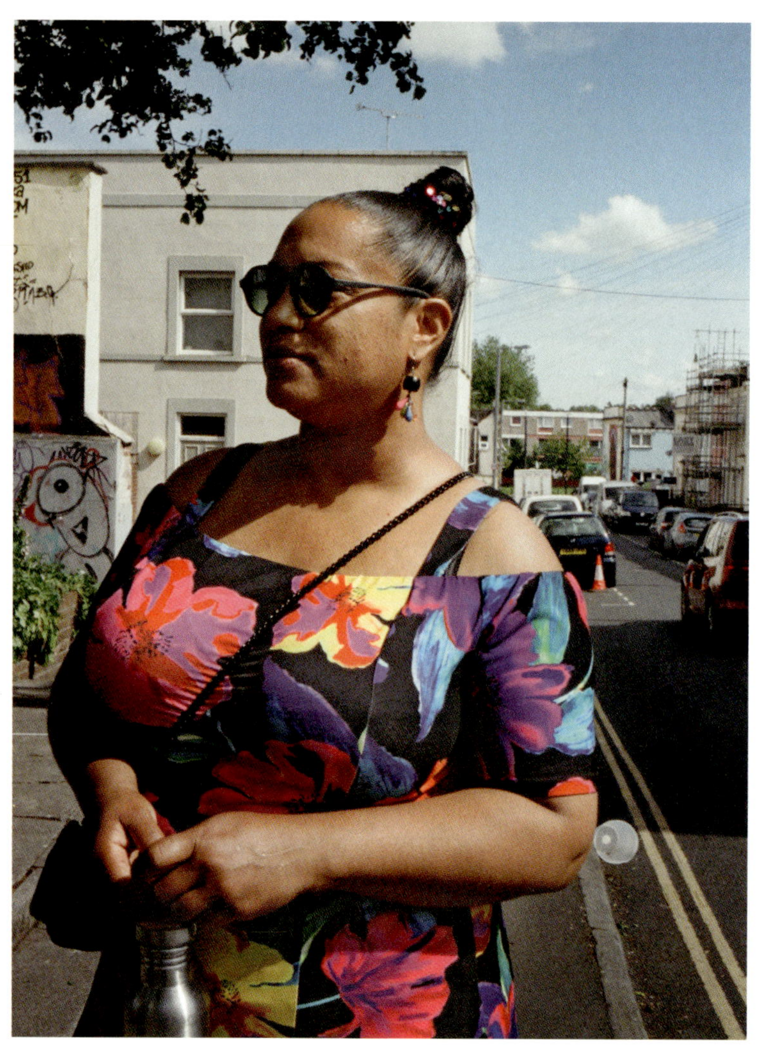

The bright lights are on you, Janet.
And as you sing I wonder
who has hurt you so,
who has kept your heart in stasis,
pierced you so that we can't tell
the sung from the screamed,
as your voice seeps through the TV
to my aunt with her gold hoop earrings
already beginning to sway,
she taps her itchy, too-tight
cornrows and tries to smile
to keep her voice from cracking,
singing, to not to give in
to the feeling, but we all know
in that living room who my aunt
is seeing behind those closed eyes,
the man, broad-shouldered and broad-nosed,
hewn as if from a mountain, who'd visit
each and every fortnight, but after a year
would remain in pregnant silence
when asked to name this thing they shared,
but just then she tries to hit the highest note
in the chorus, misses its mark
by a long, long way, her voice breaking,
and she leaves the room
and does not return until long
after the song has been sung.

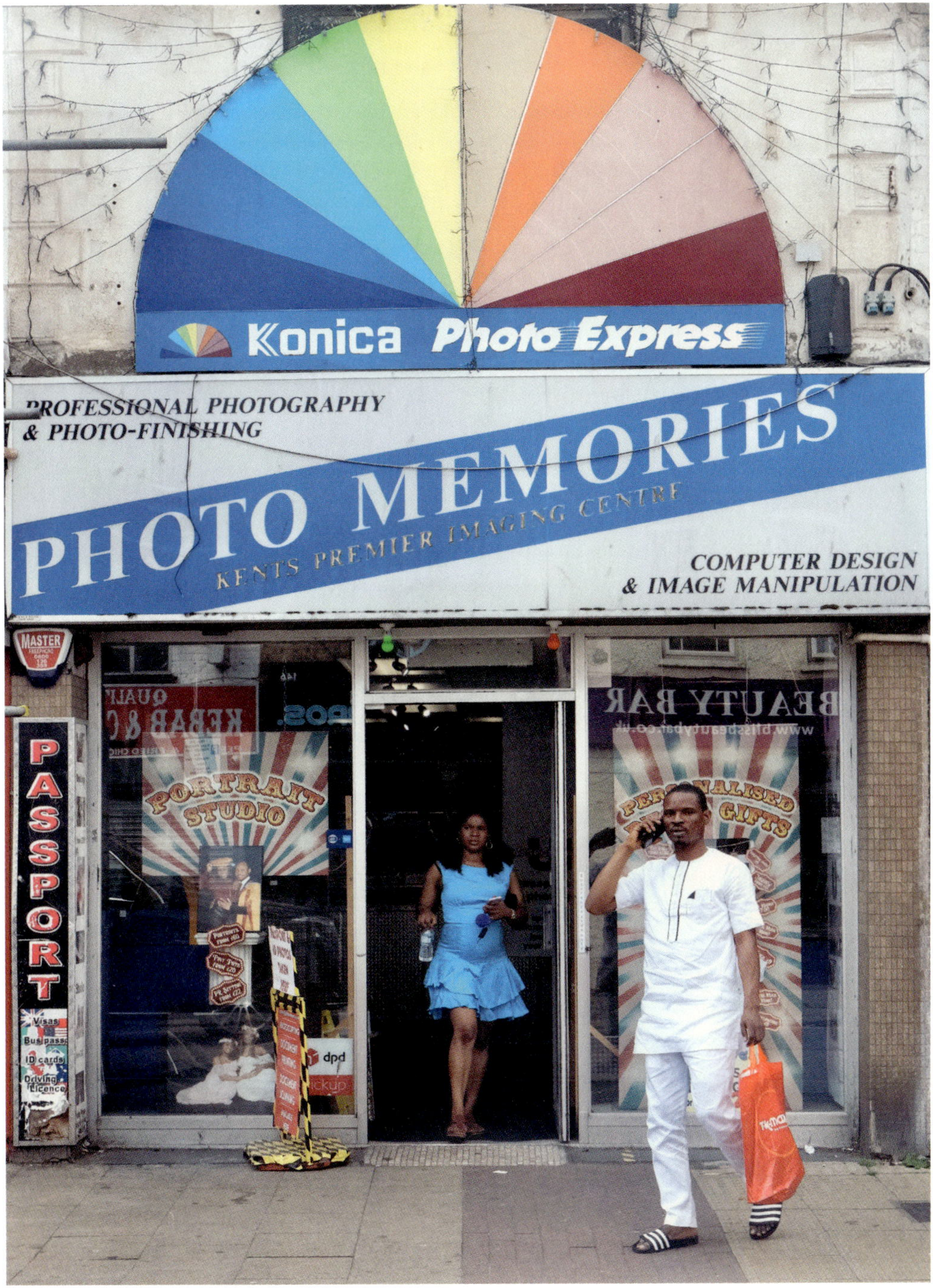

Konica Photo Express
PROFESSIONAL PHOTOGRAPHY
& PHOTO-FINISHING
PHOTO MEMORIES
KENTS PREMIER IMAGING CENTRE
COMPUTER DESIGN
& IMAGE MANIPULATION
MASTER
PASSPORT
Visas
Bus pass
ID cards
Driving
Licence
PORTRAIT
STUDIO
PERSONALISED
GIFTS
BEAUTY BAR
dpd
pickup

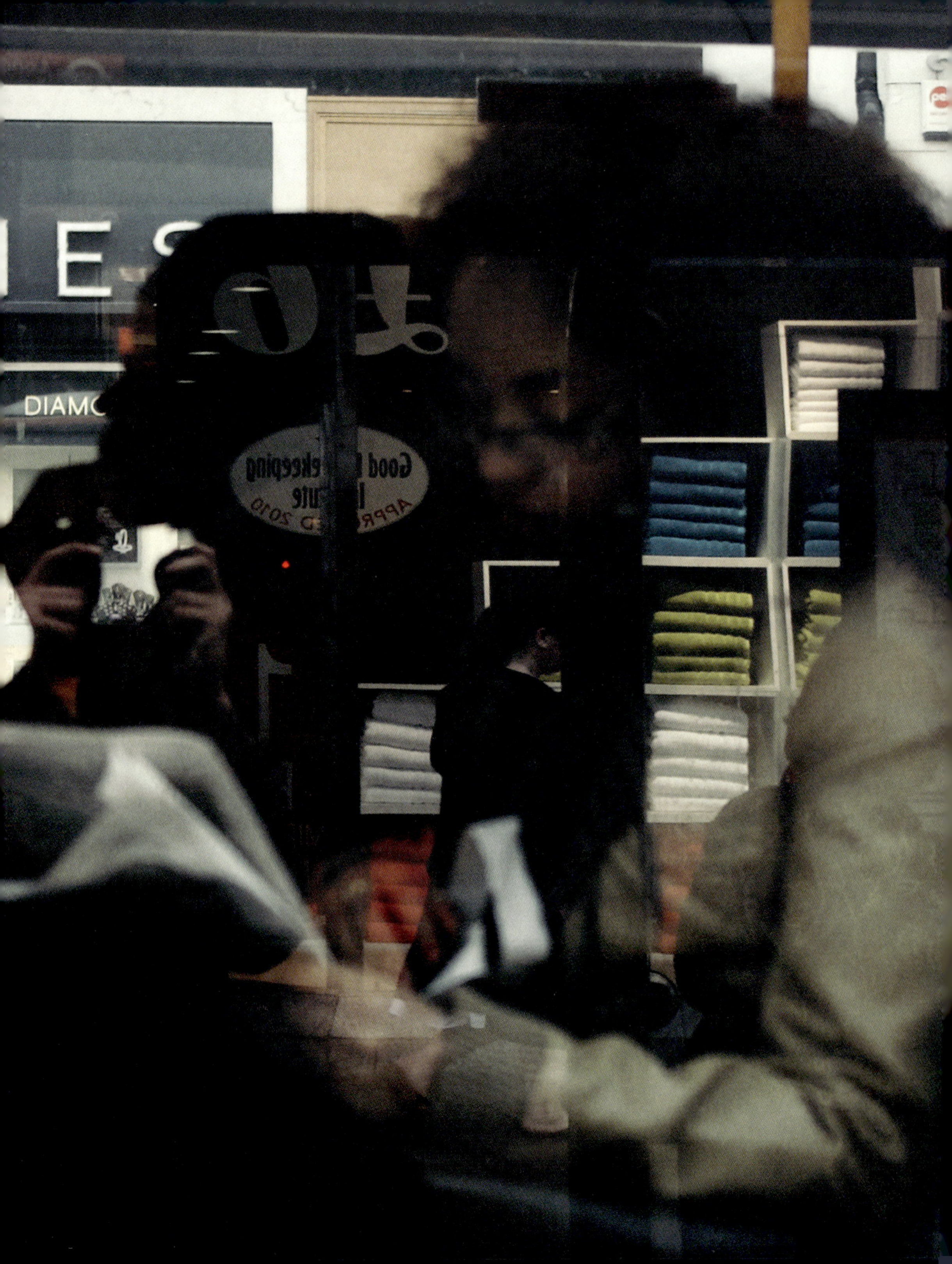

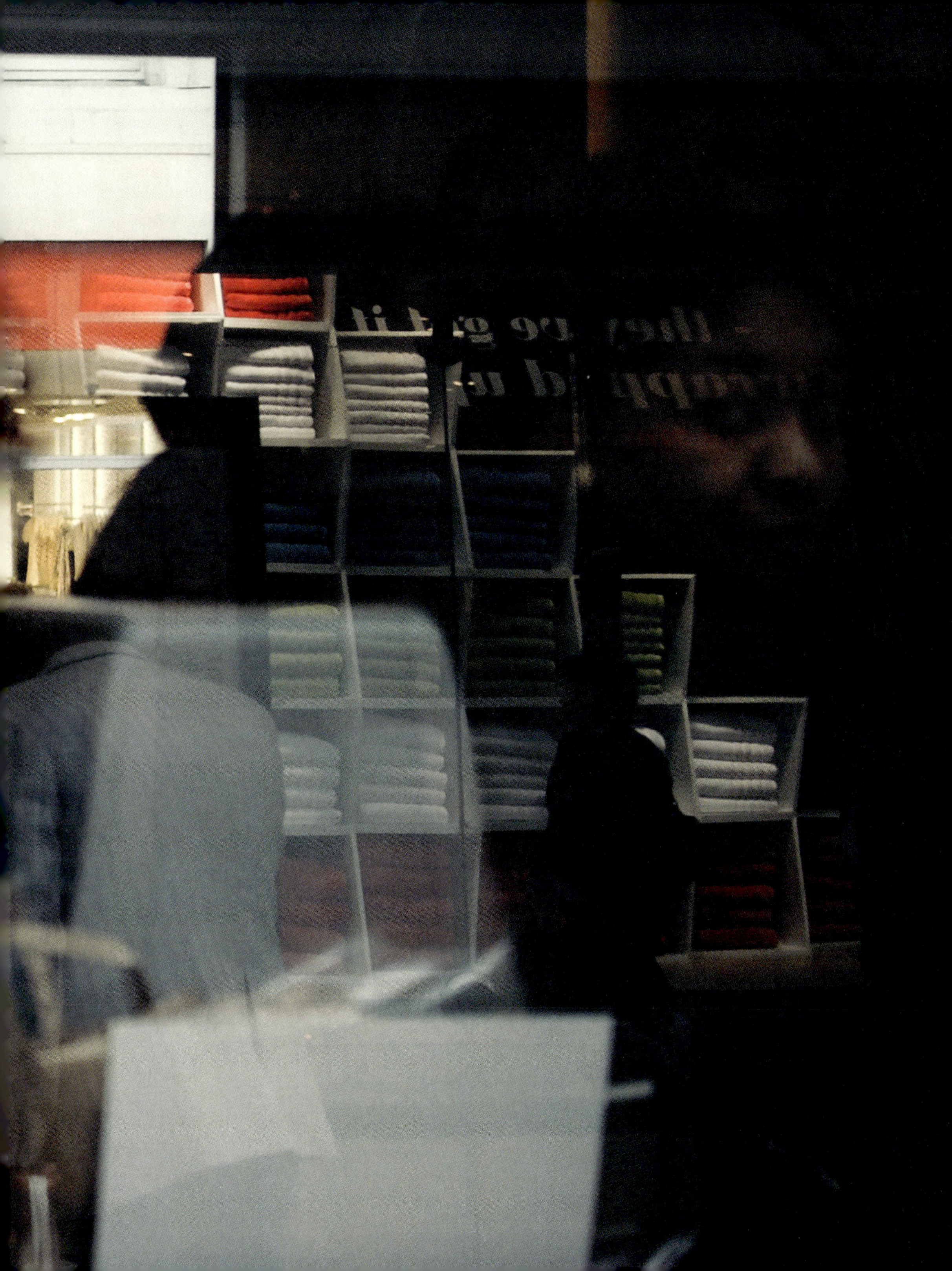

Ode to a Female MC

Here's to you
who kept the culture
centred and sensible.

You were never rare
just held back, ignored
in a world of masculine microphones.

Even now a beanie and a hoodie
gives you more cipha space
than dresses.

A lyrical third rail.
Beefs being nothing
you'd give space to

on this open-mic list
you just argued to get on
in the small club of sweaty

young men intent on battle
while only you can gain a unity
of headnods and hands-up.

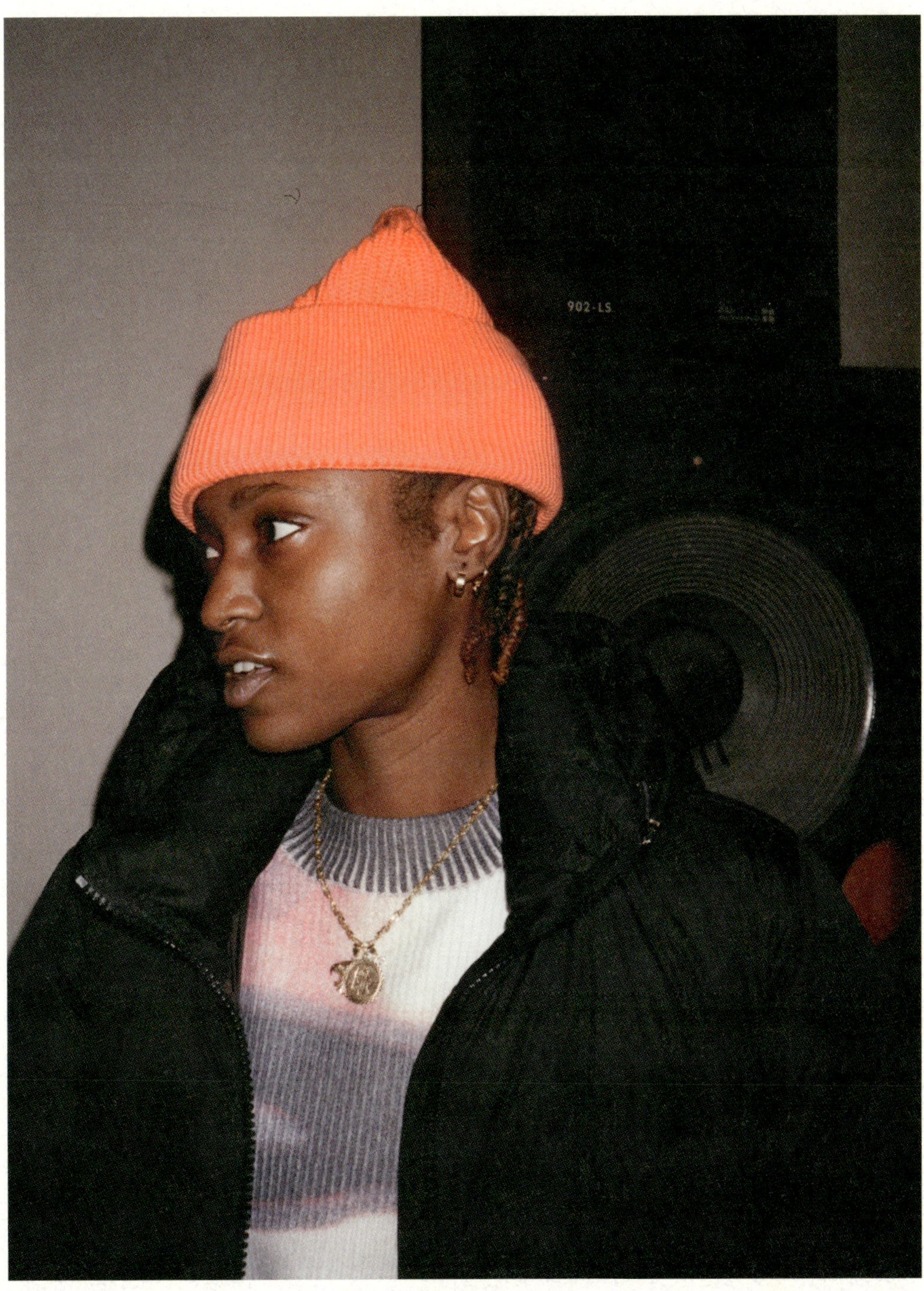
902-LS

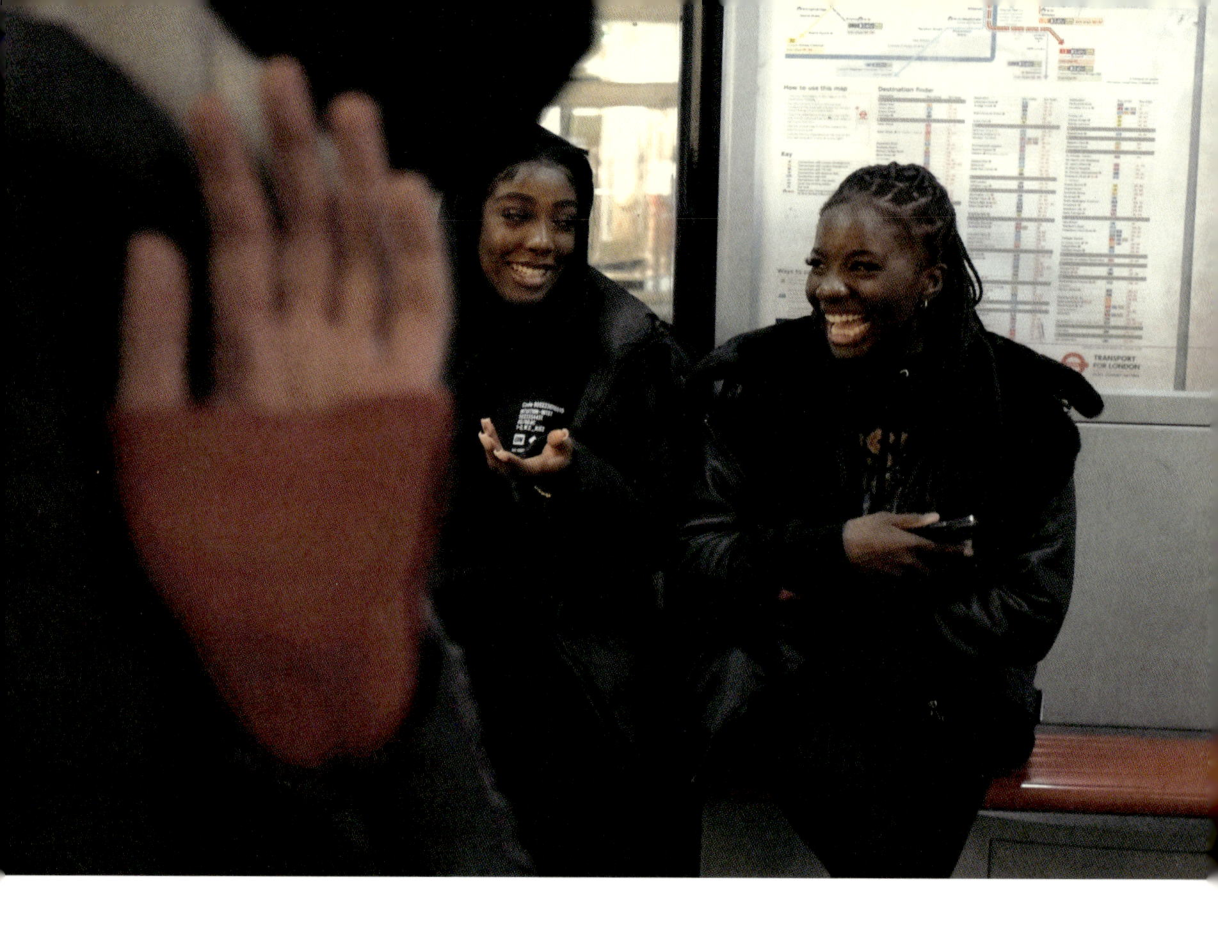

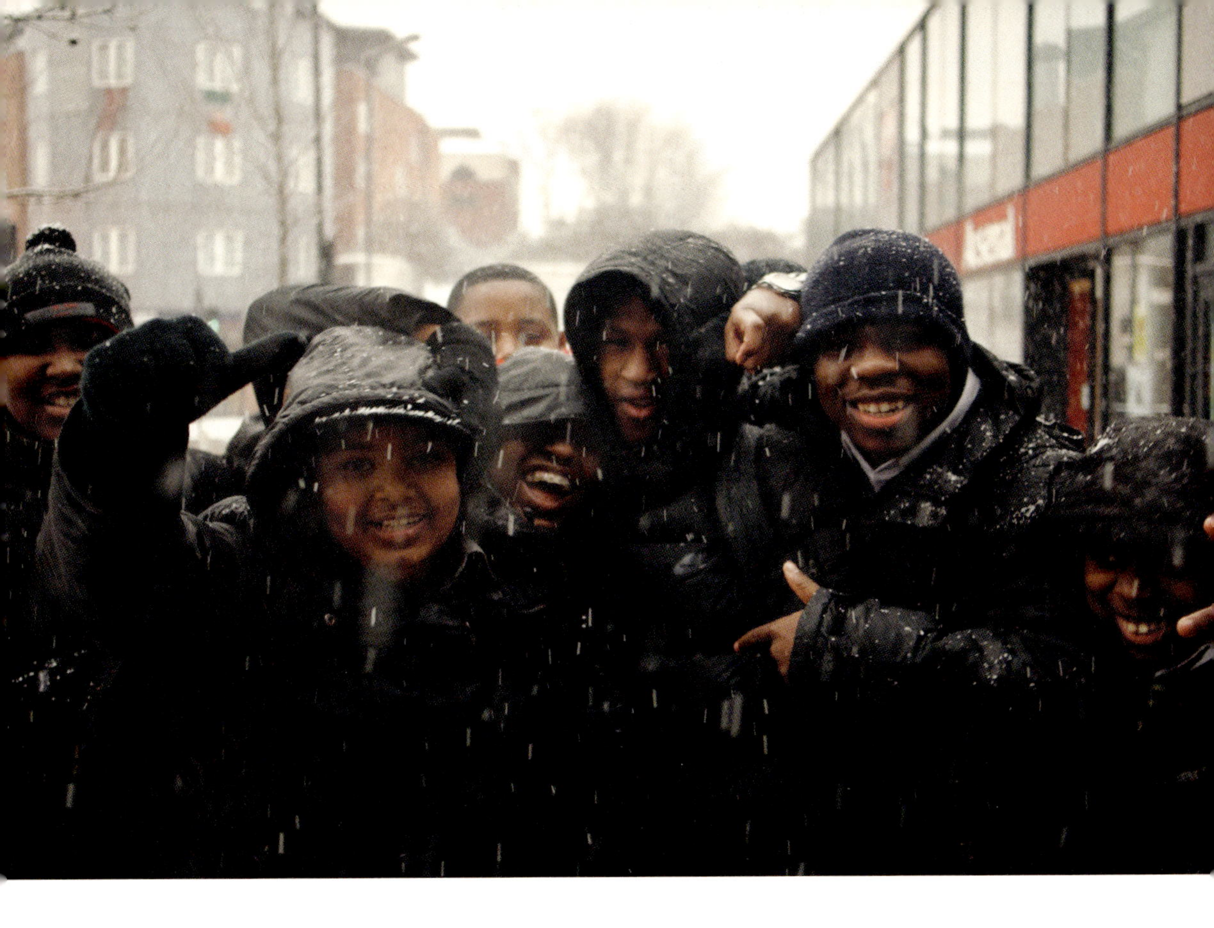

Endnote

1. *Saye lived on the twentieth floor with her mother.* Channel 5 News on Twitter, 2017
2. *Saye exhibited her photography at the prestigious Venice Biennale.* Another Mag 2020, 'Khadija Saye's Powerful Photography Is Now on Show in London'
3. *Saye's self-portraits contained elements of mystery and melancholy.* Good Therapy, 'Self-Portrait as a Form of Therapy'
4. *To make her pictures she used the wet-collodion process, which involved a long exposure on a metal plate coated in silver nitrate.* Chemical Pictures – The Wet Plate Collodion Book: Making Ambrotypes, Tintypes & Alumitypes: Volume 1, Quinn Jacobson, pp. 52-53
5. *It can be said there was a spiritual element to her pictures.* onlinevictoria-miro.com, Khadija Saye: 'in this space we breathe'
6. *The headties featured in the photograph would transcend ideas of culture or fashion and they'd become symbolic of protection.* Cornell.edu, The African American Woman's Headwrap: Unwinding the Symbols
7. *She'd often stand collaged with plants and other household or religious objects; the last time I saw her was at the Tate Museum and she seemed happy and enthused with life.* www frieze com, 'In Memoriam: Khadija Saye'
8. *Surrender and ancestors were ongoing themes in her work.* www.galdem.com, 'Grenfell: a Reflection on the Homecoming Work of Gambian–British photographer Khadija Saye'

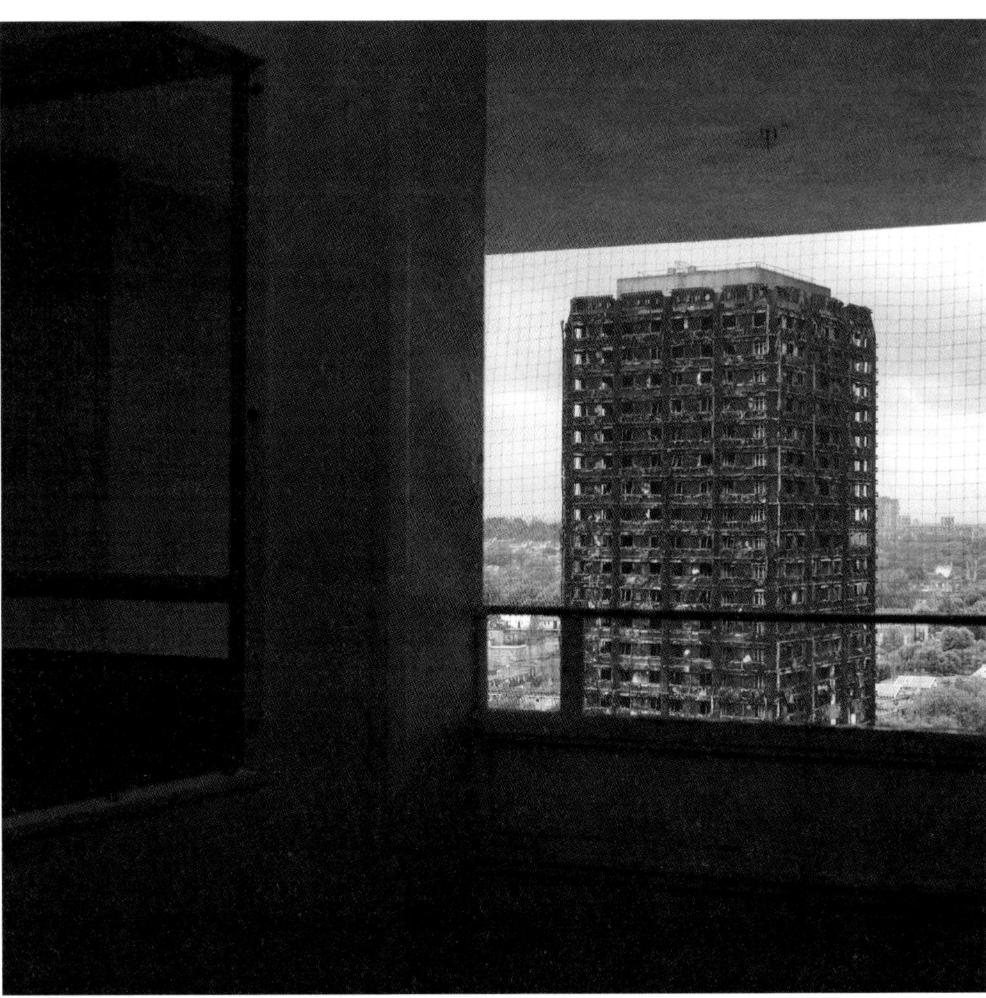

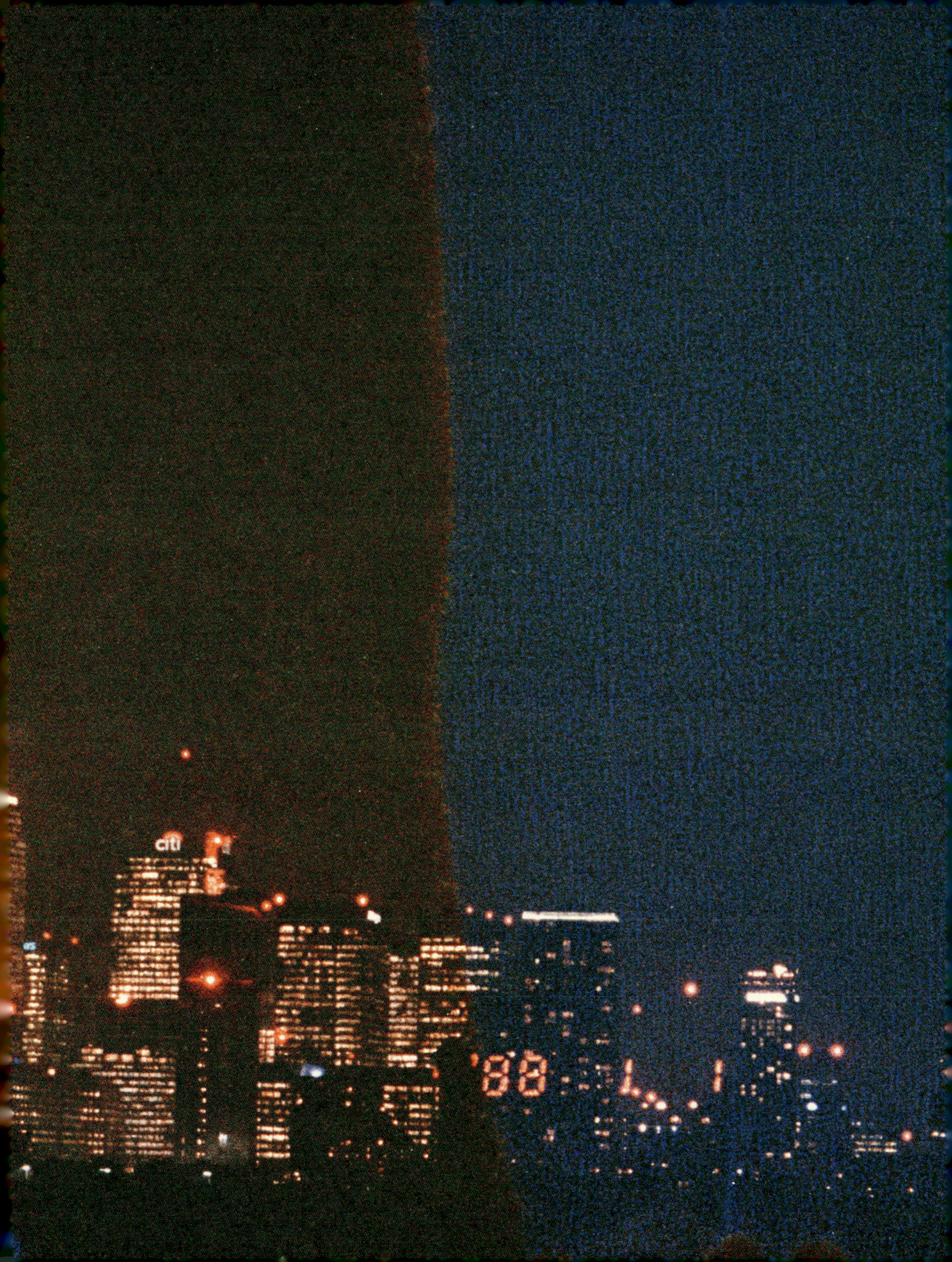

citi

Dear Haters

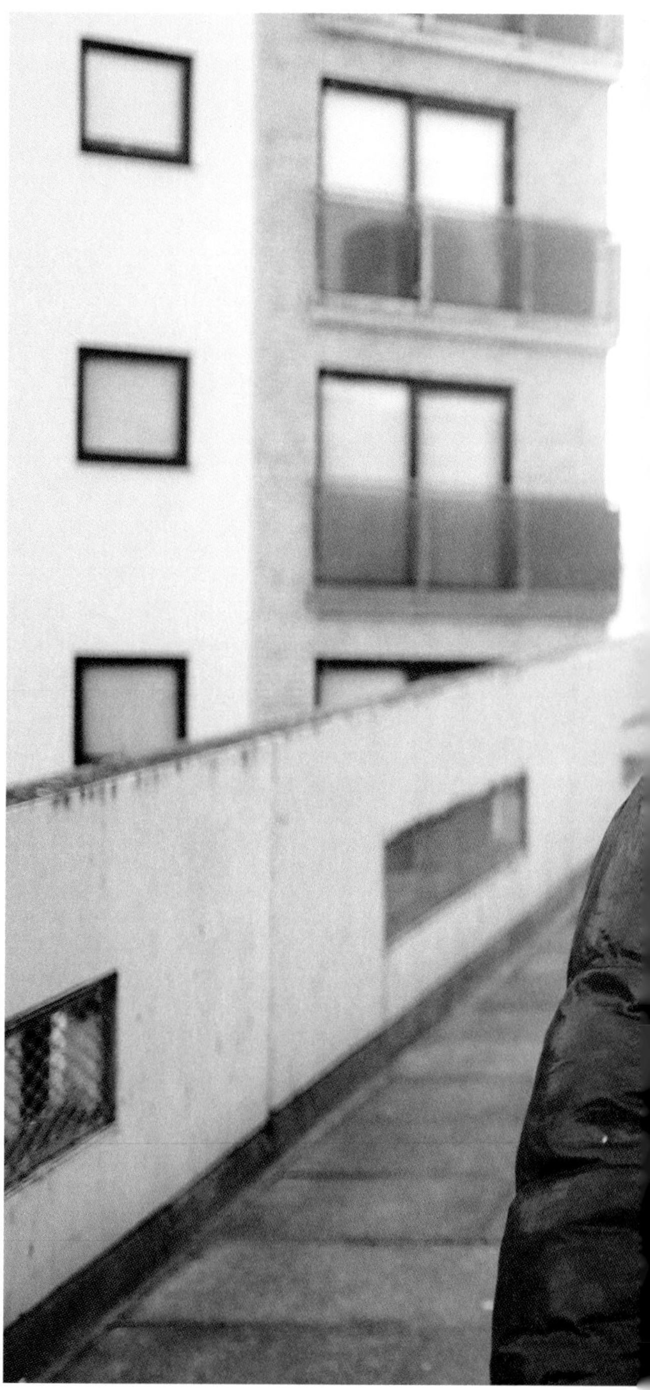

Is it my skin? Is it yours?

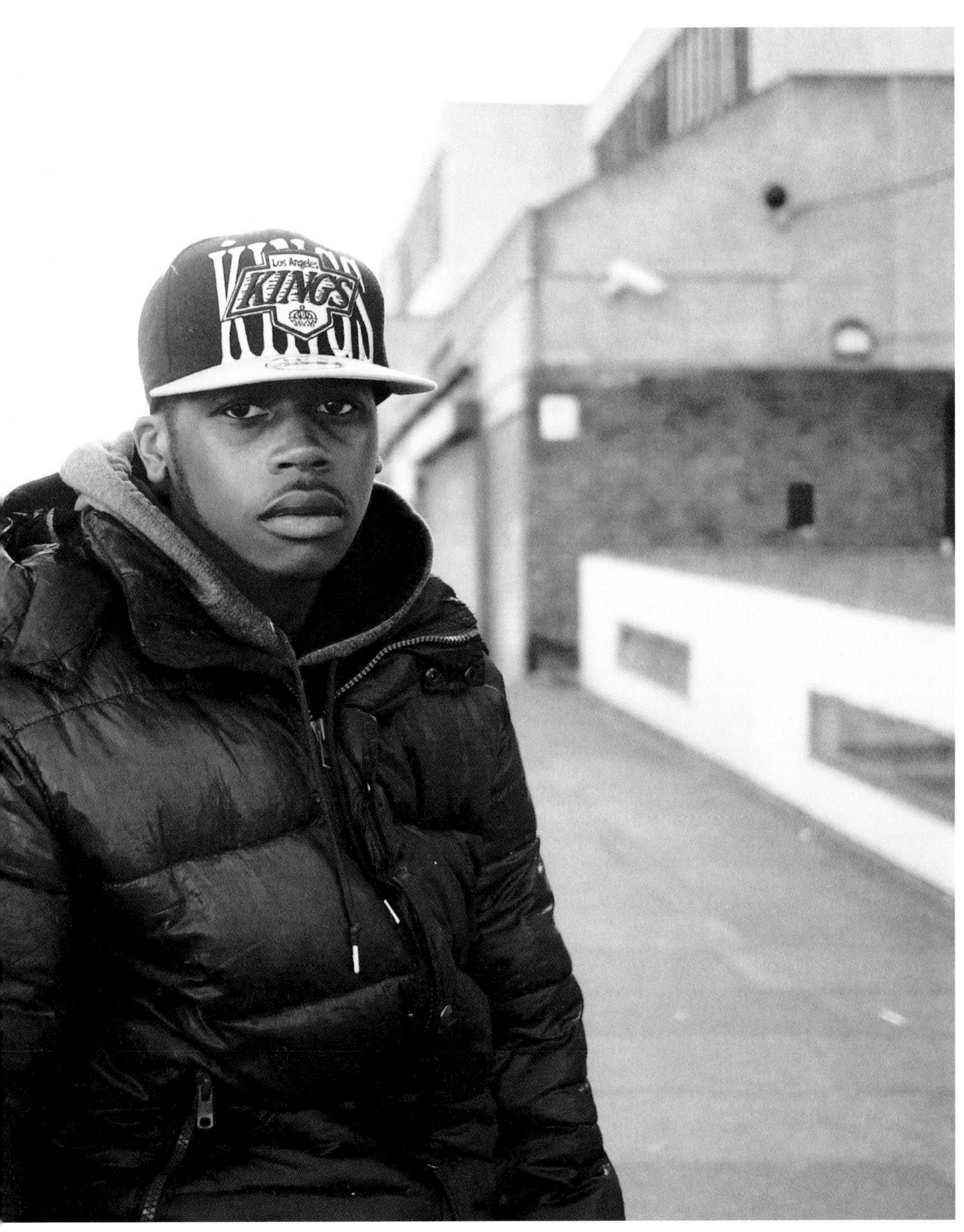

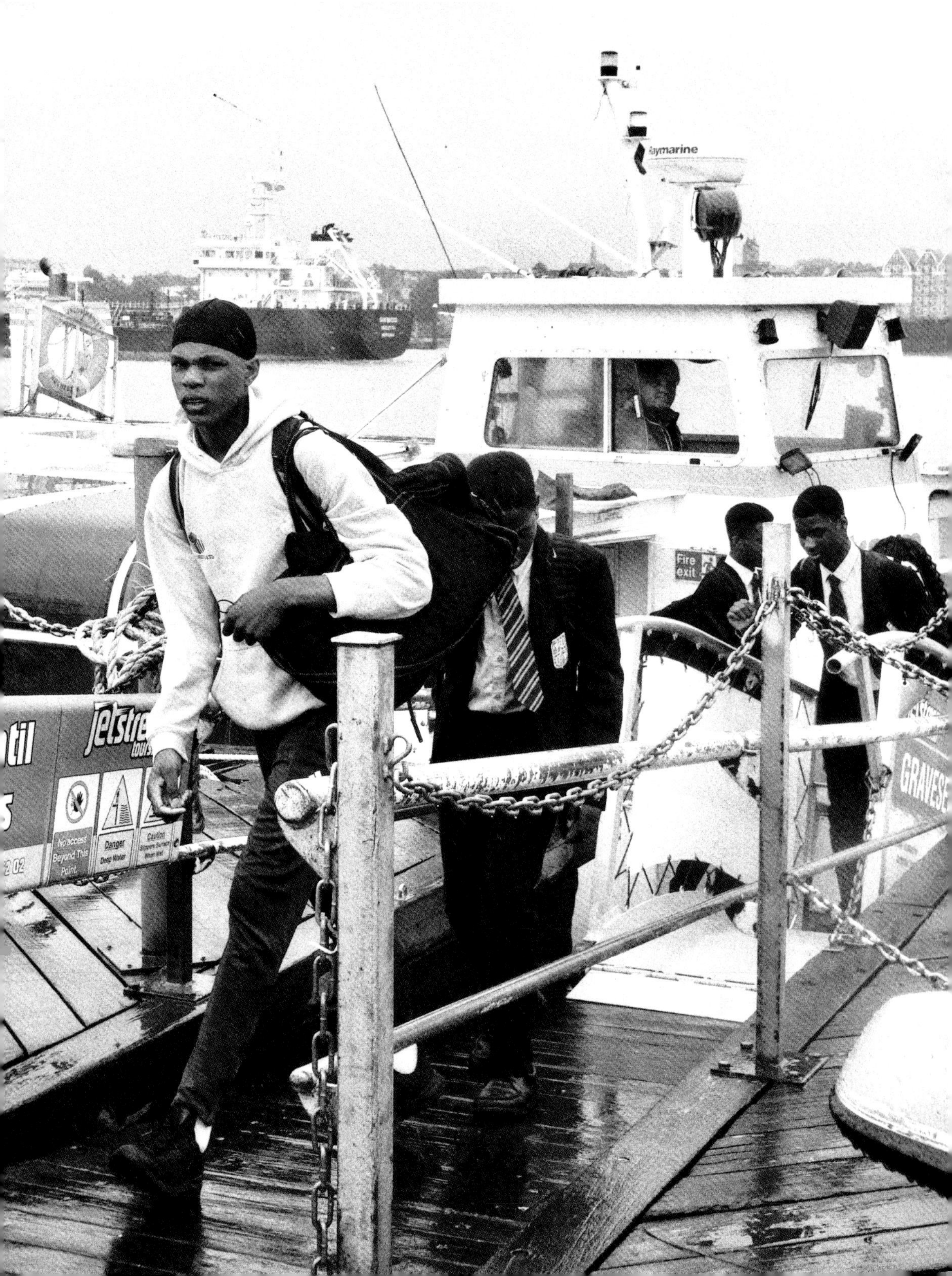
jetstream
tours
til
No access
Beyond This
Point
Danger
Deep Water
Caution
Slippery Surface
When Wet
Raymarine
Fire
exit
GRAVESE

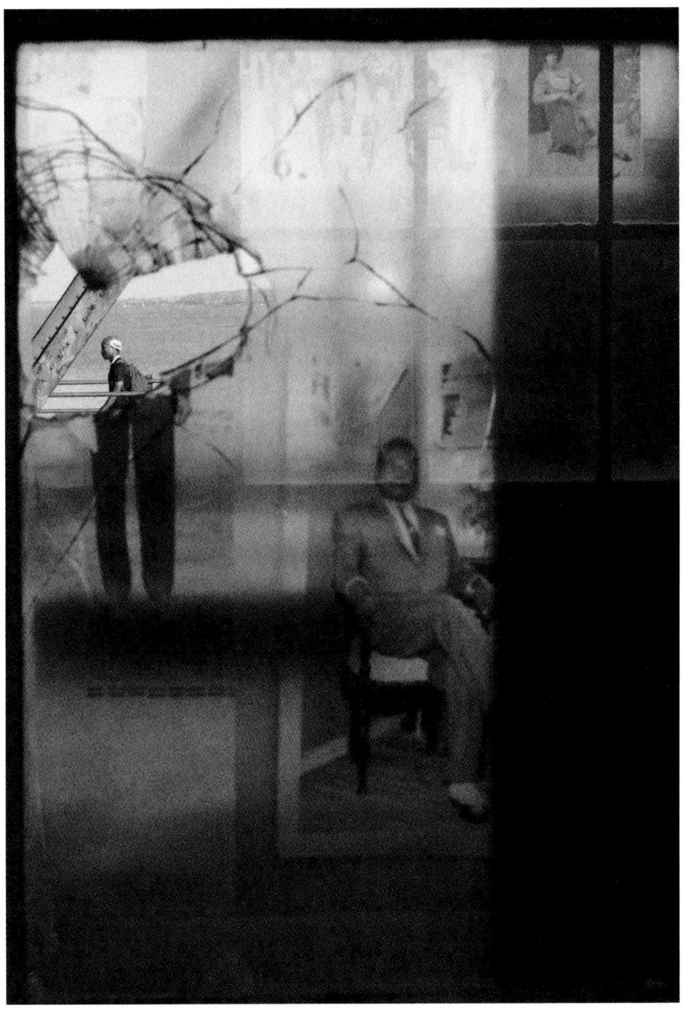

Story

My body is the shape of my journey.
Babies? Yes, I've had a few,
and the stretchmarks on my stomach and hips?
Designed by God, they are beautiful.
The flare of my nostrils is my grandmother's
(which skipped a generation to centre my face).
Two fully grown men still prefer my food
over their wives' cooking. It's not my problem
their wives can't cook; and I crave no man
who doesn't adore this storied body,
because it's mine and it's the only one I've got
and it has no space for shame, mine or yours.
If your body isn't telling your story
it means someone else is using your body to tell
theirs, and you better solve that problem.

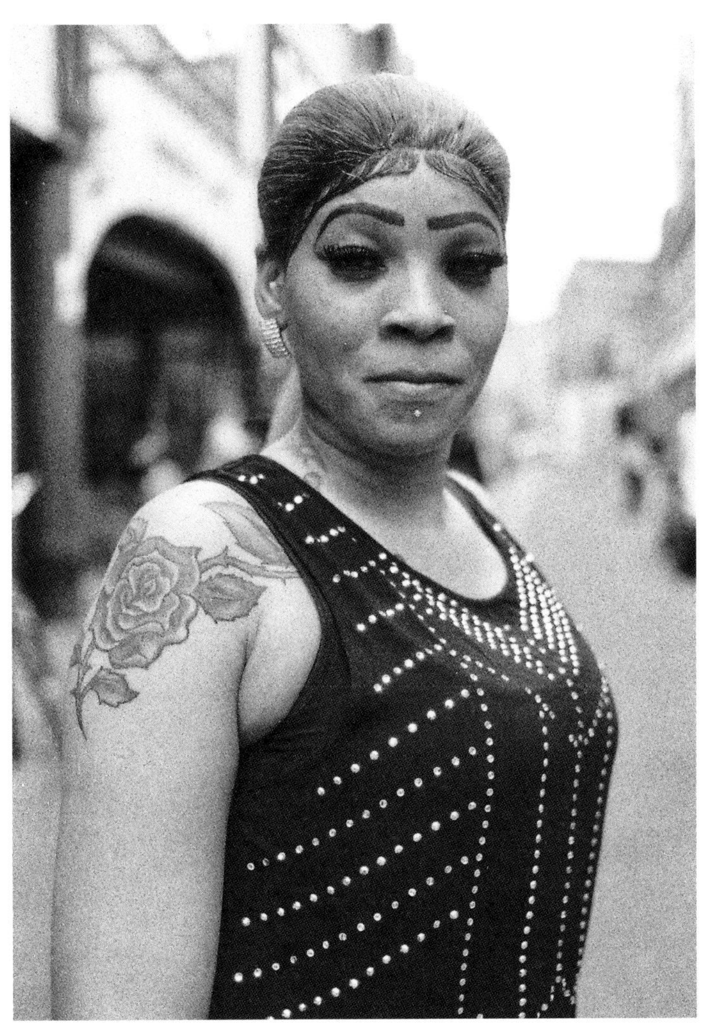

Real Pain

is transcendent.
It puts you into another realm;
not of conversation or entertainment
but the torturous circle of your own head,
if only because no one else can feel it.

Around here everyone
was either hooked
on pain, selling pain or died
from pain and I became a part
of pain's chain as it was placed

in my hand, in my body
and mind. O pain, O pain you've hidden
yourself O pain, you've hidden yourself inside.
You've hidden yourself inside my life.

Pain filling my stomach
so I can't eat, pain filling my head
so I can't think, pain in my speech
that offends the genteel

and I cannot get you out, pain,
for I fear there'll be not much left
of me without you and though
I've held you inside, contained
you within the borders of my skin,
I'll not lose this weary game of living.

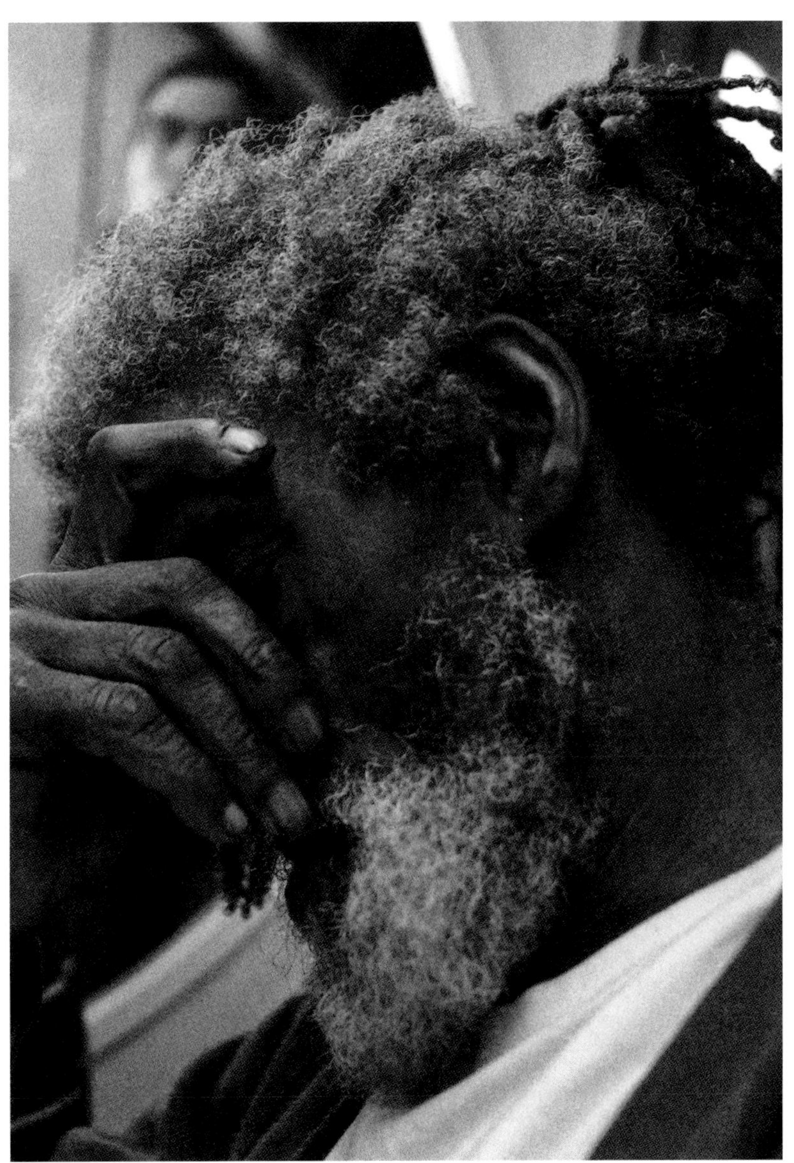

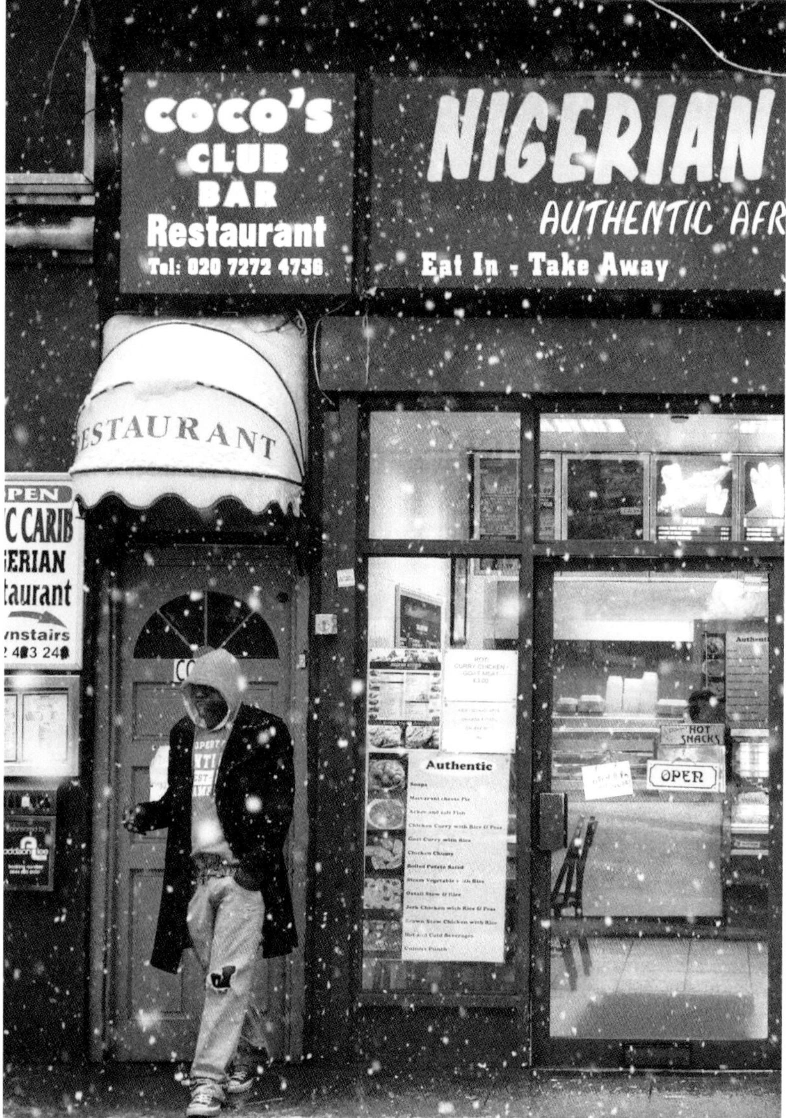

COCO'S
CLUB
BAR
Restaurant
Tel: 020 7272 4736
NIGERIAN
AUTHENTIC AFR
Eat In - Take Away
RESTAURANT
OPEN
C CARIB
GERIAN
taurant
nstairs
HOT
CURRY CHICKEN
GOAT MEAT
Authentic
Soups
Maccaroni cheese Pie
Ackee and salt Fish
Chicken Curry with Rice & Peas
Goat Curry with Rice
Chicken Cheasy
Boiled Potato Salad
Steam Vegetable with Rice
Oxtail Stew & Rice
Jerk Chicken with Rice & Peas
Brown Stew Chicken with Rice
Hot and Cold Beverages
Guiness Punch
HOT
SNACKS
OPEN

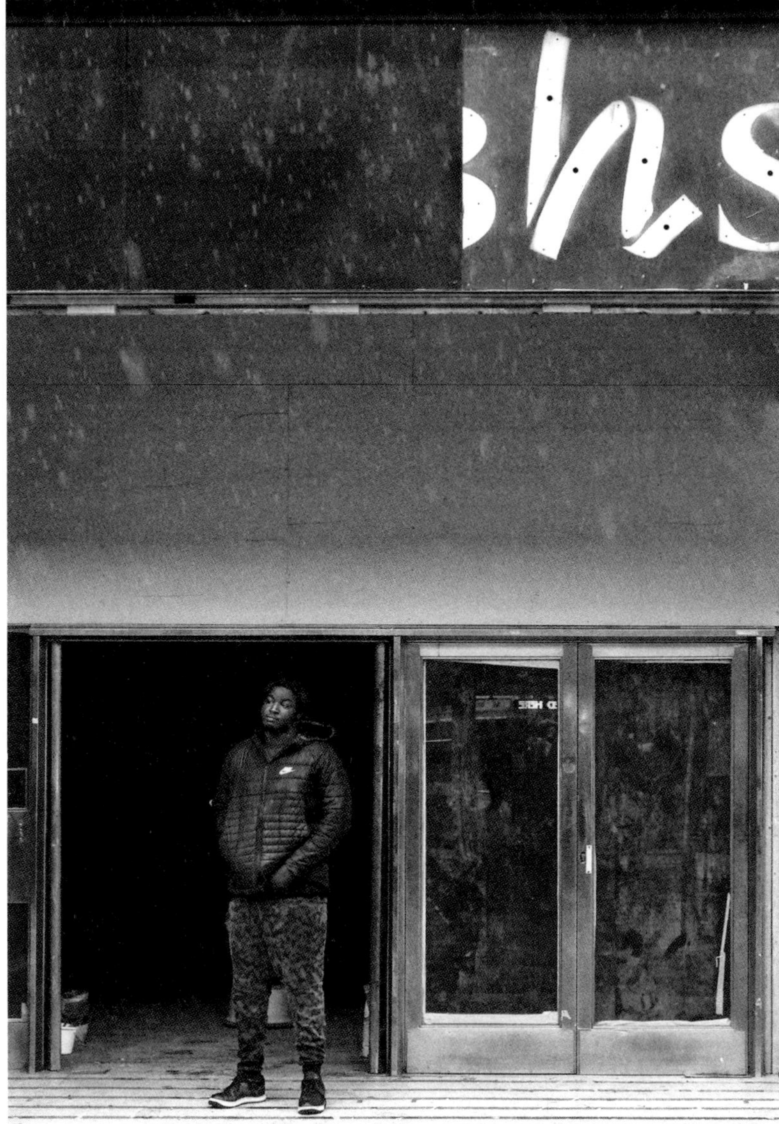

Bhs

Thirty-Second Exposure

Turn off the red light and transfer
the print to the water tray; notice the detail.
See her sunken caramel face first,
the perfect flare, sheen and symmetry
of her hair (maybe she had it done
for the shoot). Then notice his raised
eyebrow and furrowed forehead
(a slight discomfort, perhaps?),
how he stands with his arms
behind his back, how she sits
with one hand spooning the other.
He with one jacket button done up,
she modestly covered up to her neck
(church children for sure).
The mahogany of his skin,
the pride of his Afro.
Her eyes a private dignity
at once an existence and a longing.
And if you find yourself staring,
wondering what's their story,
perhaps falling a little in love
with their awkward innocence,
prissy independence and shyness,
then sit with that unfolding
feeling for a while, let it lead
you to a memory of yourself
at that age (with your thumping
heart) too frozen to ask a girl
you like to slow dance;
while the music played on
and the unafraid danced around you.

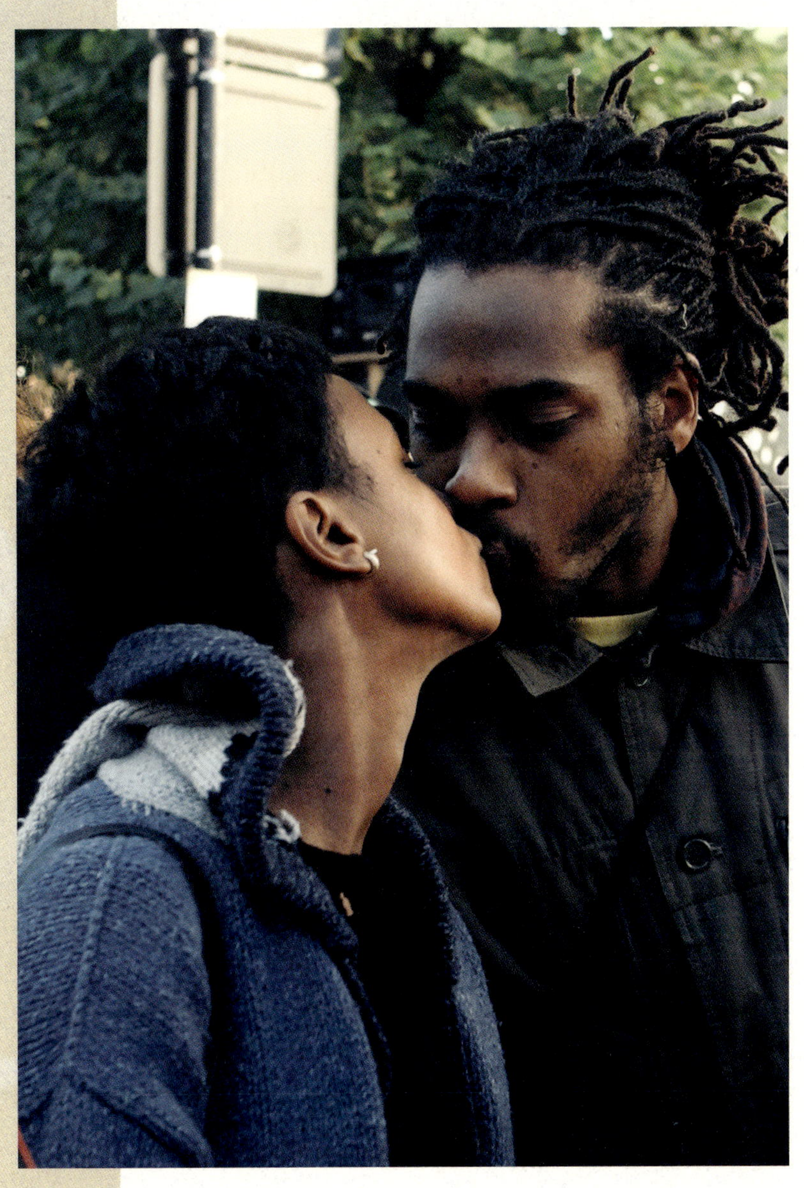

Survivals

Don't fall into dreams
of other men who don't care
that you wake screaming.

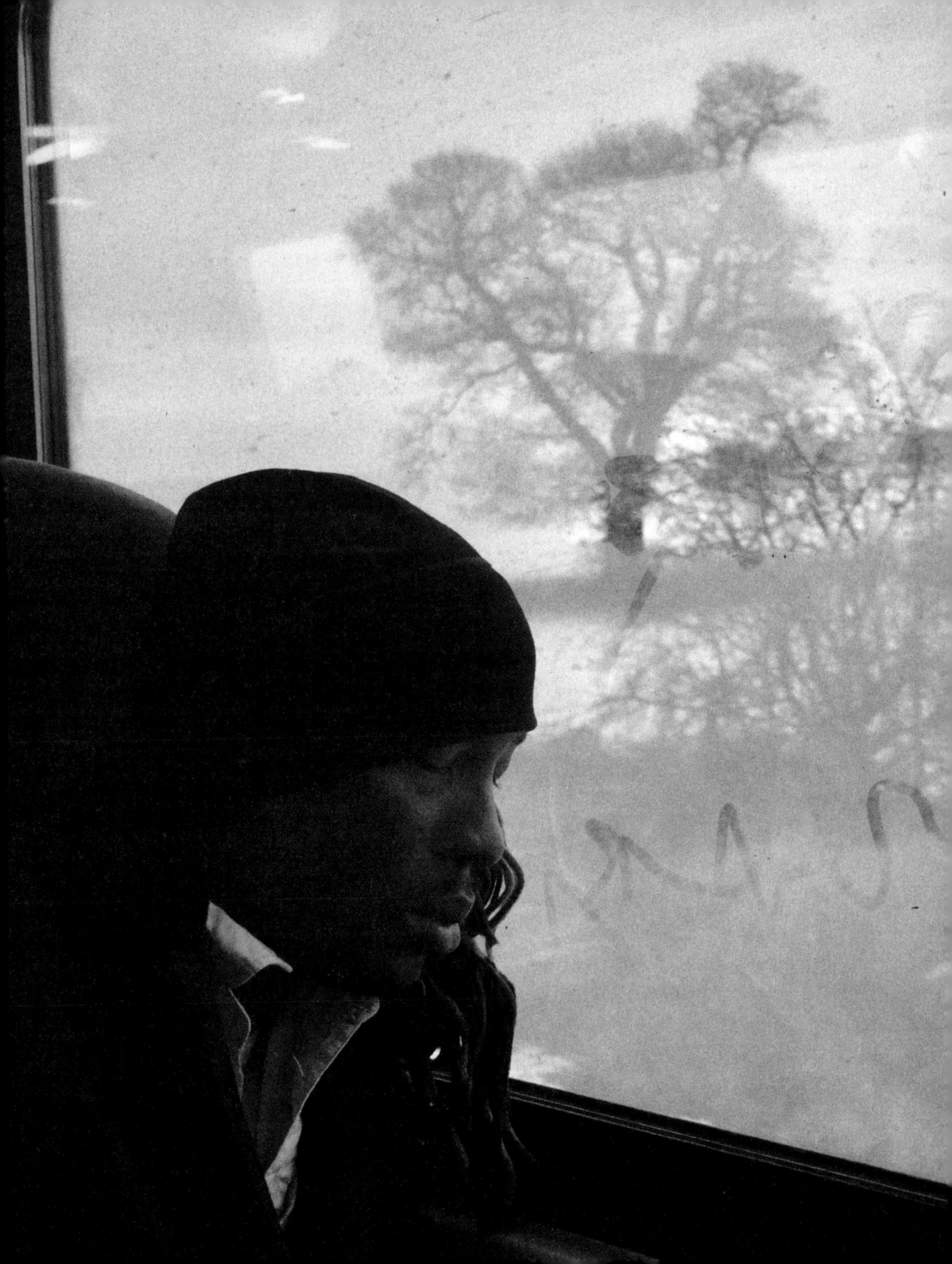

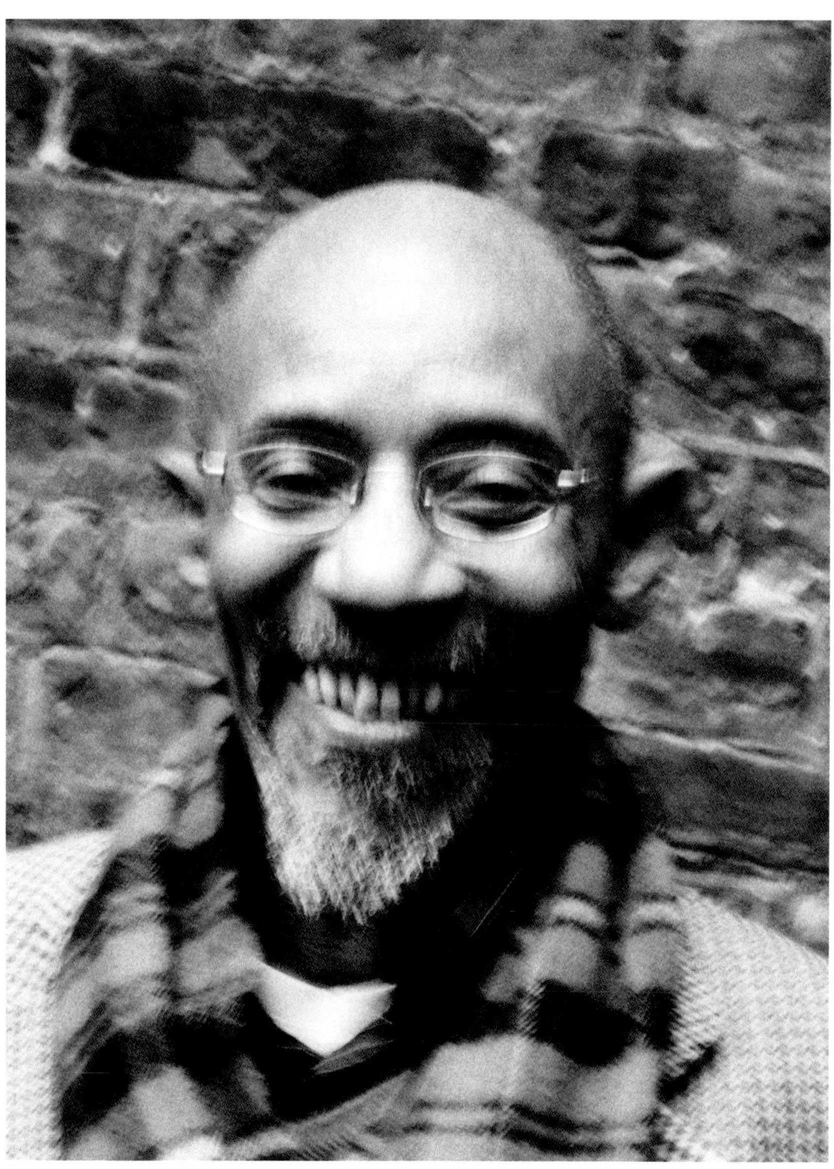

On Black Joy

The Malian photographer Malick Sidibe ran a fairly rustic studio in Bamako in the late sixties. It was a time of transition, where through the magic of television American images were being beamed into Bamako's homes, driving massive change away from traditional modes of fashion, music, dress, behaviour and presentation. Malick Sidibé was there to capture that transition in pictures. At times he would even assist in the styling of the pictures, because he was beginning to pick up on what the young upcoming generation was trying to portray.

Besides his studio work he also shot reportage-style pictures in the nightclubs and parties of Bamako. It was a heady new time; the Mali Federation had gained its independence from France and there were new freedoms in the late sixties and early seventies. People wanted to express themselves differently, they wanted to mark this new era with a rejection of past restrictions and behavioural modes. Sidibé says, 'We were entering a new era, and people wanted to dance. Music freed us. Suddenly, young men could get close to young women, hold them in their hands. Before, it was not allowed. And everyone wanted to be photographed dancing up close.'

Sidibé was documenting the newly liberated consciousness of Mali and its joyful expressions of independence. In all of his nightclub shots there are different levels of performatively expressed Black Joy, but none so much as in a picture called 'Nuit de Noël: Happy-Club'.

The picture 'Nuit de Noël (Happy-Club)' or 'Christmas Eve (Happy-Club)' contains much of what I believe Black Joy consists of; a metaphor, or perhaps more an ideogram of Black Joy. The picture itself is simple but not simplistic. There are two Black dark-skinned people dancing, close enough to share each other's space but not touching; they are looking at each other's movement as if to continue in synchronicity. Though frozen in the shot they look like they are in step with each other. He has on a light-coloured summer suit, she has on a light-coloured sleeveless dress that reveals her long, sinewy arms. Her dress is pleated and ruffled from her waist down and stops just above her knee. If you look further down you will see that she is dancing barefoot on the cracked poured-concrete floor of the club (you get the feeling she's taken off her fancy shoes just off camera so she can really enjoy this dance) with some empty chairs and bottles of drink watching on in the background. He is tall, slim, dark-skinned, handsome and clean-cut. From the picture you feel that these are two people at the moment of falling in love. That could be my own bias. But if you look really closely at their faces, and the way they lean into each other, and mirror each other, you can see it. A kind of joy, a Black Joy.

There are ideas I want to extract from this picture as an ideogram that will help to illustrate the idea of Black Joy. The first is the idea of synchronicity.

Synchronicity is so much a precondition for Black Joy we nearly ignore it. Whether it's the strength of Kanye West's choir moving and singing in unison, or people together listening to a massive sound at Carnival swaying and swaying to Ms. Dynamite's 'Booo!'. Black people getting together en masse, and united by a tune, a song or a dance is always a precept for Black Joy.

Another idea is that Black Joy is often not deliberate or complex but there is a complexity to the feelings it might elicit. In fact, for me and a lot of other Black people I have spoken to, being Black and making a living is such a constant struggle that we are sometimes not ready when joy overtakes us. It can result in a flood of tears or a feeling of ecstasy, or an epiphany that you are universally connected to the world and other Black people. The feelings of Black Joy are so rare that you sometimes don't know how to react other than to retreat and settle and get yourself together, only to find Black Joy is often uncontrollable.

Black Joy can often be captured by some type of technology or artist, from a DJ on turntables to a poet, a dancer, or a photographer, all of whom can, through their technology, replicate the feelings of Black Joy in other Black people who choose to participate in the process, either as makers or audience. This can sometimes be several decades later, as in the recent case of the *Summer of Soul* film by Questlove, which had Mahalia Jackson gearing up Gospel after taking the mic from Mavis Staples and hitting tones that evoked every female ancestor known and unknown from aeons of generations before me and which had me in floods of tears. Through a computer screen, this affected me as much in 2021 as it had others in 1969.

Black Joy can also be seen in terms of the Zulu idea of Ubuntu. Ubuntu suggests that a person is a person only through other people. This is what predicates the joy of family gatherings, or the joy of your friend group coming together for birthdays or getting ready at midnight to go to a house party. The joy isn't only in the party itself, the joy is in the joint anticipation, the preparation, the journey together. The joy is in being part of something, a crew, a family, a football team winning your Sunday league, and that type of Black Joy you can only experience through other people. Going back to the Sidibé photograph; it would be a very different picture if he was dancing by himself. In fact, part of the deep sadness about Covid isolation is that for long periods of time we were not able to access many preconditions or facets of Black Joy, leading to a dissolution of identity and the onset of low-level trauma which ultimately Black Joy is an antidote to.

I want to conclude with a personal reference to a form of Black Joy that I've experienced or observed, which, though not obvious at the time, really shaped what I think of as Black Joy.

In 1993 I saw it on VHS (remember that?) the Black Art film *Daughters of the Dust,* whose sumptuously lush cinematography by Arthur Jafa pulled me into the lives of three Gullah women from South Carolina. As well as the name for the people, Gullah was the language spoken in the film; a mixture of Mende Ibo Yoruba and Twi. As I understood it at the time, in order to avoid the then-illegal trafficking of slaves across the Atlantic, from 1 January 1808 the plantation owners of the South let some slaves live amongst themselves on St Simons Island and other islands off the coast of Georgia so that they would have children who could be born into slavery. The effect of that was that on St Simons Island there was a high retention of African culture, much more than in any other part of America (which more or less banned traditional language, culture and beliefs by replacing them with the so-called civilising beliefs of Christianity).

Around 1998 I had been invited to a residency at the University of South Carolina, the major part of which was to work with the Gullah community, and I jumped at the chance. Even though the organisation of the residency had room for improvement I was nevertheless incredibly happy to be there. Where I stayed in Georgia held all the rippling-heat mysticism of the American South I had seen in films. The Black people who lived there for the most part seemed happy but extremely poor. I had several transformative experiences there, like seeing Reverend Frazier (the boxer Joe Frazier's brother) at 90 years old sing a type of gospel blues with only his stomping boots on the stage for percussion that brought me out in goosebumps. But the experience that sticks in my mind the most is being taken to the PEN centre to supposedly meet other poets, only to be led into a room of five-year-old children. (Did I say the organisation of things wasn't great?) Anyway, resigned to making the best of my situation, and faced with 25 shiny, anticipating Black faces, I grabbed the nearest storybook and opened the pages so they could see (by the way, I can read upside down) and began my best theatrical storytelling. By page 8 all the children had jumped up and started running round the room like a mosh pit at a rock show. I looked to their teacher to find out what was going on as the children continued circling, shouting and laughing. She came across with her head in her hands saying, *Mr Robinson, I don't think these kids have had anybody read to them like that before; they may have got overexcited.* As their teacher and I watched them running around in a circle of pure freedom I realised that this was Black Joy, the smile on their faces, the synchronicity, the shrieking, the freedom.

As these examples were occurring I often didn't see them as Black Joy, because I was wrapped up in the moment of the experience, but I remain full of gratitude for Black Joyful experiences because they remind me of the richness and purpose of life. As we go through life full of mundanity and inevitable struggle it's these reflective moments of Black Joy that will stay in our memories, no matter how big or small.

Ultimately my lasting definition of Black Joy is when Black people come together, whether it be in celebration or communion, and are able to celebrate by shrugging off the rigours of Black living in racist societies or under economic and social hardships. When this happens we synchronise, we associate and identify, we purge trauma, we laugh and we move and create Black Joy.

I have bought the Malick Sidibé picture as a poster and I have it hung in my study. Every time I or my work feels too bleak it always reminds me of the steps I need to bring specifically Black Joy back into my life.

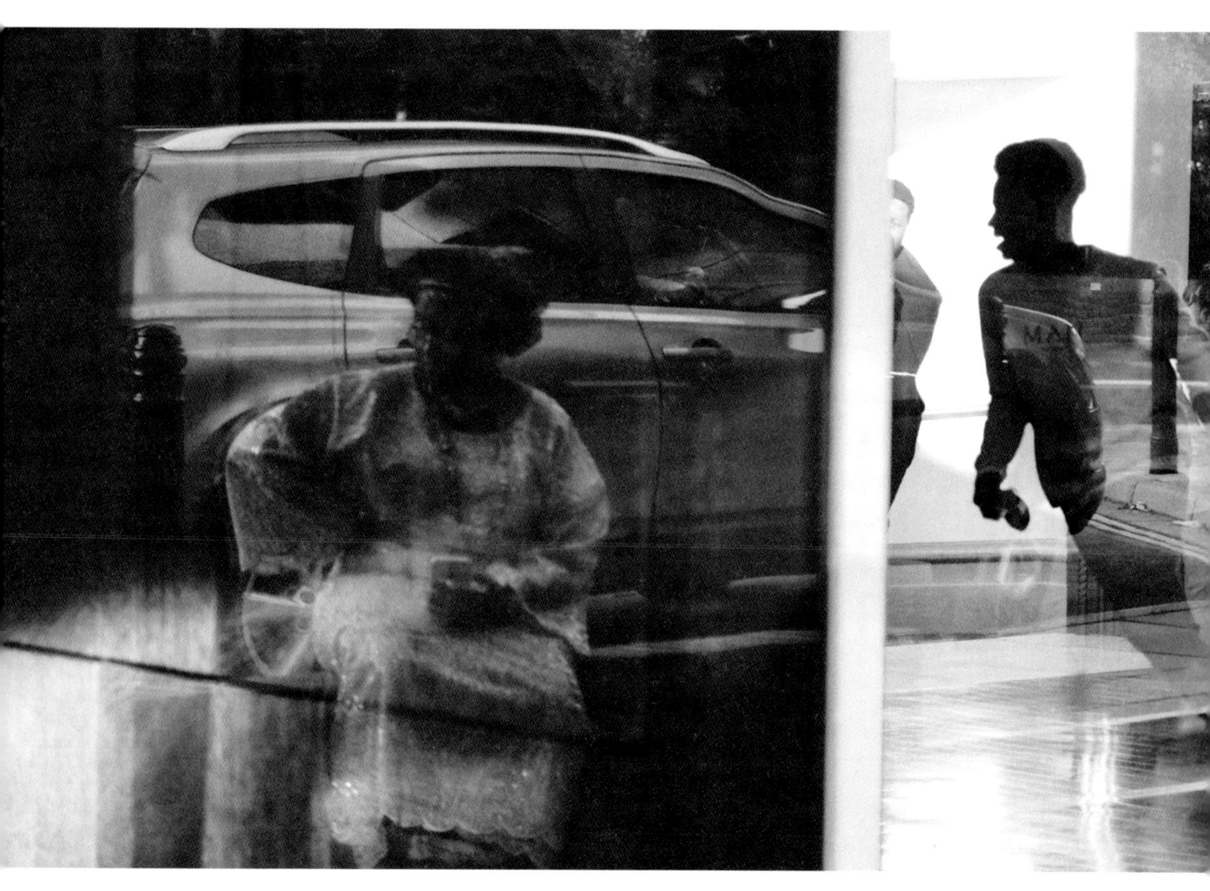

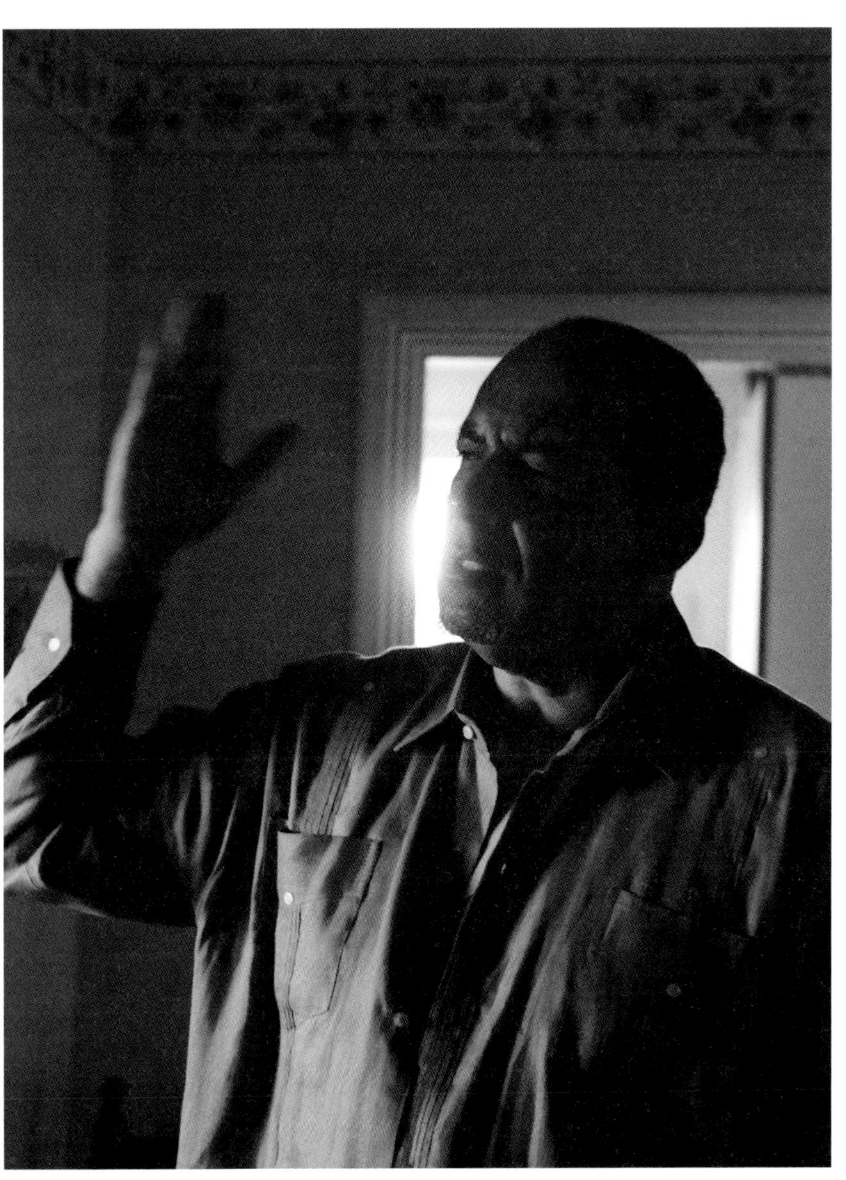

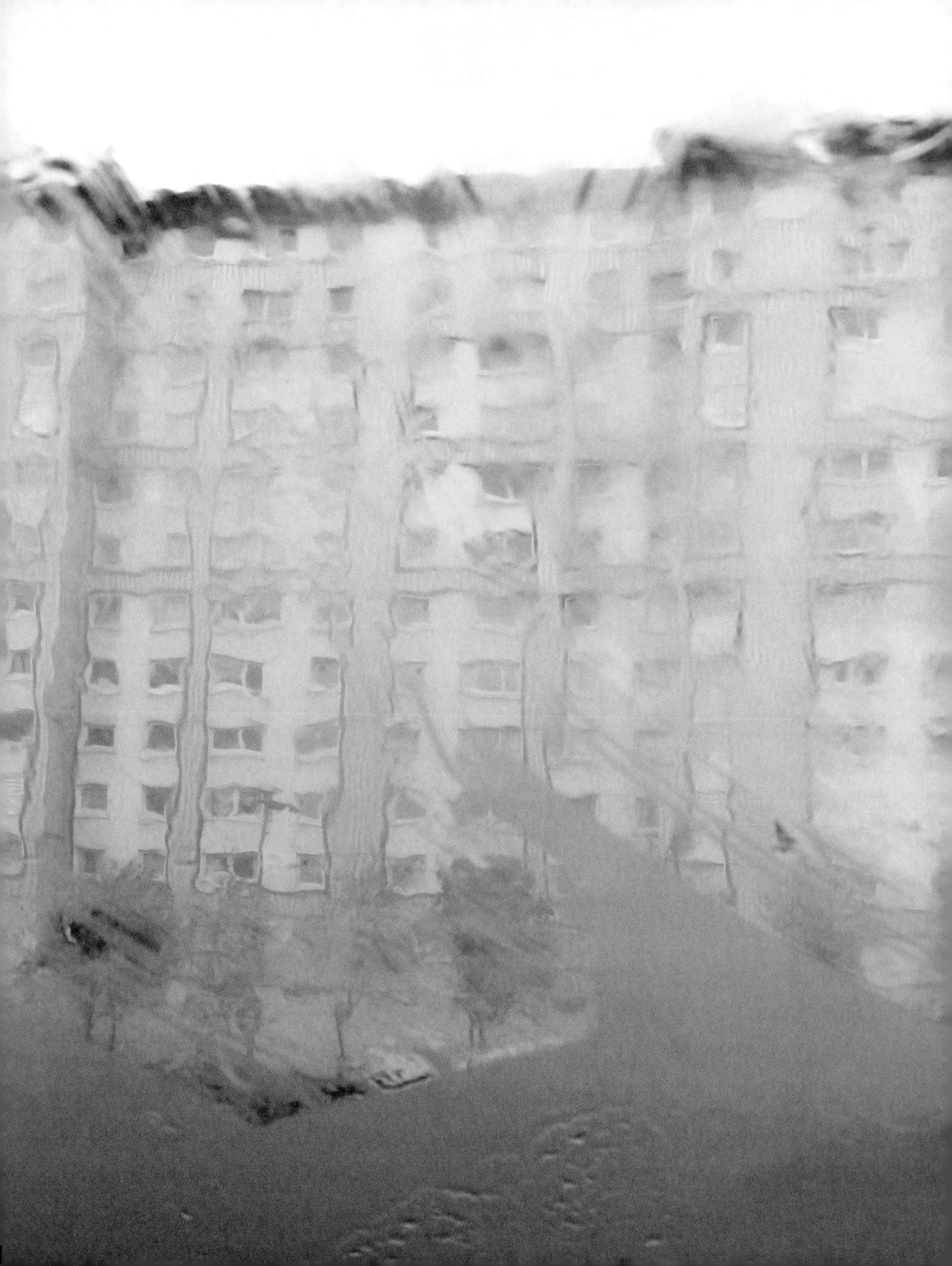

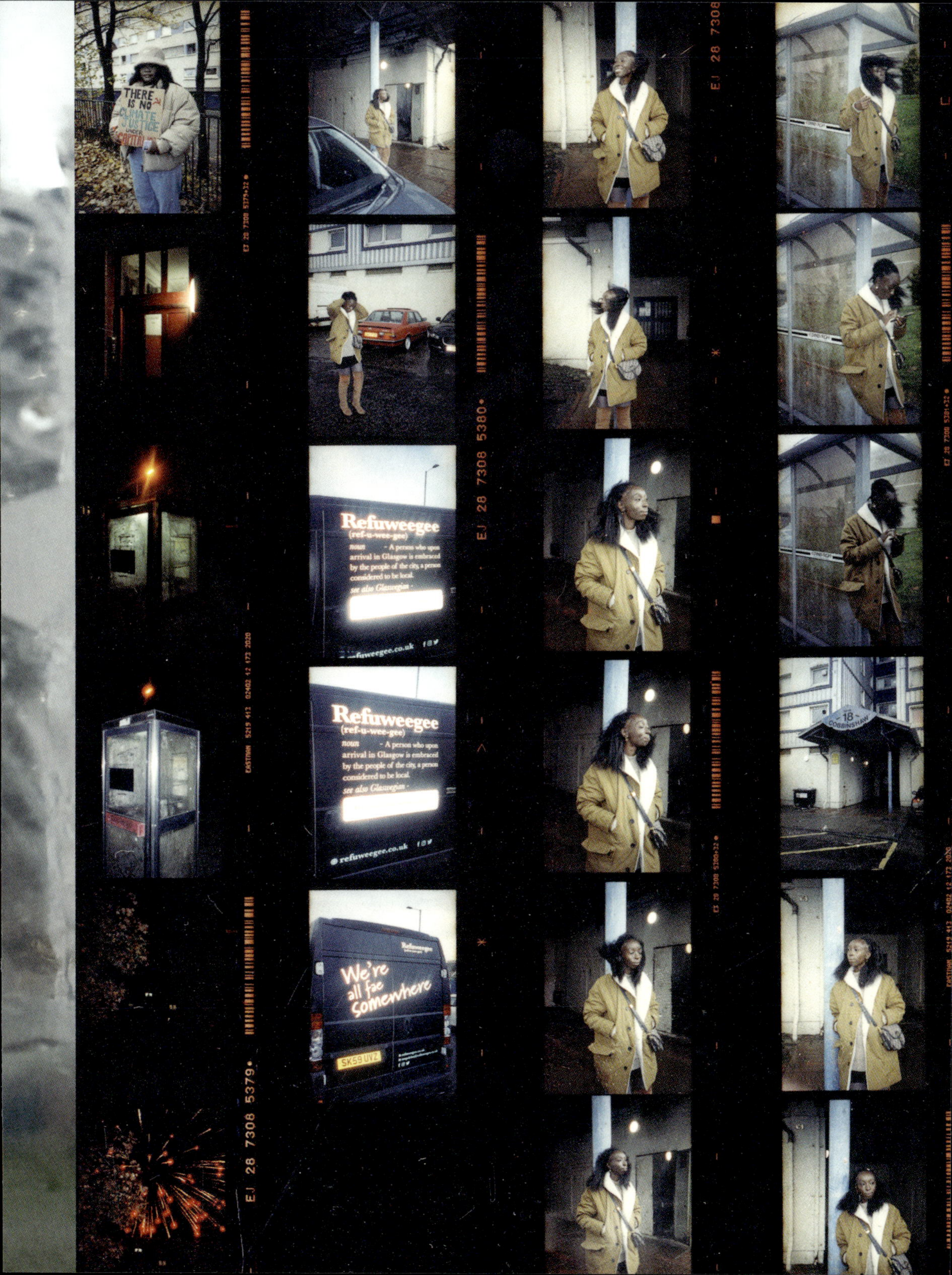

THERE
IS NO
CLIMATE
JUSTICE

Refuweegee
(ref-u-wee-gee)
noun   - A person who upon
arrival in Glasgow is embraced
by the people of the city, a person
considered to be local.
see also Glaswegian -
www.refuweegee.co.uk

We're
all fae
Somewhere

SK59 UVZ

18

EJ 28 7308 5379
EJ 28 7308 5360
EJ 28 7308 5380

The Black Activist

The Black activist's right shoulder muscle is strained from trying to keep her black fist raised in the air for too long. If she was going to protest she was going all the way, with berets, shades, leather jacket, gloves and a megaphone. When the megaphone ran out of batteries she shouted until her voice went hoarse. She walked until there were huge rubbed-raw sores on the back of her heels, and when the pain was too much she folded down the back of her sneakers and continued as if she were wearing slippers. She was going to actively work against racism with all she had in her, as she handed out her backpack of flyers about the problems of intersectional racism and took cards and numbers from other people on the march. When she got home her housemates told her that if she didn't take care of herself she'd drop dead from exhaustion before the revolution even got here. They ran her a soapy bath to get her to relax, but as she sat in the bath the film in her head of Black men and women being shot and choked to death in broad daylight captured on mobile phones kept coming to her, one after the other, and she felt like she was just wasting time. She jumped out the bath and wrapped in her towel she lay on her bed replying to racists on Twitter way into the night.

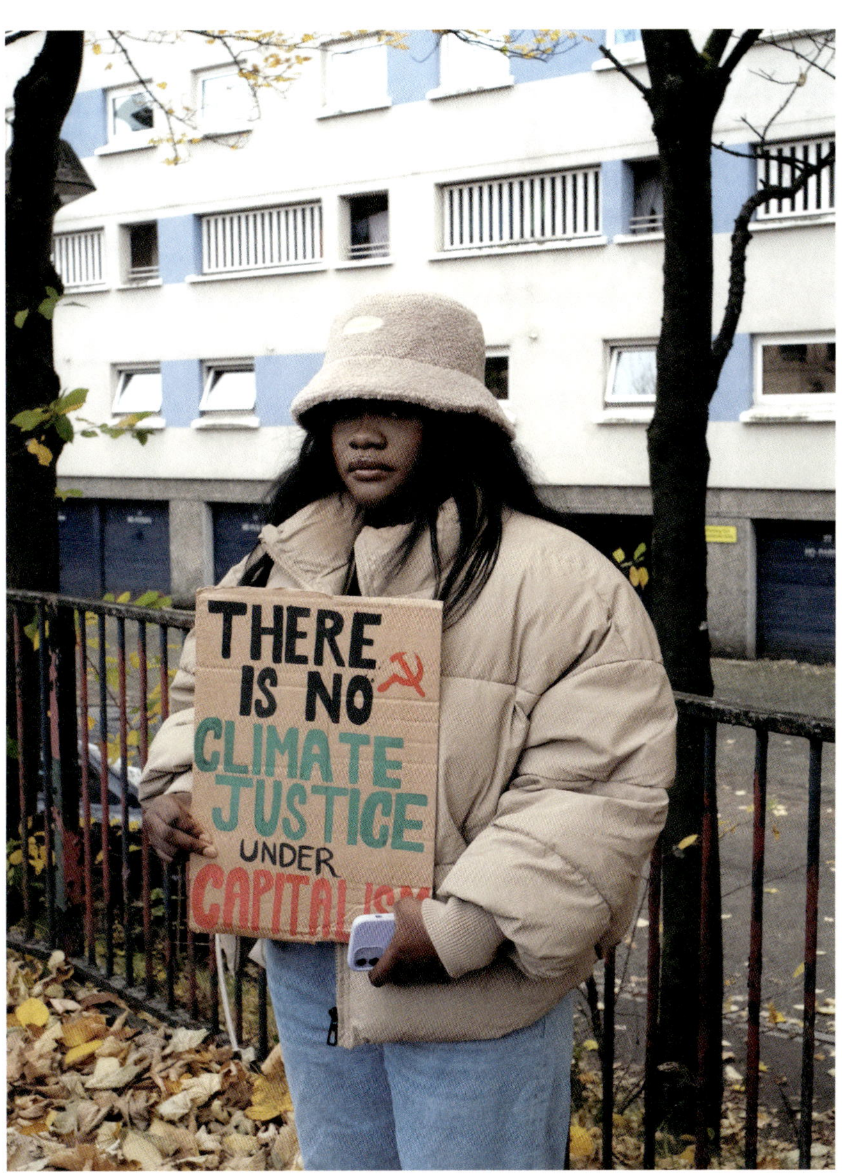

THERE
IS NO
CLIMATE
JUSTICE
UNDER
CAPITALISM

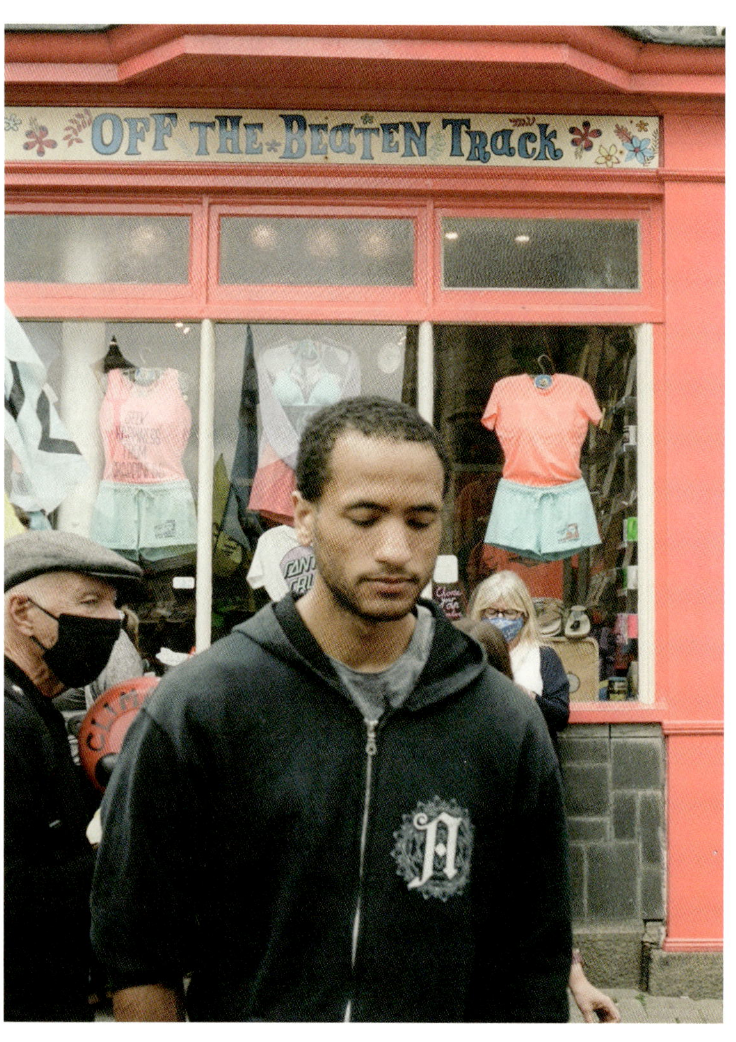

OFF THE *BEATEN TRACK

Refugee and Migrant Justice
Please Pull to Enter
NO SMOKING.
It is against the law to
smoke in these premises

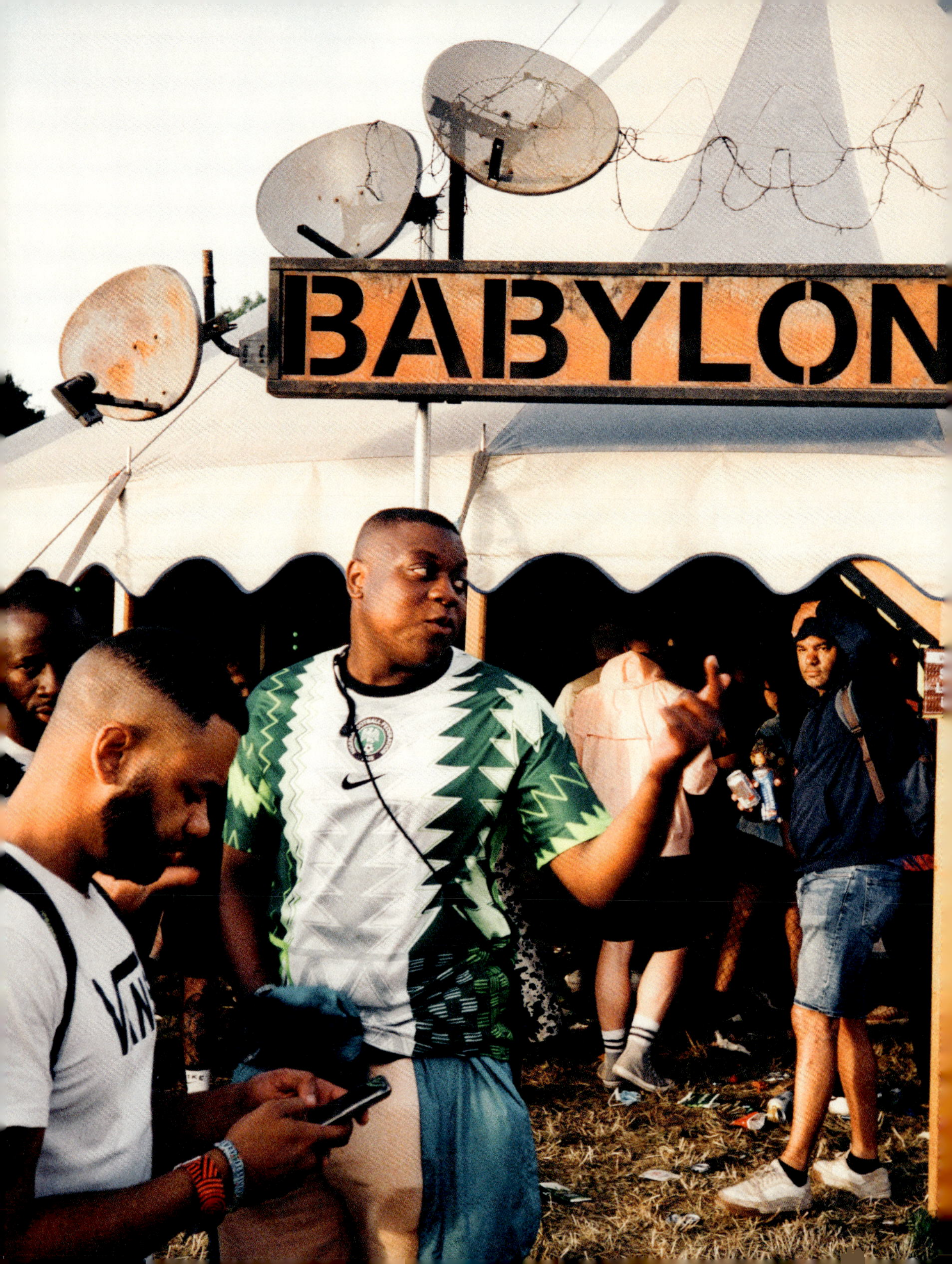
BABYLON

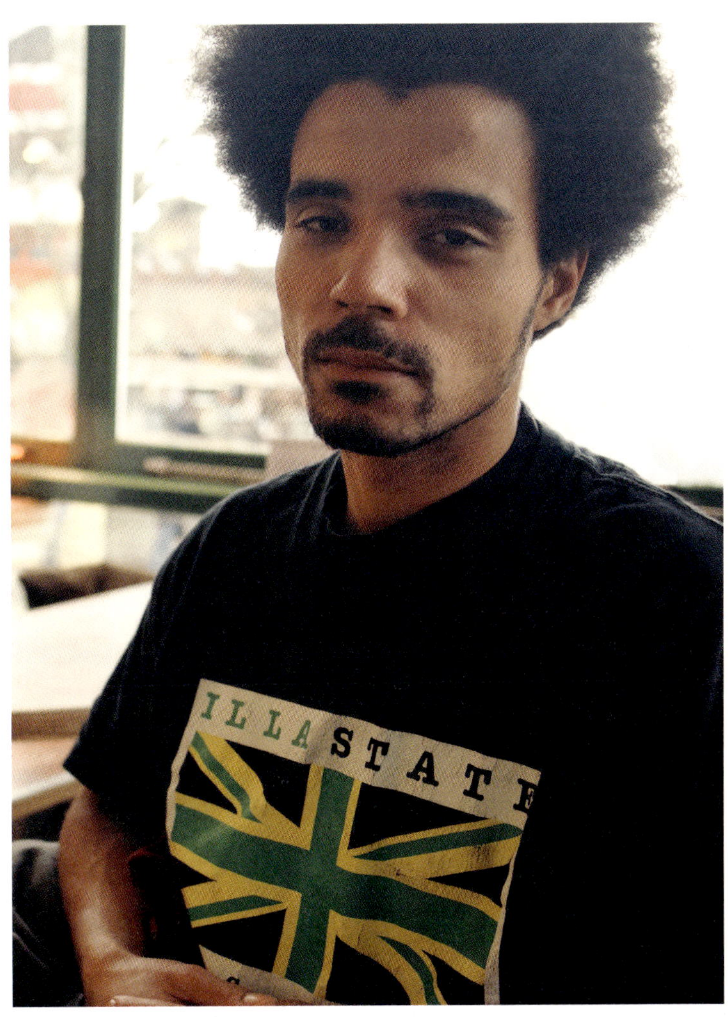
ILLA STATE

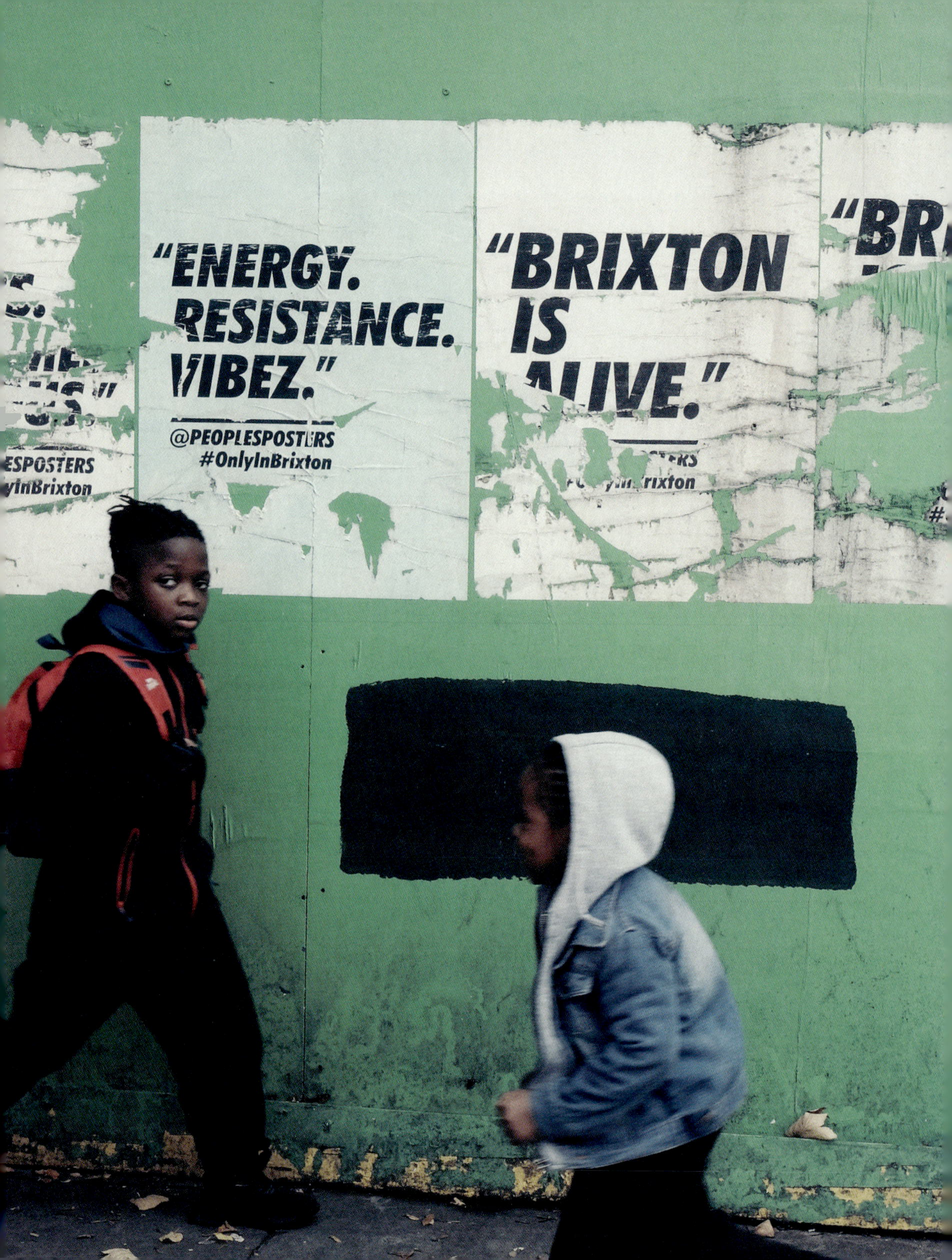
"ENERGY.
RESISTANCE.
VIBEZ."
@PEOPLESPOSTERS
#OnlyInBrixton
"BRIXTON
IS
ALIVE."
STERS
yinBrixton

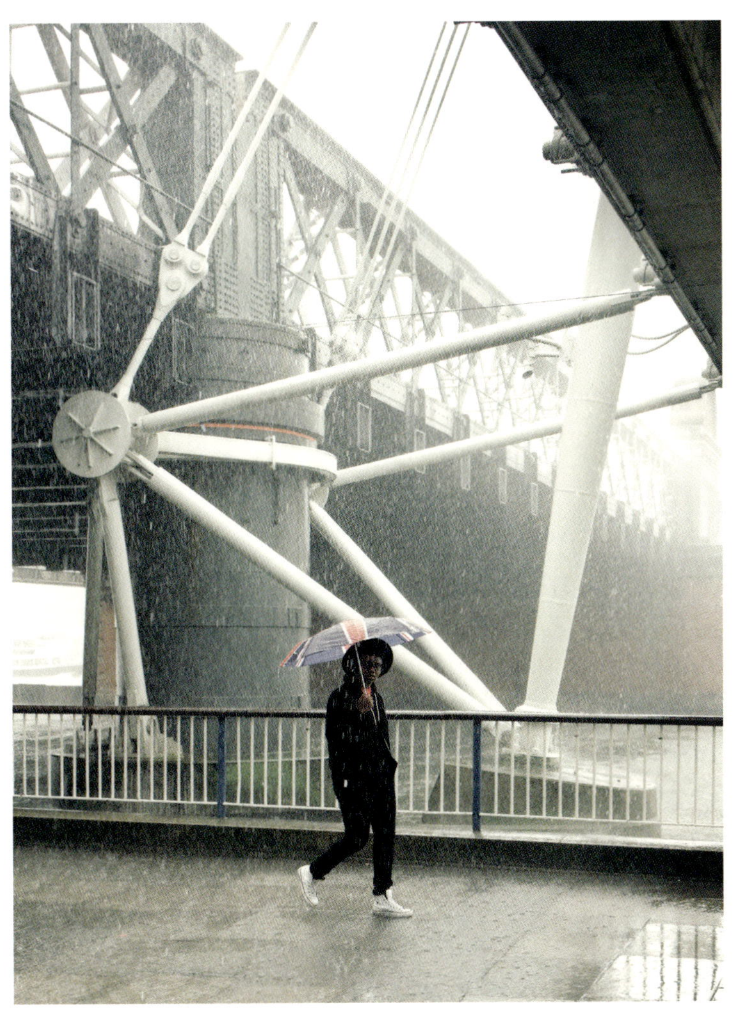

Nineties Soul Soundtracks Make Everywhere into Somewhere

Even stopping at the gas station is better when you're listening to Keith Sweat singing 'Make It Last Forever'. Johny is running the music for this hour-and-a-bit-long trip. We head out on the motorway to the sounds of D'Angelo's iconic Rhodes piano introducing 'Brown Sugar', and by now we are both singing the lyrics, and then *boom* Erykah Badu's 'Appletree' kicks in and the sky is full of grey, bruised cloud and the leaves of the trees look a deep moss-green and the vibe continues song after song. We talk a bit about European soul; I talk about Omar and Johny introduces me to Stephen Simmonds. The lane markings are passing us at speed, the trees look in through the windshield at us singing Jodeci's 'If You Believe in Love' at the top of our voices. Until the trees open out into the stone-grey buildings of Edinburgh with Zap Mama's 'Bandy Bandy' and we're there.

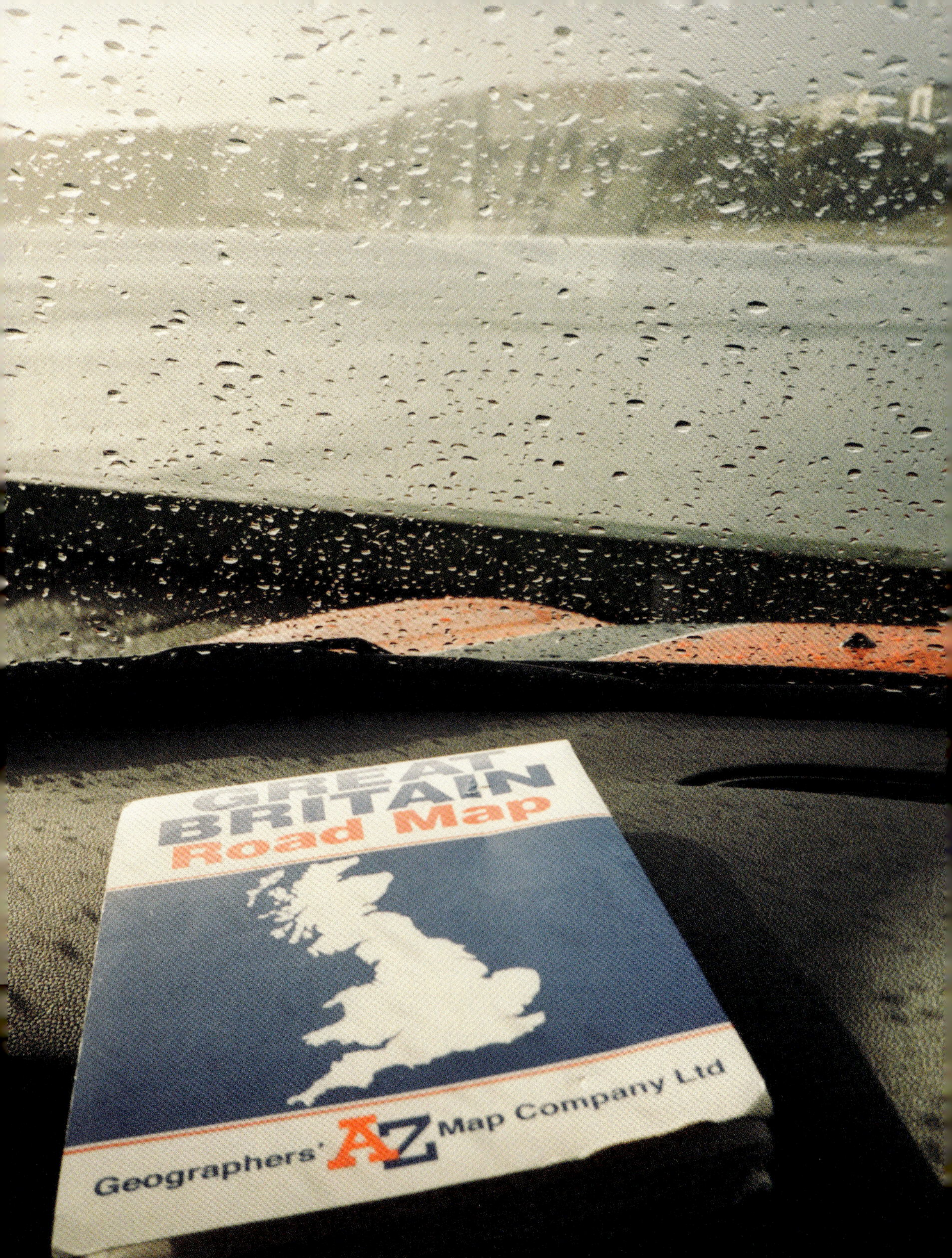

GREAT
BRITAIN
Road Map
Geographers' AZ Map Company Ltd

Deal

The long flat beach of Deal is a five-minute walk from Deal train
station, through a few cramped streets that widen into a vista
of sea, all watched over by beach houses of the quirkiest colours
and shapes, which are mostly empty.

And with thoughts of starting a family
where you can raise kids by the coast
I came out here for the ocean's beauty,
but even beauty has its compromises.

Historically speaking, writers seemed very critical towards
Deal. Dickens in his novel *Bleak House* called it 'as dull an
appearance as any place I ever did saw'; William Defoe wrote
in 1704 that 'The barbarous hated name of Deal should die'.
William Cobbett in 1823 called Deal 'The most villainous place'.

The seagulls here seem to have no fear of humans as they soar
and glide.

There is a sense of staring, here – or should I say glancing.
It's noticeable, but not malevolent, more surprised or curious.
I am told it's to be expected because only five Black men live
in Deal and perhaps they thought that I was to be the sixth.

The water, too brisk for even the hottest of summer days.

Deal Pier is a brutalist concrete structure that stretches out from the shore for three hundred and eleven metres. It feels like strolling into the water, walking on it.

The wind is so blustery that it would be wise to take off your cap because it willl soon be lost.

There are fish in these waters. There are fishermen in boats.

You can get genuine jerk chicken in the courtyard of The Astor Community Theatre from a Jamaican during the summer play season.

Living here is the new frontline of race relations. Everyone will know you because being Black here you can't hide. So you'll be confronting stereotypes, both positive and negative.

Even these smooth stones on the beach can twist your ankles into painful angles.

Deal beach is one of the Cinque Ports, which means it's calm sea. The Vikings landed here because it was easier to come onshore. Traffickers now take advantage of the calm waters but they don't come ashore. They drop the people off as far out as the pier and let them swim their way in. Daily, people wash up on the beach.

On the Underground

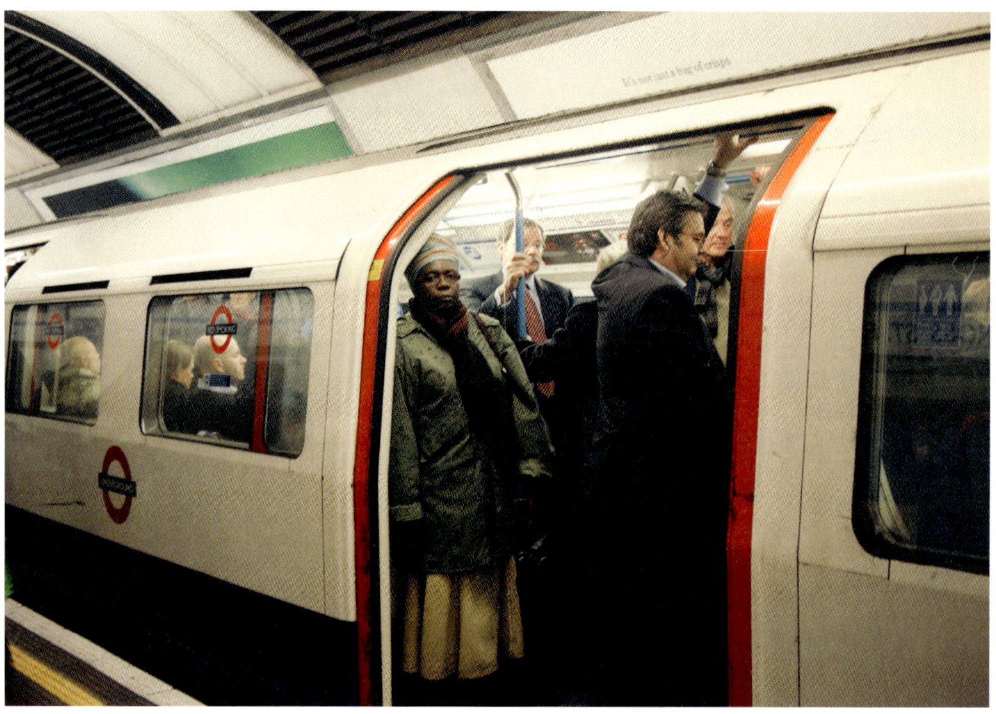

Some people will stand
the whole length of their journey
than sit with Black men.

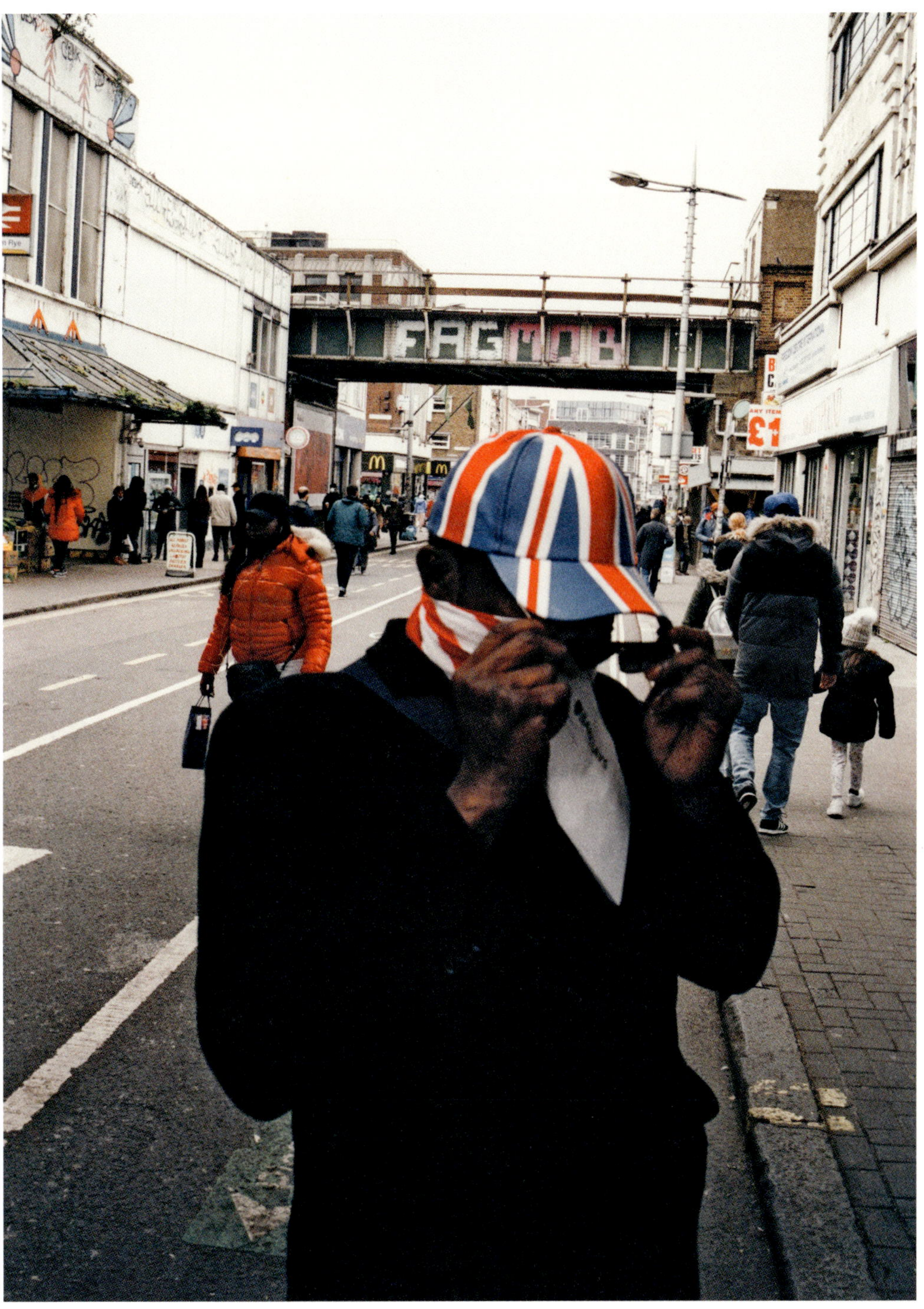

FAGMOB
ANY ITEM £1

Coast

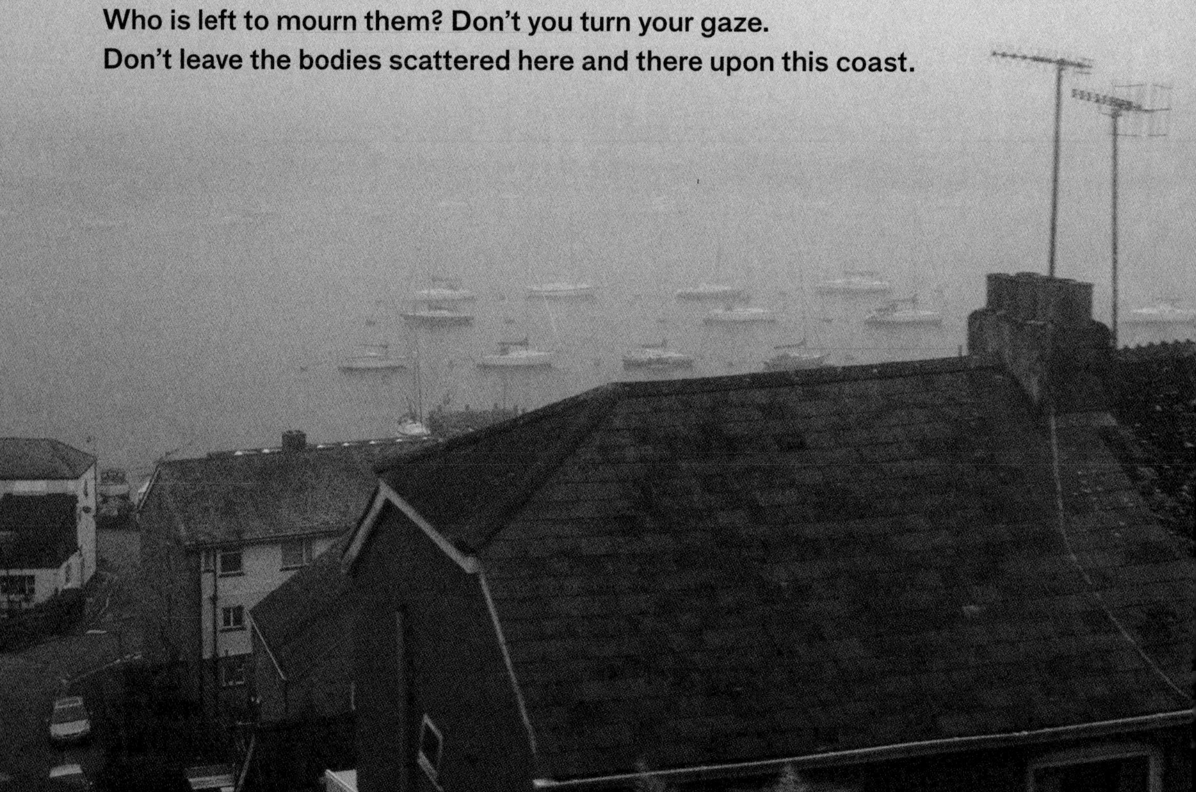

I stand here still, like a guardian on this coast,
I remain but sometimes life is hard here on this coast

This frosted bitter wind and me in too-thin clothes,
some things are still too much for me to bear upon this coast

I'm staring out to sea from the jagged pale white cliffs
hoping I don't fall, but I am scared up on this coast

I've nowhere to hide when the slow drifting tides come,
that's the time I feel in constant fear upon this coast

A sinking in my stomach, an upturned rubber dinghy,
those people were so close, they nearly made it to this coast

How quickly they were washed away, pulled below, with the tow.
Does anybody really care upon this coast?

Who is left to mourn them? Don't you turn your gaze.
Don't leave the bodies scattered here and there upon this coast.

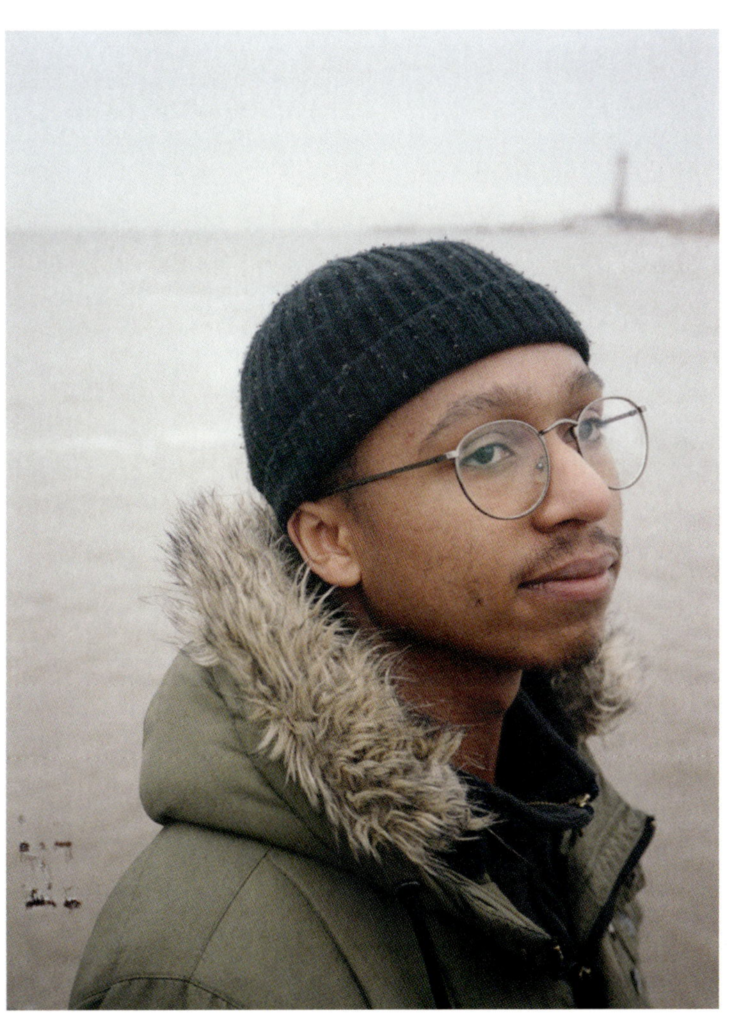

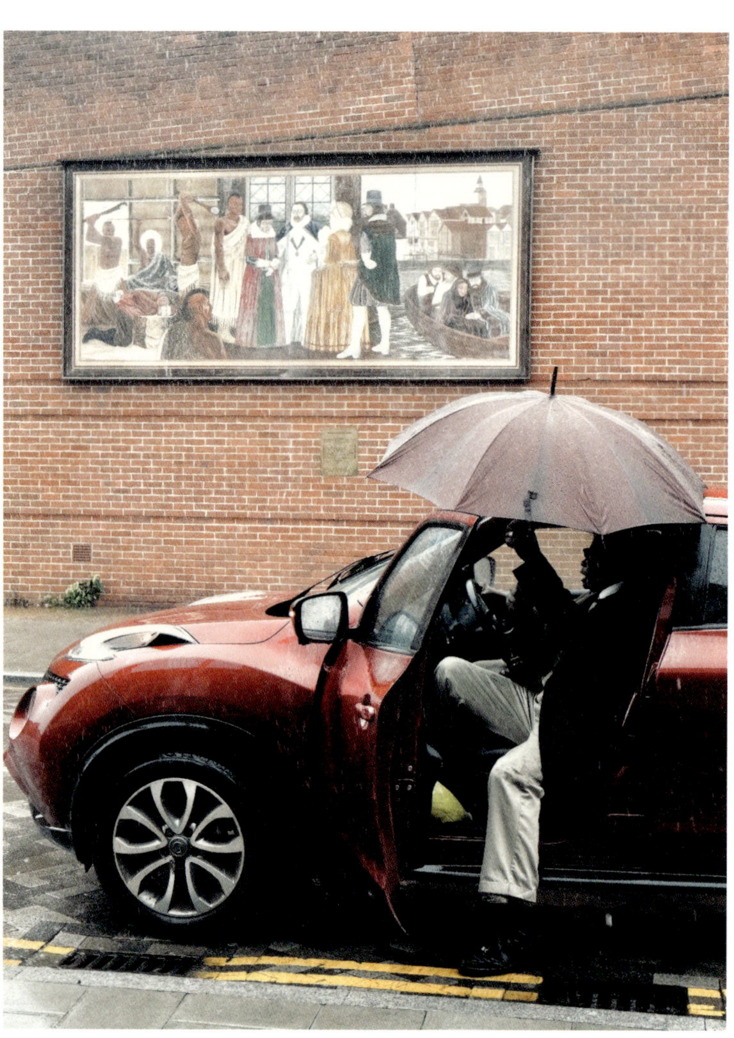

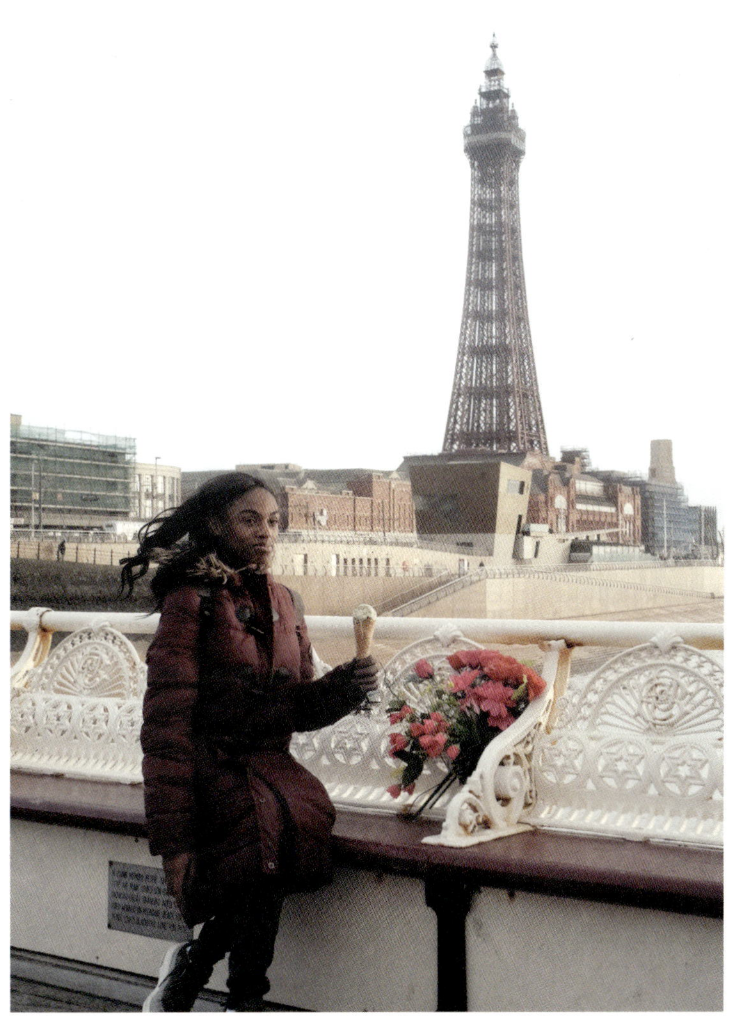

Flâneur

/flaˈnəː, French flanoeʀ/

Someone who walks without aim, looking for the energetic vibrations of a city, needing to walk, needing to get out of one's flat, out of one's own way, to feel some sunlight on your skin, even in winter when the sunlight is weak; to look for energy or fresh air; to clear one's head; to get some external energy into the body; a moving meditation; to commit only to what is discovered while walking with no prior plan; to observe a city on foot; to get lost; to feel re-inspired; to find oneself again. Usage: The photographer walked aimlessly, trying to find new images of the city like a flâneur.

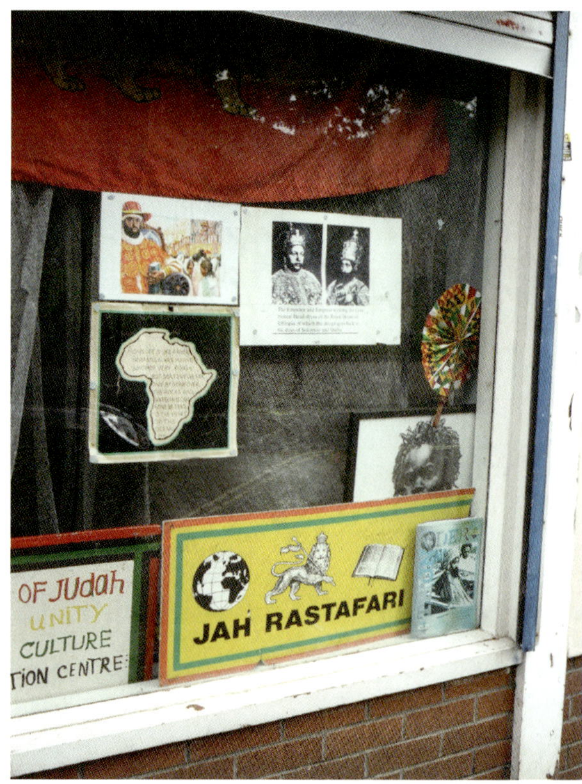

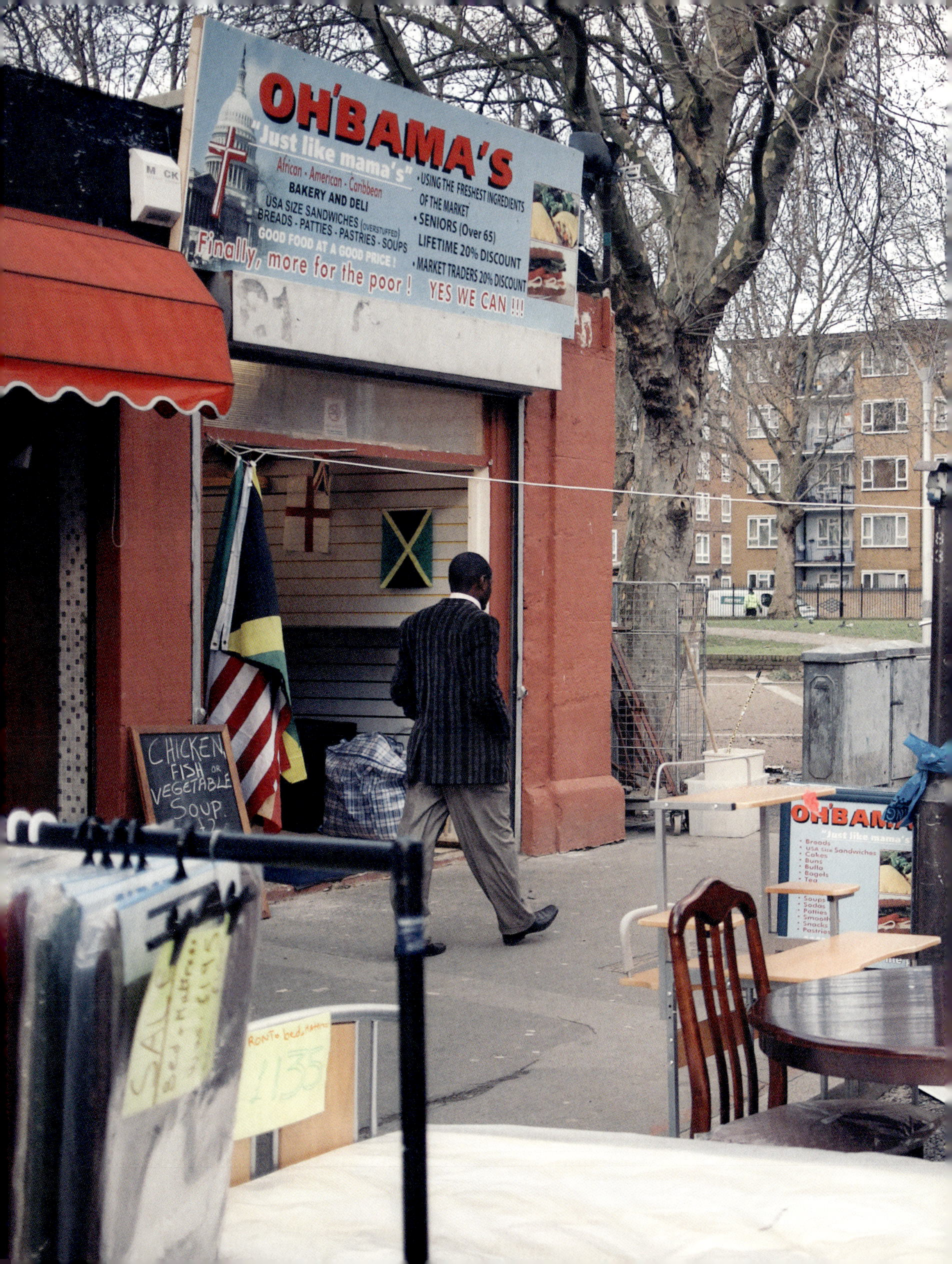
OH'BAMA'S
"Just like mama's"
African - American - Caribbean
BAKERY AND DELI
USA SIZE SANDWICHES (OVERSTUFFED)
BREADS - PATTIES - PASTRIES - SOUPS
GOOD FOOD AT A GOOD PRICE!
Finally, more for the poor !
• USING THE FRESHEST INGREDIENTS
OF THE MARKET
• SENIORS (Over 65)
LIFETIME 20% DISCOUNT
• MARKET TRADERS 20% DISCOUNT
YES WE CAN !!!
CHICKEN
FISH OR
VEGETABLE
SOUP
OH'BAMA'S
"Just like mama's"
• Breads
• USA Size Sandwiches
• Cakes
• Buns
• Bulla
• Bagels
• Tea
• Soups
• Sodas
• Patties
• Smoothie
• Snacks
• Pastries
SALE

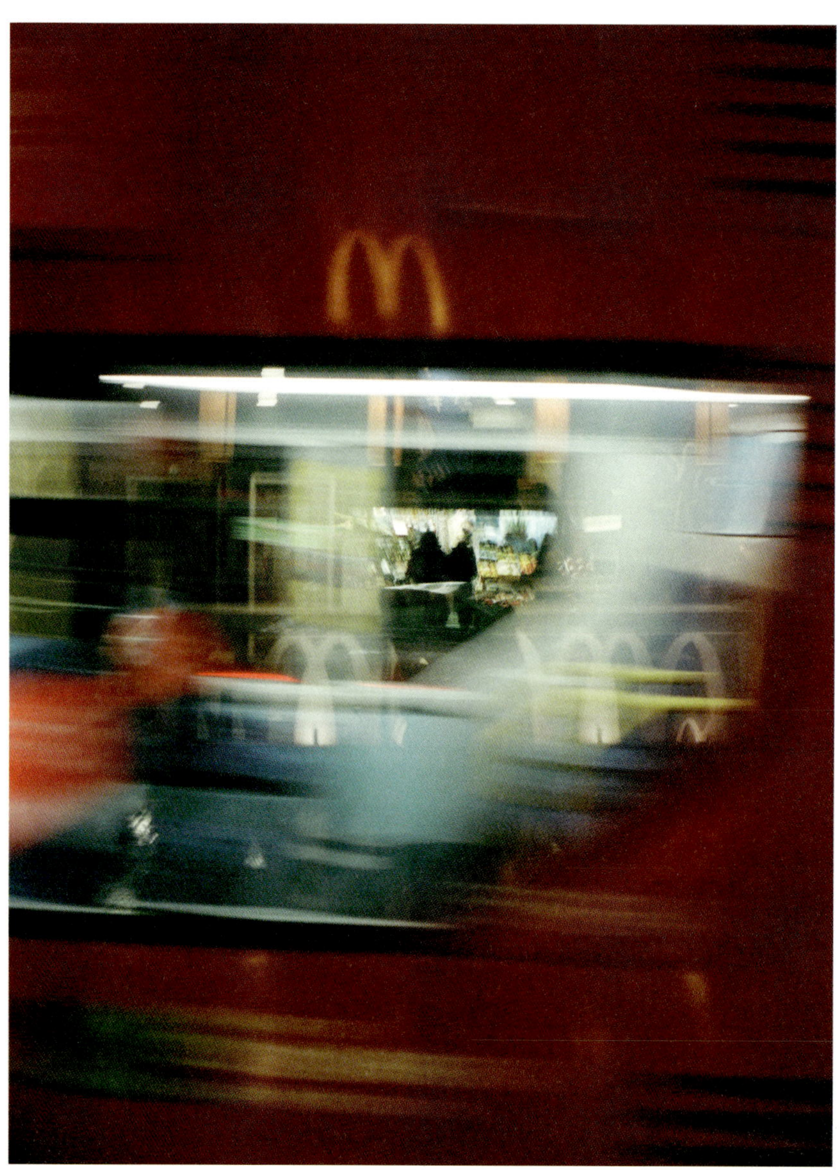

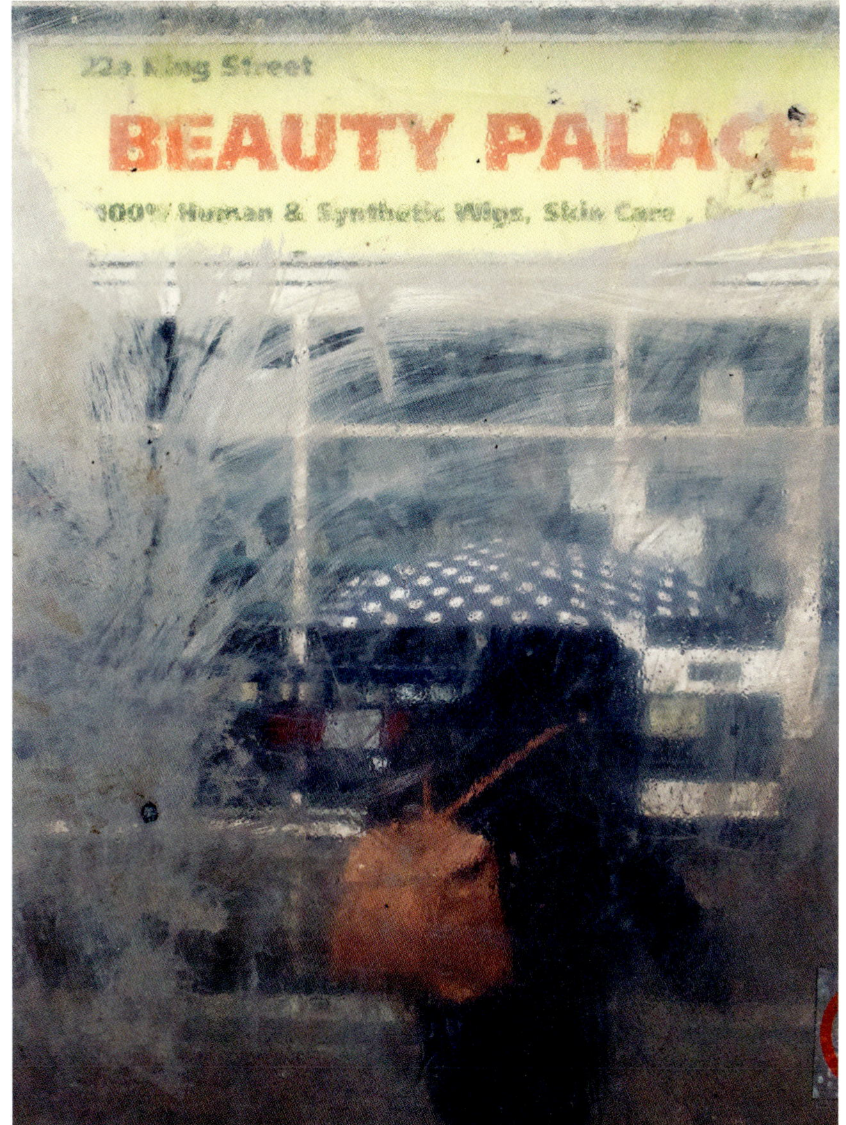
22a King Street
BEAUTY PALACE
100% Human & Synthetic Wigs, Skin Care

Loving Myself in a Land That Does Not Love Me

When hatred like seasons shifts from chill to bitter, I cocoon, I oil my scalp, I stretch, eat greens and grease my skin.

Each day will bring its battles so I must be prepared. Even now I'm barefoot, earthed in backyard grass, watching my griefs seep into soil to come rushing back as positive charge.

I set up camp, light vanilla-scented candles, listen for myself amongst my Stevie Wonder tapes, find the top range of my vocals in 'Another Star'.

I read myself in James Baldwin books, use my best pen in empty notebooks and write 'Do not test me today, I have no white flags.'

I remind myself their unhealthy minds must not infect mine. I read my Bible, I pray, I ask for forgiveness, for wisdom, for clarity, for insight and foresight. For what is ritual without renewed vision?

I paint my nails scarlet, hypnotise myself with splayed fingers, I nap.

See there's this hate that intrudes on my day, unannounced by way of memory or trigger; and without the washed and strengthened temple of my body, I could quickly and easily be diverted from my divinely inspired purpose.

I rest, I read, I soak and I sing. How far are the preparations for war from the rituals of peace?

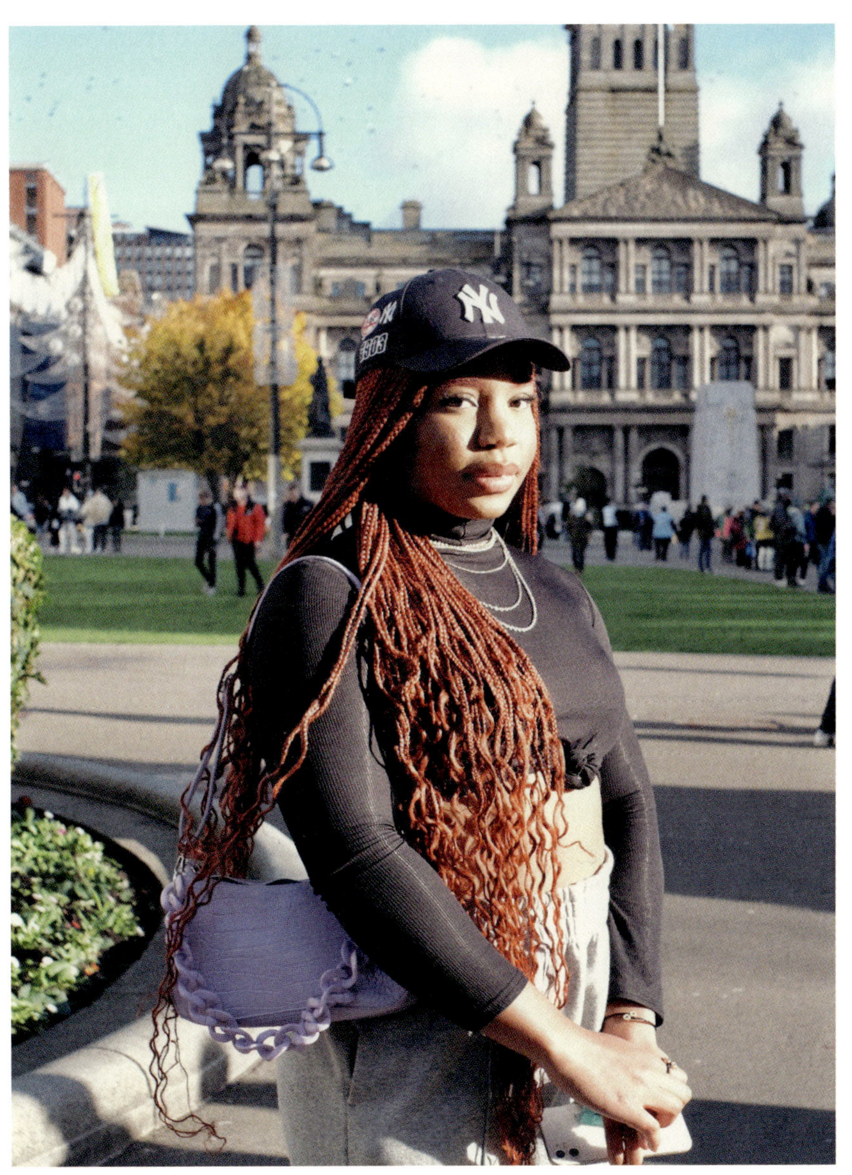

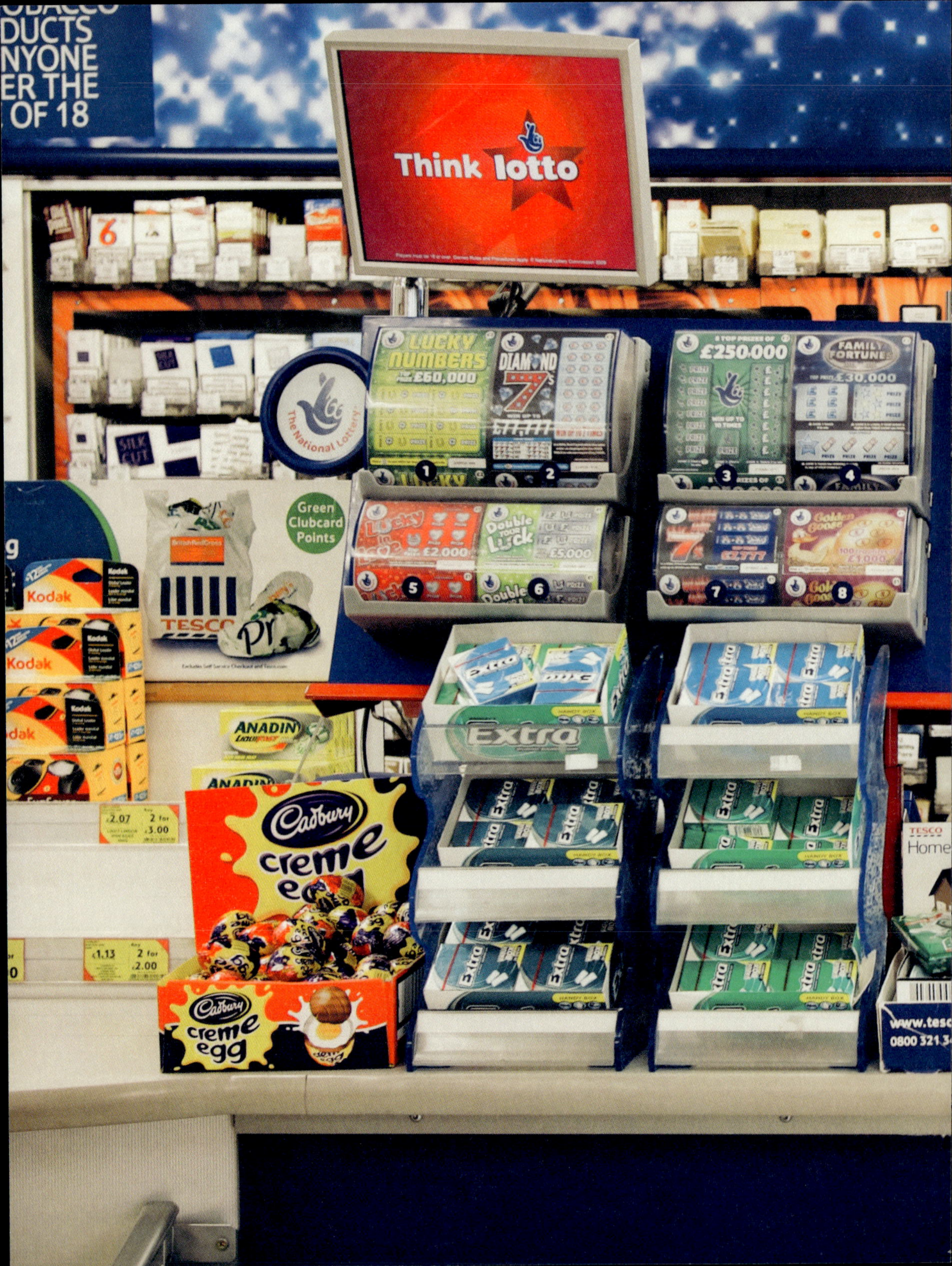
OBACCO
DUCTS
NYONE
ER THE
OF 18
Think lotto
Players must be 18 or over. Games Rules and Procedures apply. © National Lottery Commission 2009
The National Lottery
SILK CUT
6
LUCKY NUMBERS
WIN UP TO £60,000
DIAMOND 7's
WIN UP TO
1
2
5 TOP PRIZES OF
£250,000
FAMILY FORTUNE
TOP PRIZE £30,000
WIN UP TO 10 TIMES
PRIZE
PRIZE
PRIZE
PRIZE
PRIZE
PRIZE
PRIZE
3
4
Lucky in Love
£2,000
Double Your Luck
£5,000
Double
5
6
7's
WIN £7777
Golden Goose
100 PRIZES OF £1,000
7
8
Green Clubcard Points
British Red Cross
TESCO
Pr
Exclusive Self Service Checkout and Tesco.com
Kodak
Kodak
Kodak
Kodak
ANADIN
ANADIN
£2.07   2 for £3.00
£1.13   2 for £2.00
Cadbury creme egg
Cadbury creme egg
Extra
HANDY BOX
Extra
Extra
Extra
Extra
HANDY BOX
Extra
HANDY BOX
Extra
Extra
Extra
HANDY BOX
TESCO Home
www.tesco
0800 321 3

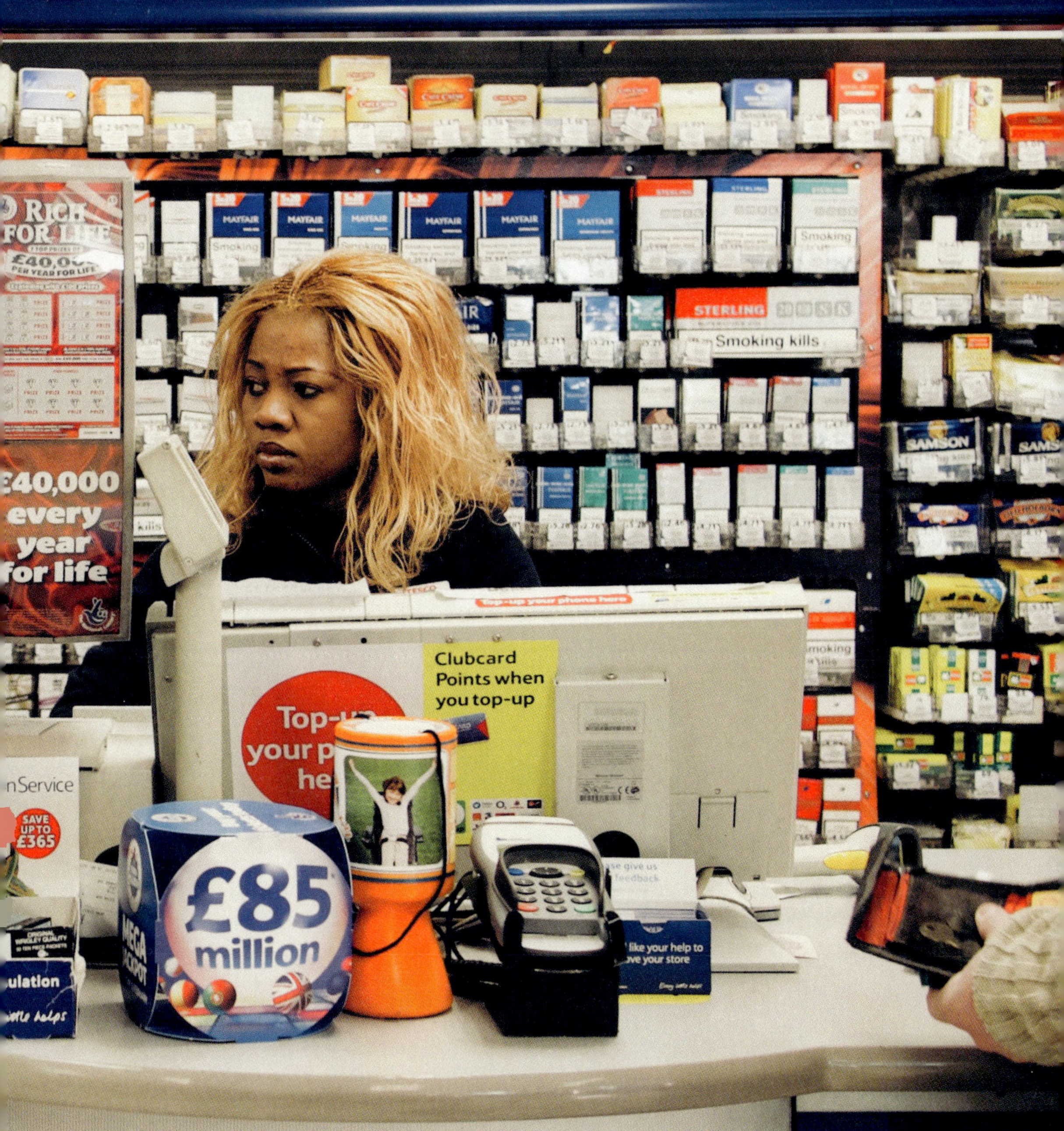
TOBA
RICH
FOR LIFE
£40,000
PER YEAR FOR LIFE
£40,000
every
year
for life
STERLING
Smoking kills
SAMSON
Clubcard
Points when
you top-up
Top-up
your p
he
Top-up your phone here
MEGA JACKPOT
£85
million
SAVE
UP TO
£365
Service
Every little helps
like your help to
ve your store

Race Report

A sampled/remixed poem from Paragraphs 3 to 5 on
page 8 of the Commission of Race and Ethnic Disparity
which state that very few impediments to ethnic minorities
are related to race.

To take the reality
the take to reality
of racial fairness seriously
fairness seriously. Seriously?
When explicitly examined
explicitly
is that too often, too too often
the system too often
is deliberately rigged deliberately.
Simply put, simply, dis/parities
do simply, implicitly and simply exist
in institutional system systemic
understanding of the reality system
of reality
of racism.
The real real force
of real real microaggressions
and deep deep-seated obstacles
for deep ethnic minorities and the rest
and rest
in the rest of Europe
and the rest
of the world. And rest.

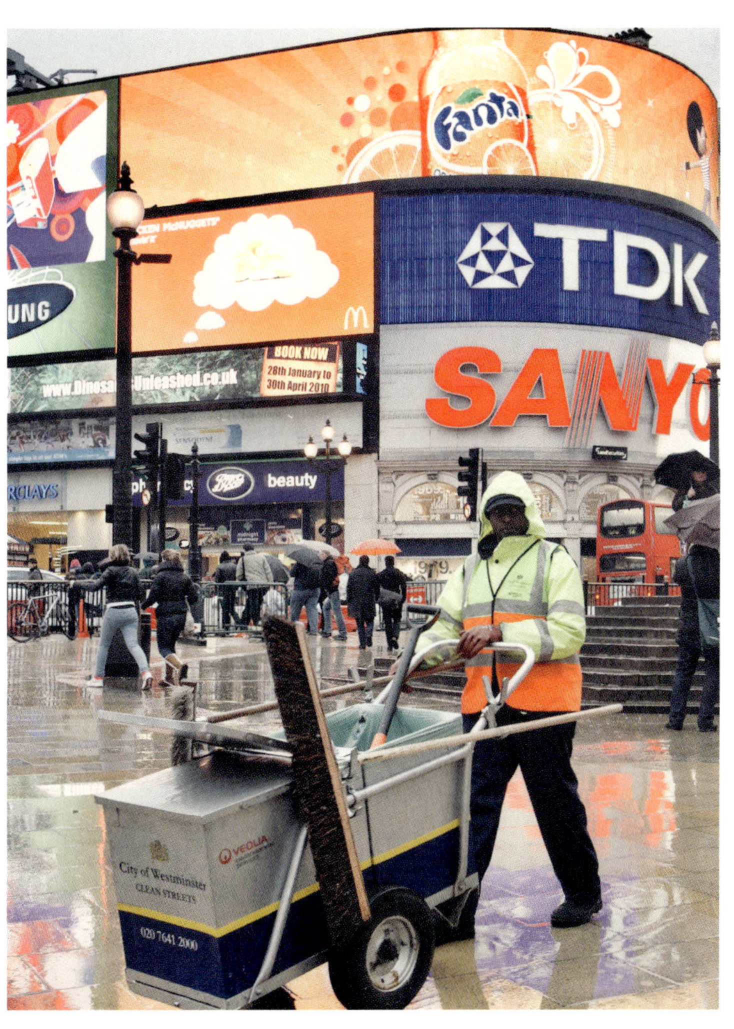

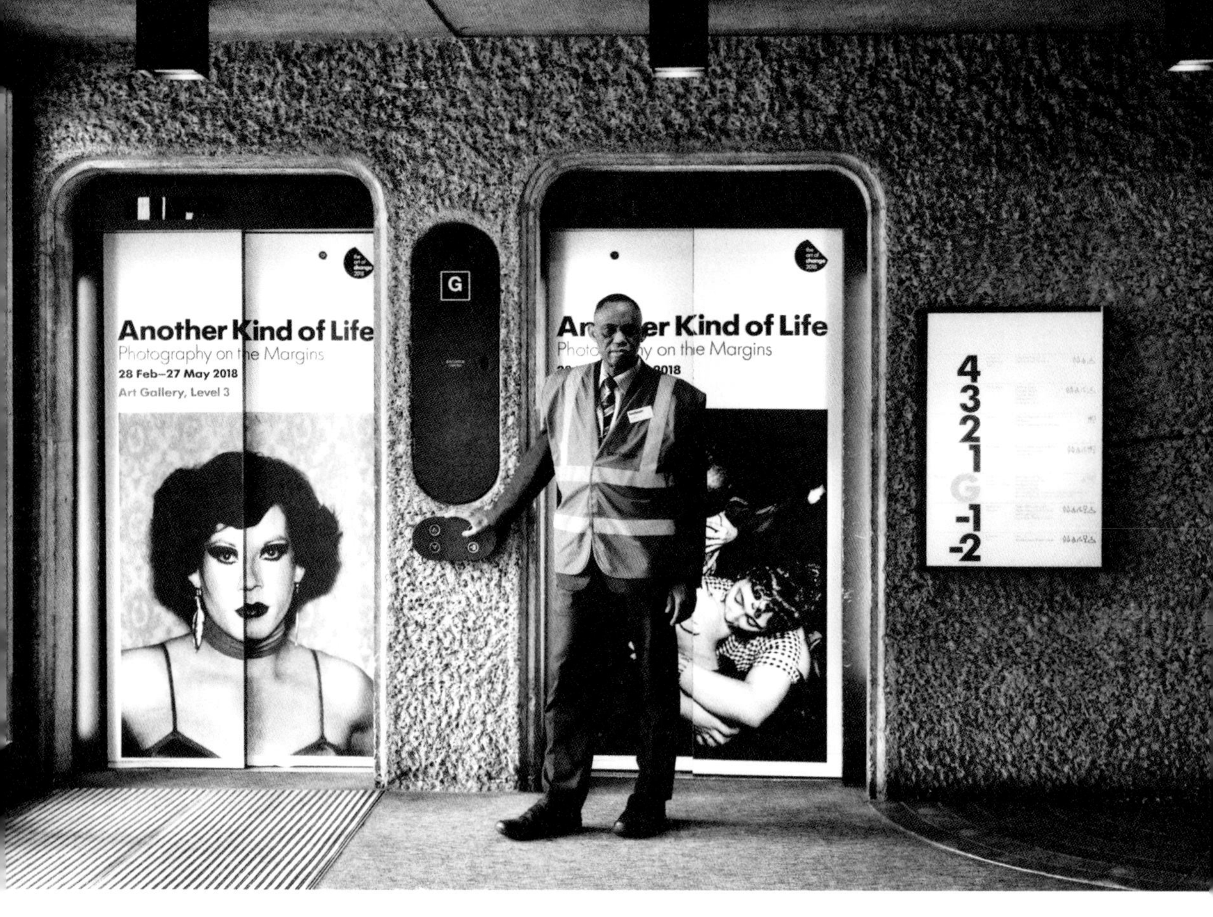
G
Another Kind of Life
Photography on the Margins
28 Feb—27 May 2018
Art Gallery, Level 3
Another Kind of Life
Photography on the Margins
2018
4
3
2
1
G
-1
-2

Benin Security Guard at the V&A

When the last visitor has left. When the chefs from the restaurant have given him some dinner in a takeaway tray to eat later. When the cleaners have donned their thick winter coats and black and purple berets. When all the display screens have been turned off, and the museum is dark and still, the security guard heads for the African artefacts room. The first thing he goes for is the Benin crown. It fits him perfectly, like it was made for his head, the rose gold against his dark brown skin. Next he picks up the wooden armband denoting a South African leader, sliding it over his security shirt. Then he takes the indigo adire cloth and wraps it around his waist and stands in front of the autumn colours of the Wissa Wassef Egyptian tapestry, pulls out his phone and takes a selfie. Tomorrow he'll be back for another shift, pulling strands of ancient African culture into a moment. It's the only thing he looks forward to.

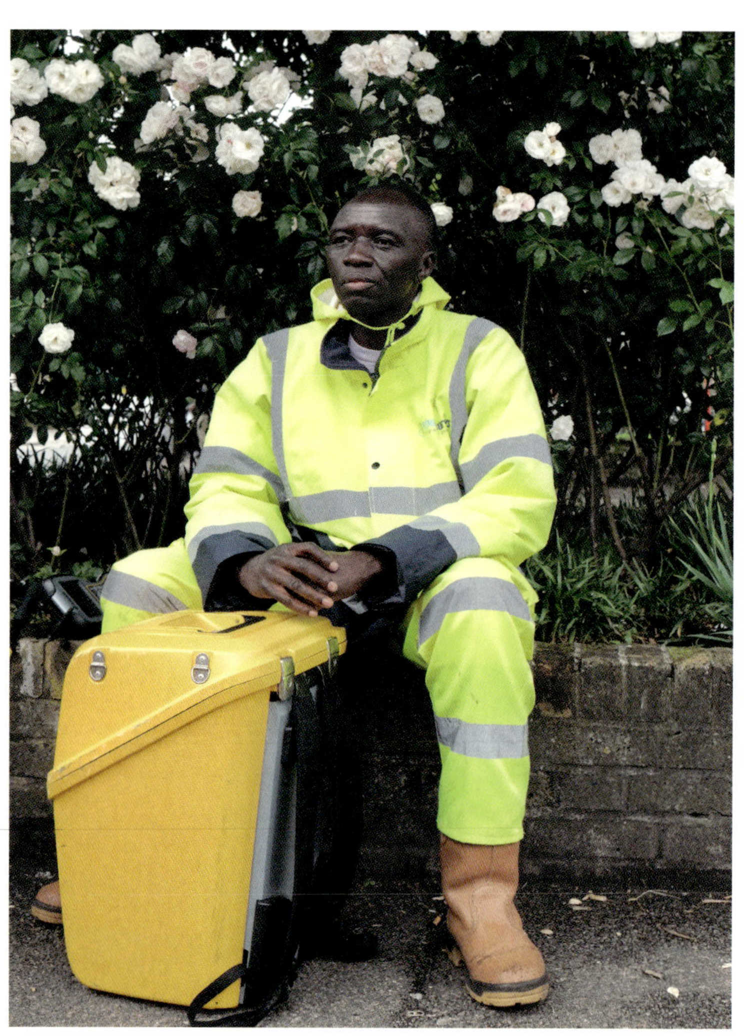

Self Portrait as King Louis XV of France

The assignment was to choose a pose from royal paintings. To adopt the posture of royalty or gentry, a pose that assigned status. To have the old and new collide, to start a South London conversation with aristocracy. So there I am, flipping through the picturebooks of paintings by van Dyck, Frans Hals and Gainsborough. Gazing at these moments caught in dried ink, oil and gouache. Poses from the French Rococo period, all pastel pinks and curvy lines. Their eyes looked straight through history at my Black face. Caravaggio's light pulled across my skin. The body's language of power, the character of status. All pomp and flattery, depictions of strength and denials of death against backgrounds of shadow, light and dust, until I came across the steel stare and pursed lips of a French king. I am Louis XV, father of ten children, well-beloved king of France from Versailles.

A First World War West Indian Soldier has doubts on the Front Line

Having answered the call to protect Queen and Country, he realised that the job was to clean up the shit of white soldiers and dig ditches on the front line. He realised that he was sacrificial. He could hear bombs exploding around him as he built bunkers to protect the white soldiers, the same ones who would gladly spit on him and call him *wog* and *nigger*. As the bombs dropped he began to see visions of children and grandchildren in the future. He could see himself in their faces, he could see their strange clothes. Babies being born, growing up and getting married. The plume and dust of every bomb brought visions of his future generations. Births, baptisms, ceremonies going on and on. He saw one hundred years of his future generations dodging machine gunfire and grenades, running towards his ditch, their faces grimacing, in fear of their lives. Children, men and women all scrambling towards him. *Come on, run!* he shouted to them. Bullets whistled past his ears and made him take refuge in the ditch he had dug. As he crouched down he realised that he had erred, volunteering for those who hate him to his core. He knew that his enlisting was a grave, grave mistake.

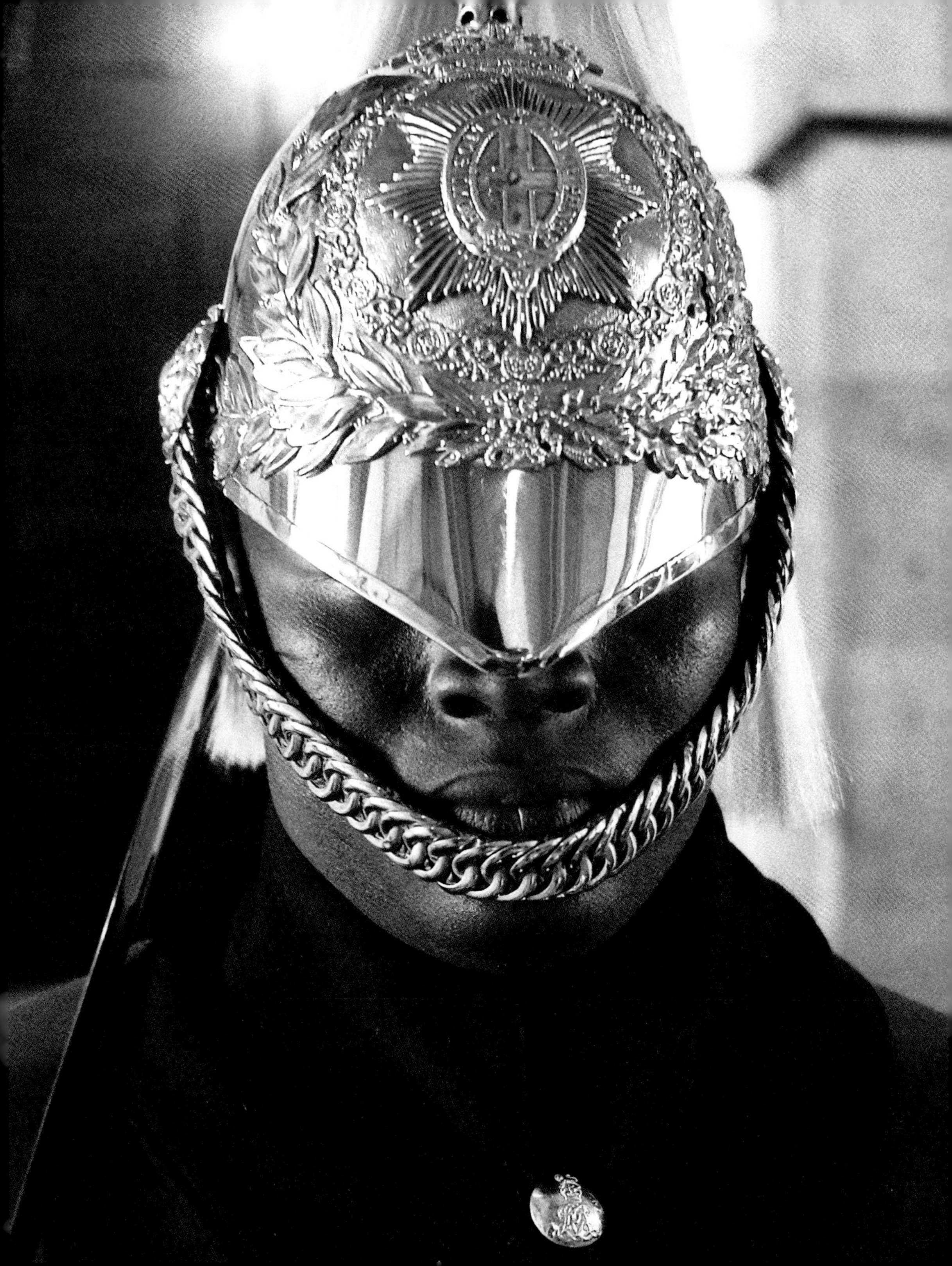

Soundtrack

From the bass and the drum
the snap and the snare
out car windows into the air
it's the sound of bass in Bristol
as they smash storefronts to crystals.
Hear the marching boots
and the shouting youths
saying Kill the Bill
we'll keep fighting till
you give us back our freedoms.
Hear the police sirens screaming
see the man-sized bins on fire
and the flames keep leaping higher.
Yet the basslines still keep bubbling
and the policemen are huddling
against a rain of fire and stones
and the crowd take back control
to pull a racist statue down
till the racist statue drown in the harbour
basslines thumping harder
and they have no fear.
Hear the snap and the snare
out car windows into the air
it's a dub soundtrack in Bristol
as they smash storefronts to crystals.

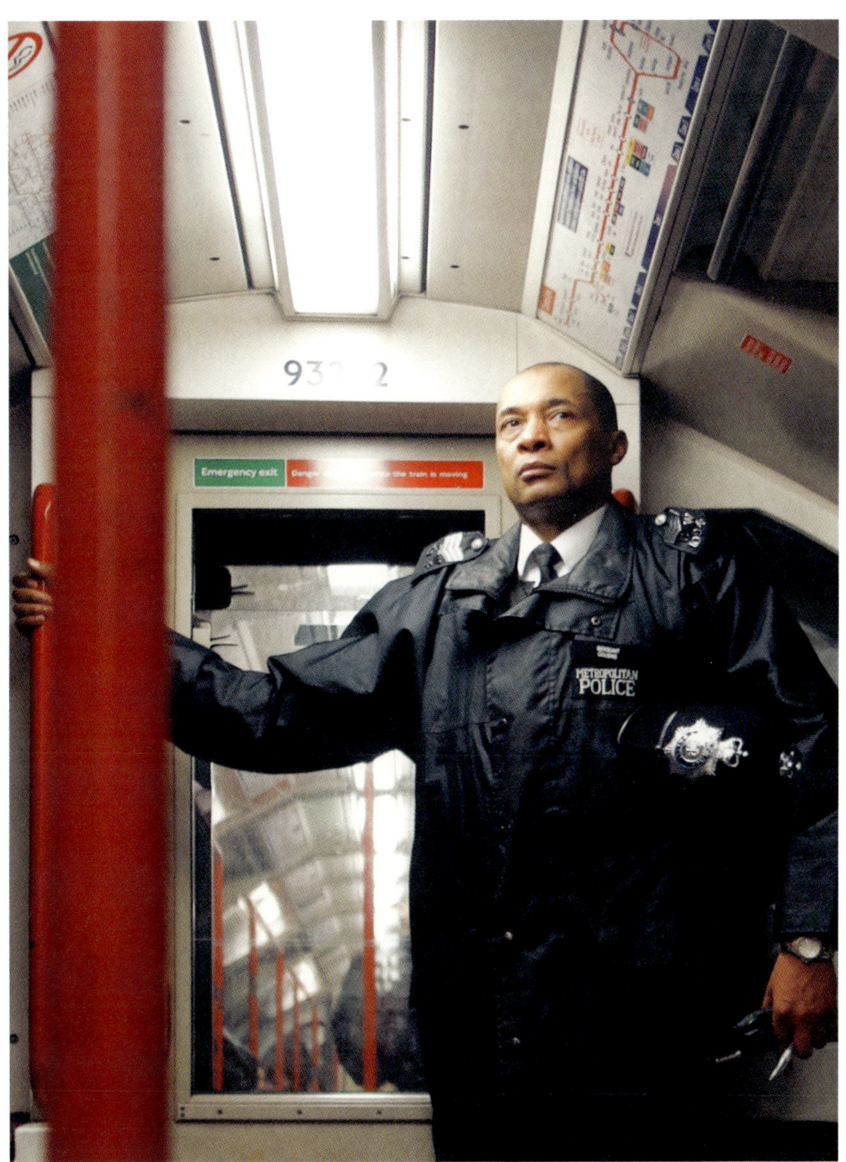
93 2
Emergency exit
Danger the train is moving
METROPOLITAN
POLICE

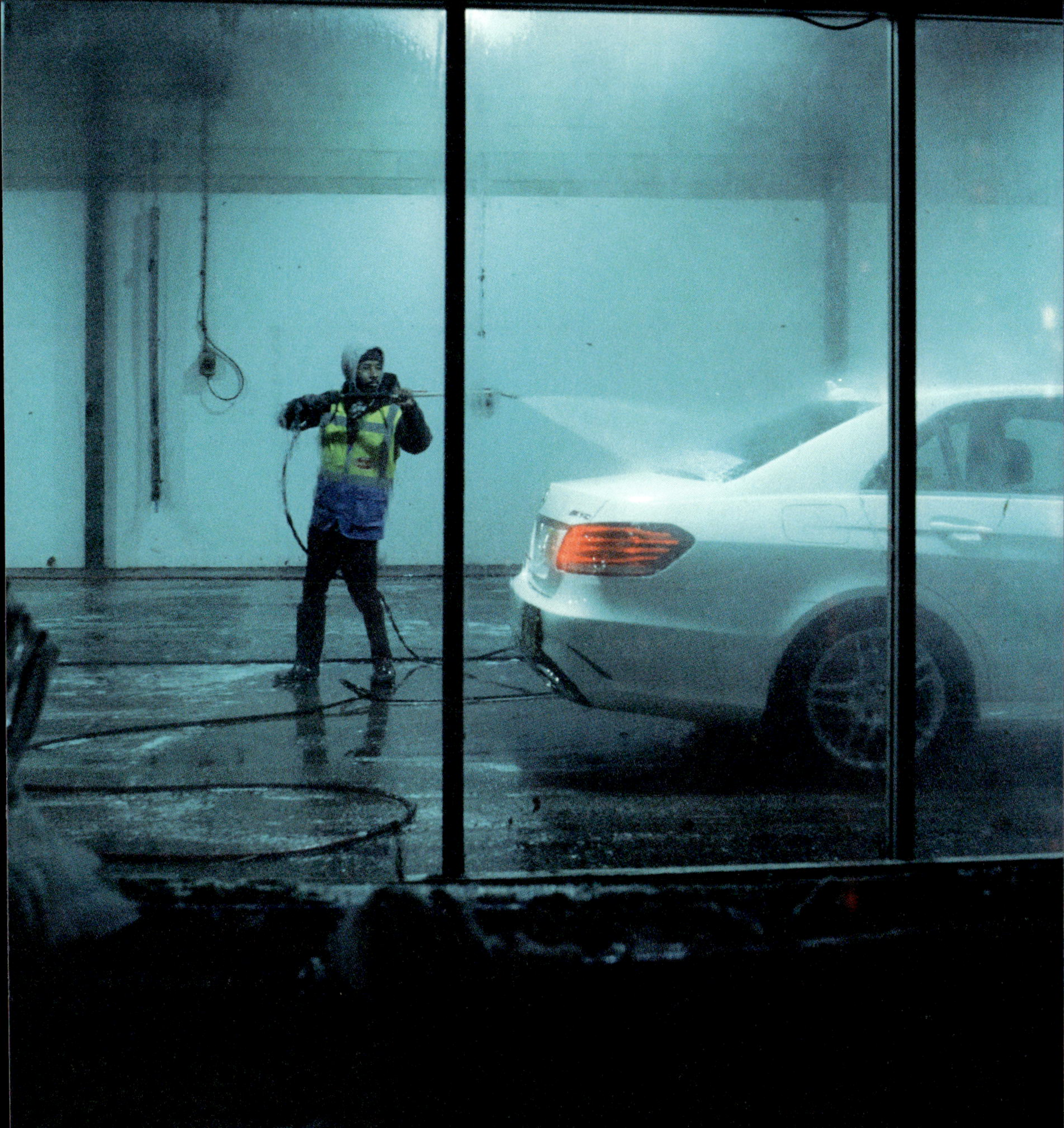

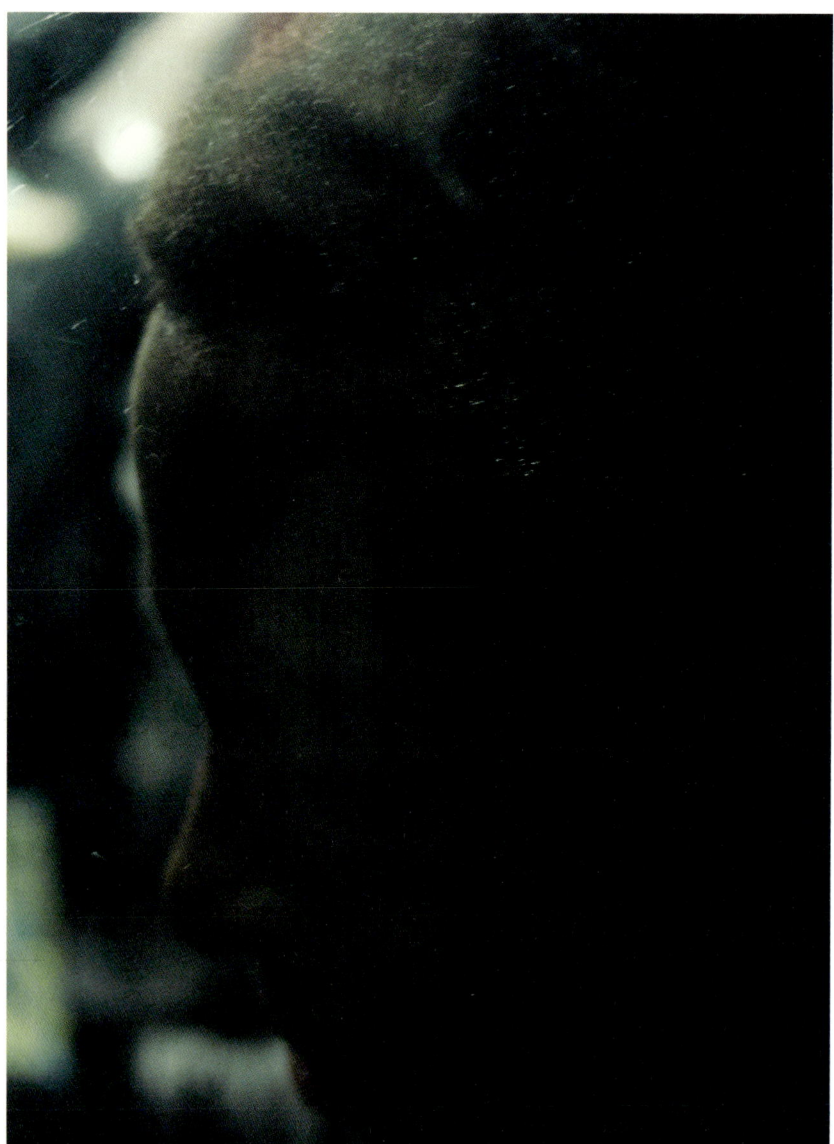

Interview

The Black man had an interview. He grabbed a pair of glasses to look less threatening. He felt silly (there was nothing wrong with his eyes). He thought perhaps a tweed jacket, something more traditional. No, no jewellery. He wouldn't have bothered, but he needed this job. A tie might have been overdoing it, he thought, as he shaved off his beard. He had been growing out his fade for weeks now, because he knew this was coming up. A short afro was the best that he could do. He was trying to present himself in a way that was unthreatening (though he knew that there was no threat there). He arrived at the building and gave his name to security, and they looked through the interviewee list. They said he wasn't on it. He asked them to look again. They refused. He asked what the problem was and to check again in case they missed it. They said that they won't be doing that. Time was passing. He was going to be late for his interview slot. There was a certain amount of anxiety in his tone. The security guard told him to lower his voice. He lowered his voice and he could see another guard near the wall talking into his radio. They asked him to leave the premises. He needed this job. He refused to leave, and asked again that they call his contact, that this could be a simple mistake. Three guards grabbed him from behind; they tore his tweed jacket, his fake glasses fell to the floor and cracked. Just then someone called out his name to see if he had arrived for the interview. He shouted *That's me*, and they put him down without an apology. He walked upstairs with his cracked glasses, the sleeve of his tweed jacket in his hand. The top three buttons of his shirt had popped off, his pristine afro seemed ruffled, and he sat and tried to answer the questions as best he could, trying to give them the impression that he'd be pleasant to work with.

Boyhood Fading

Now your child eyes dim,
and you're about men's business
on serpentine roads

and discreet alleys.
We still remember your soft
hands without callus,

and we can't forget
(regardless of squared shoulders)
the boy, in the man,

fading.

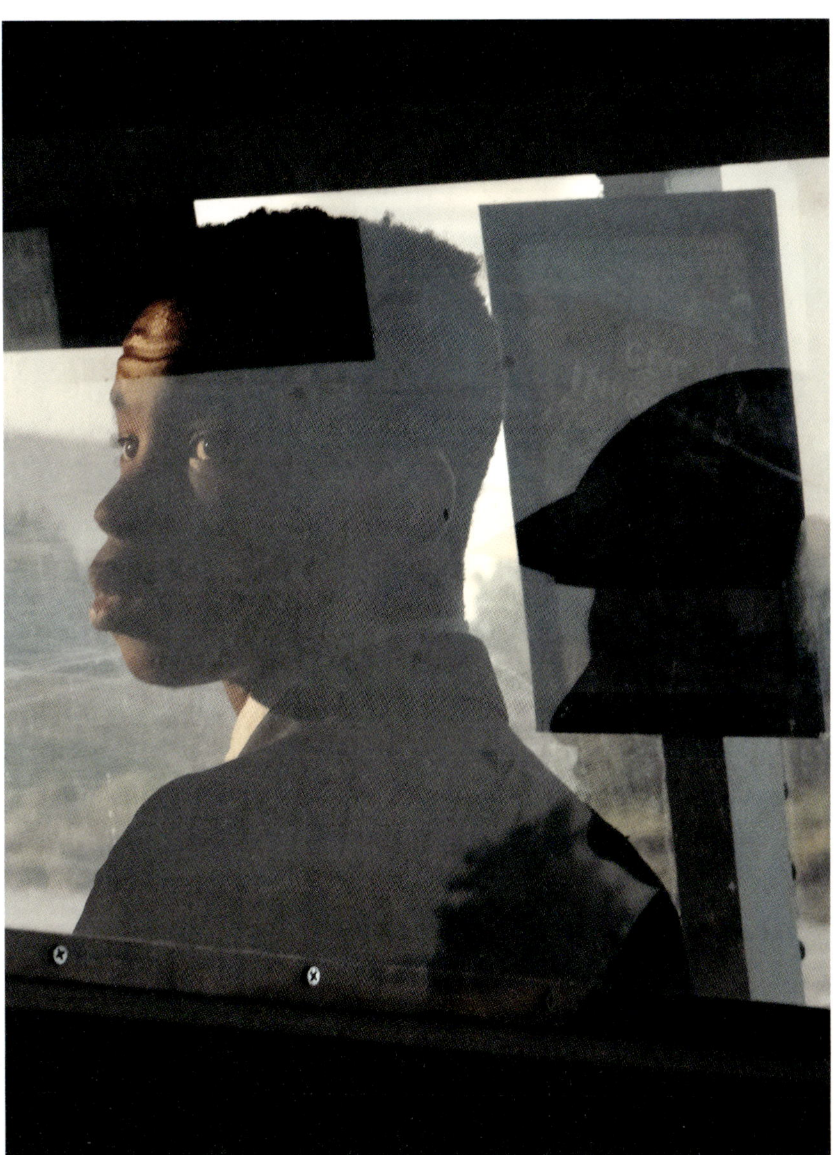

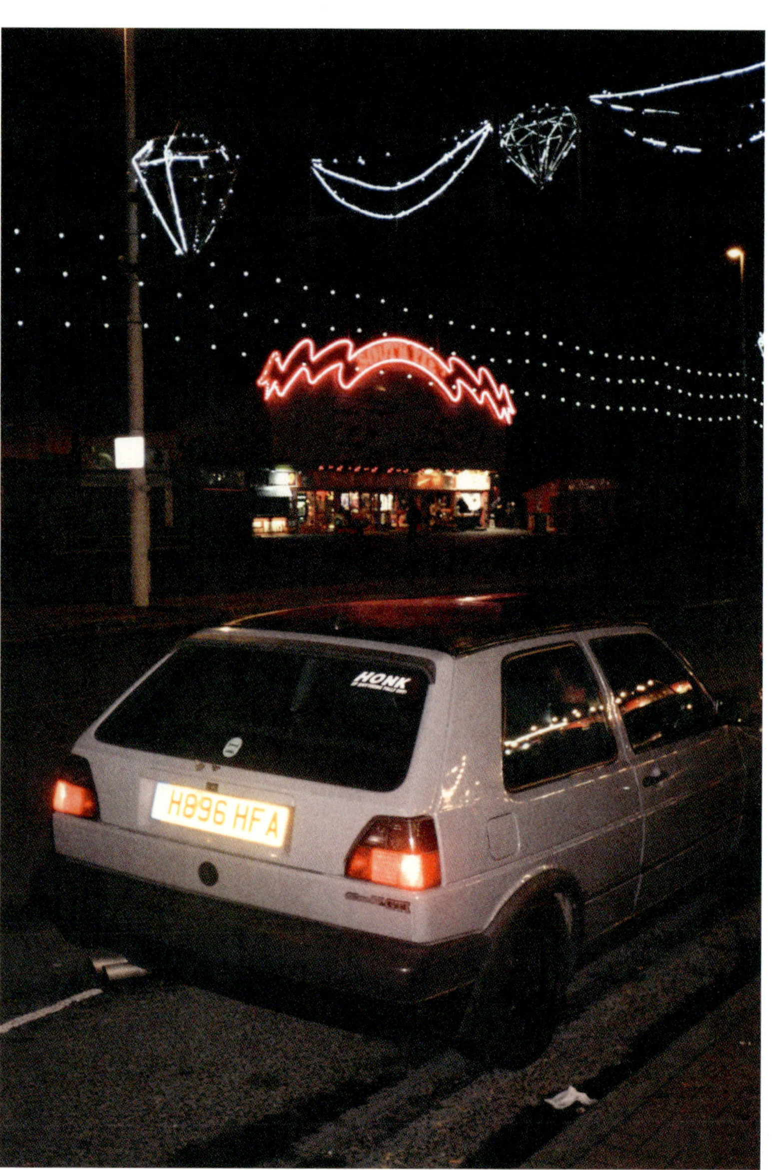

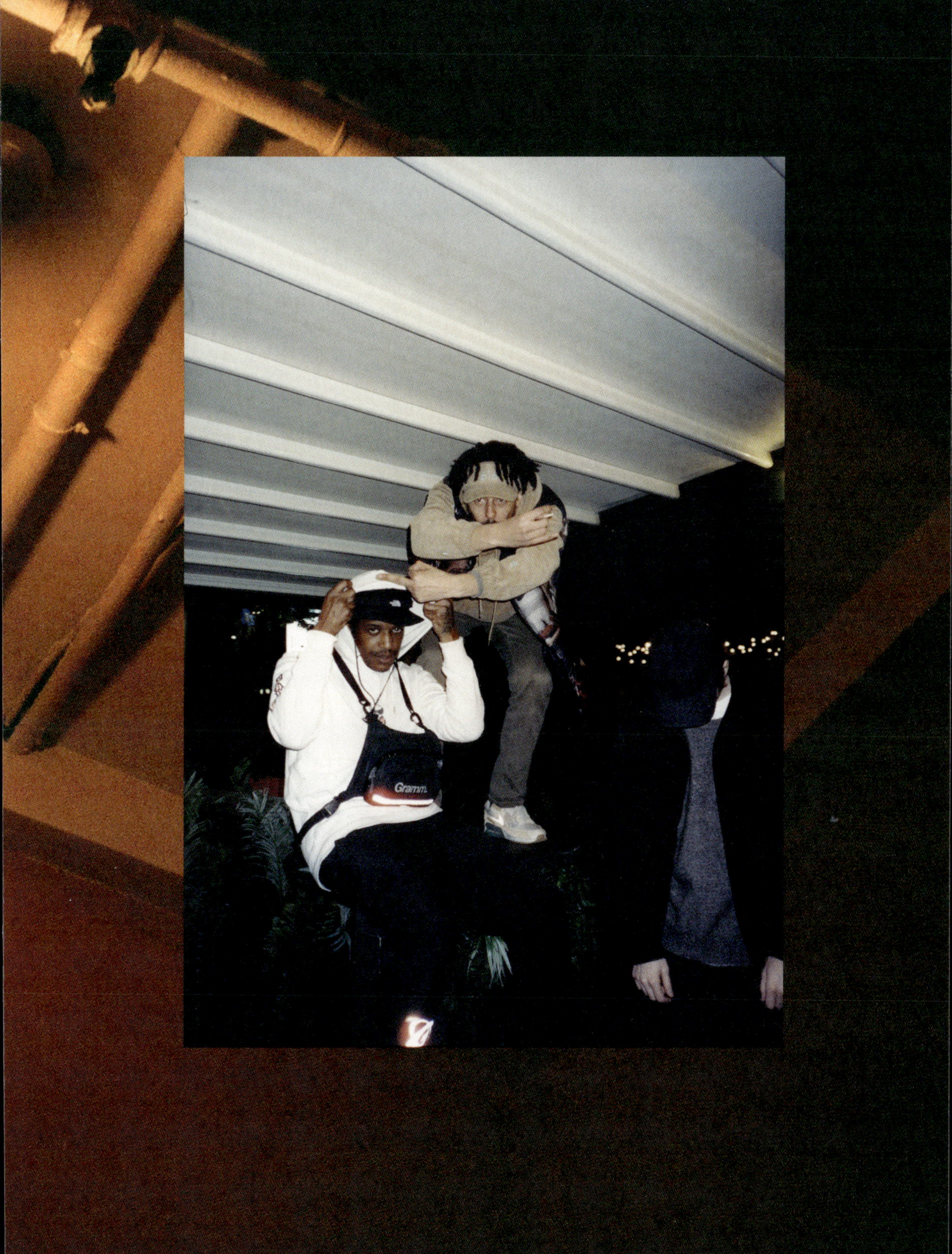

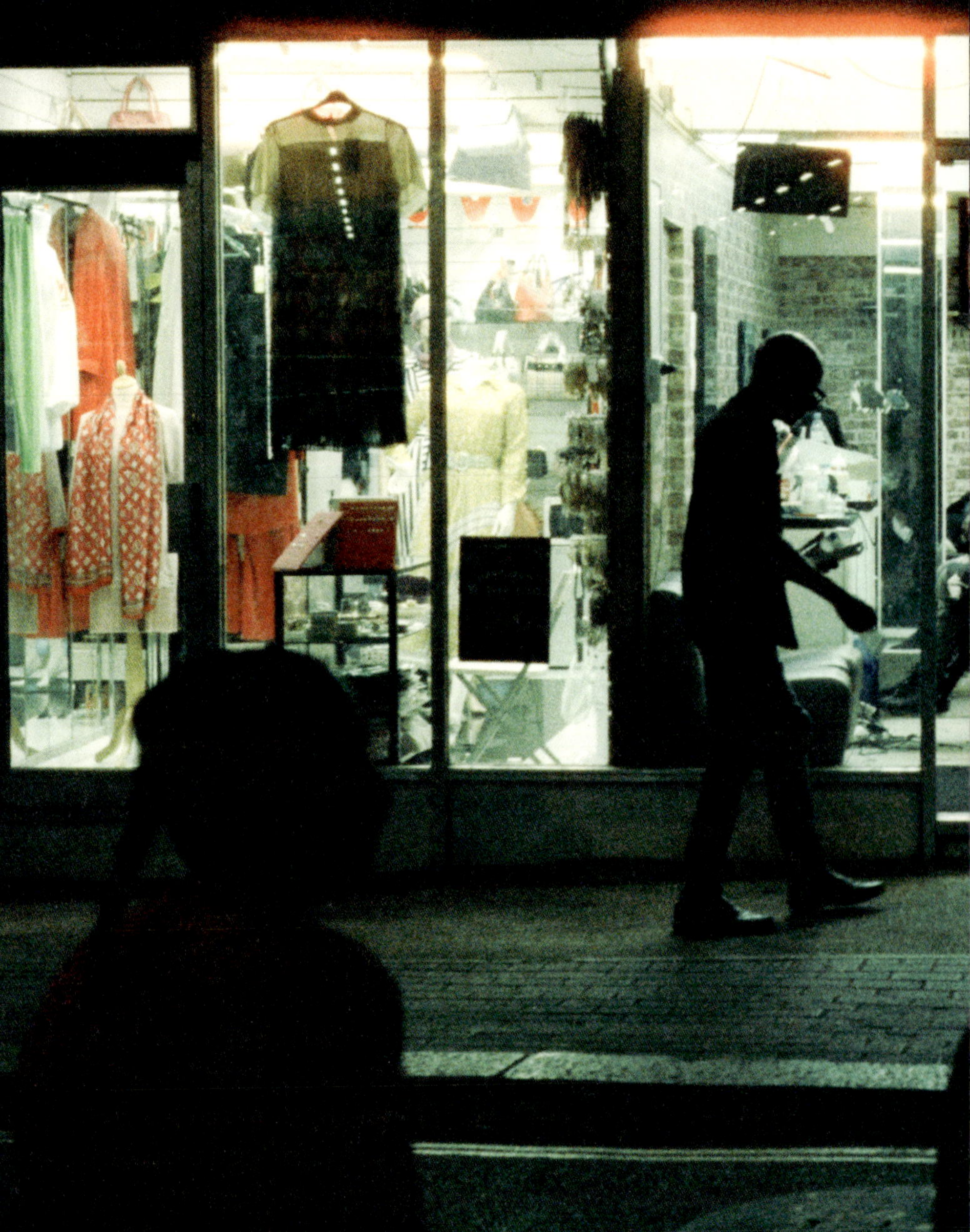

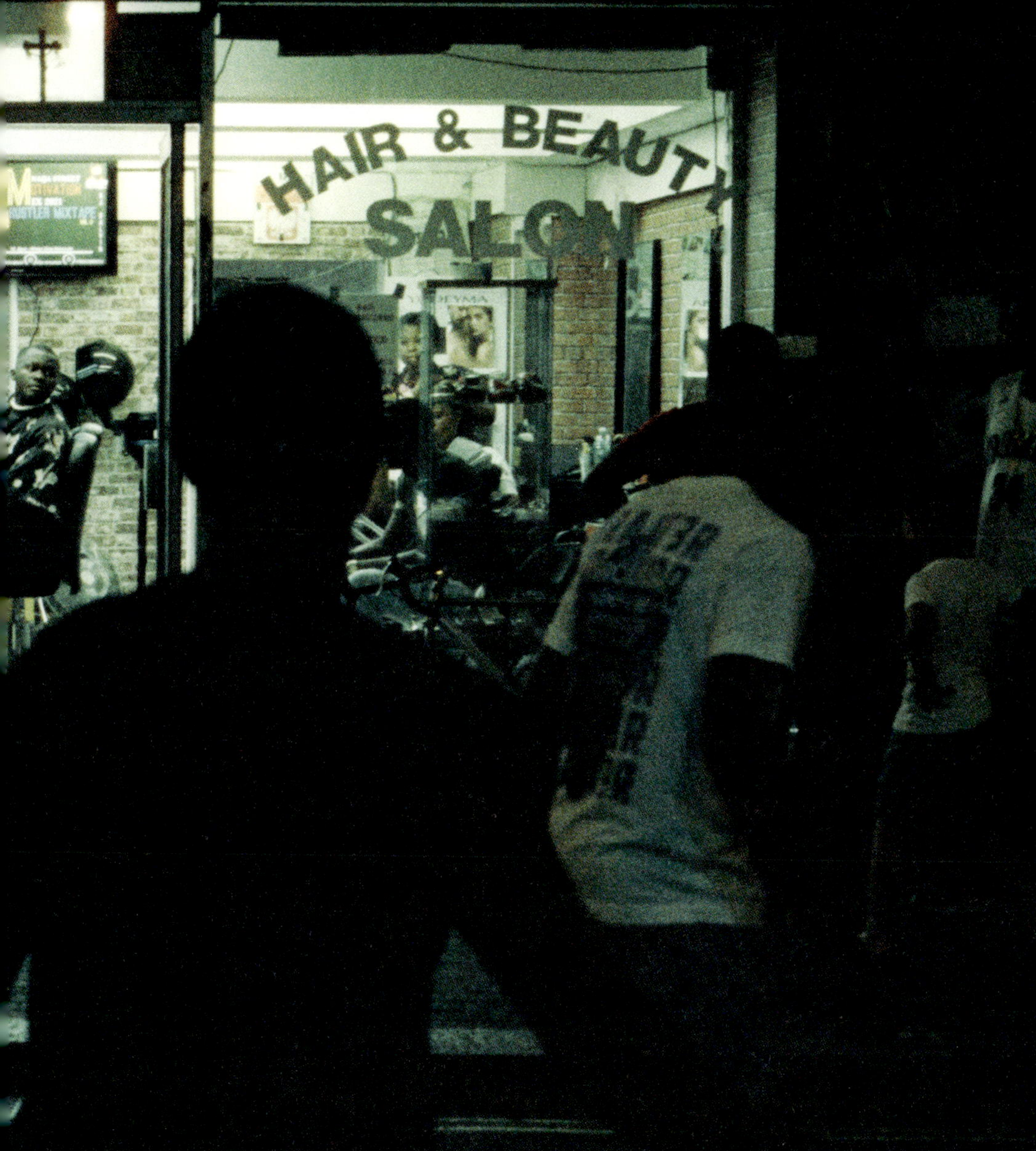
TYLIST
UTY
HAIR & BEAUTY
SALON

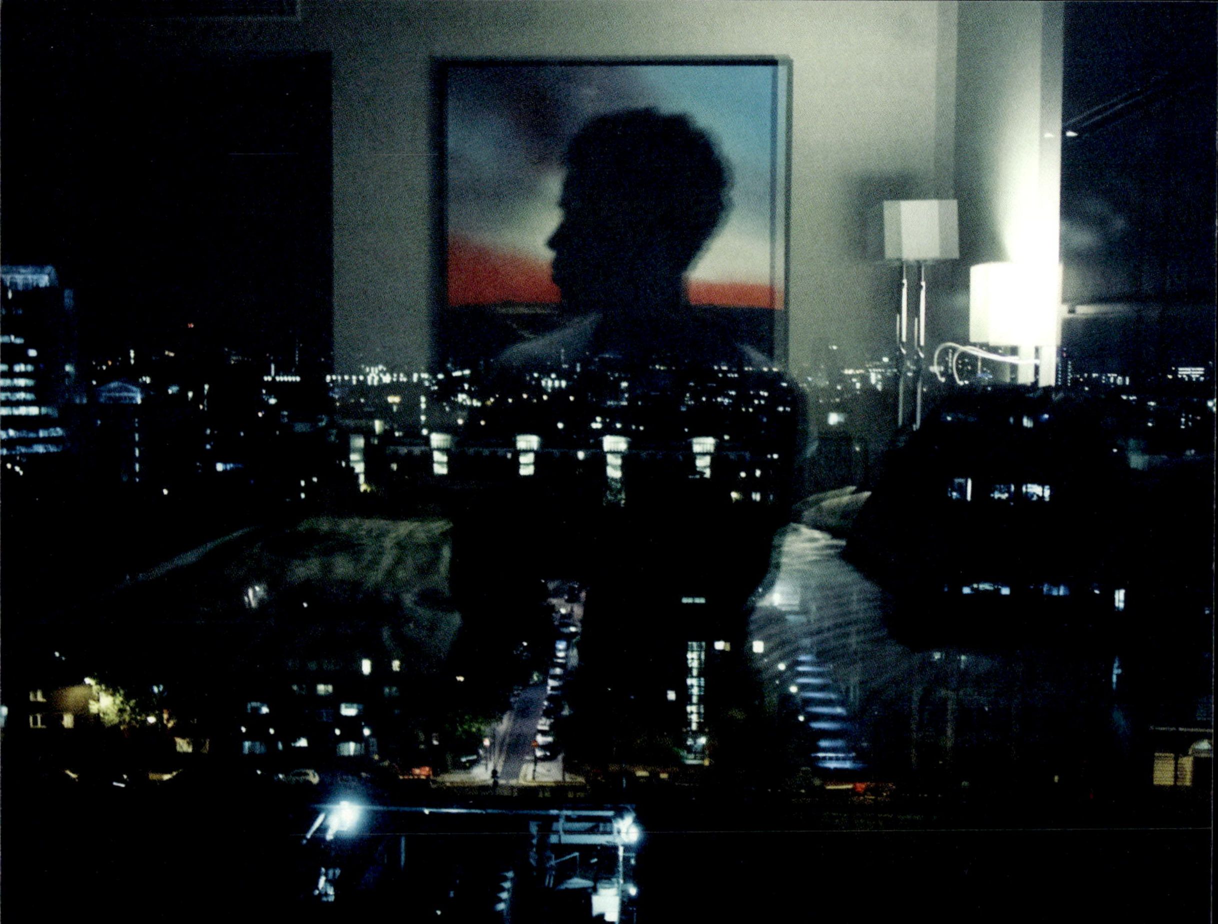

Falling Still

At times I could not even finish
a pedestrian day without getting overwhelmed.
All the energies of many strangers
made it hard to find my centre.

But then I started falling still –
I'd close my eyes, blank my mind
and relax my body for twenty seconds.
A quick vibrational reset and then
I could handle the giddying world again.

I could continue on this mortal plane
once more without wanting to fall off.

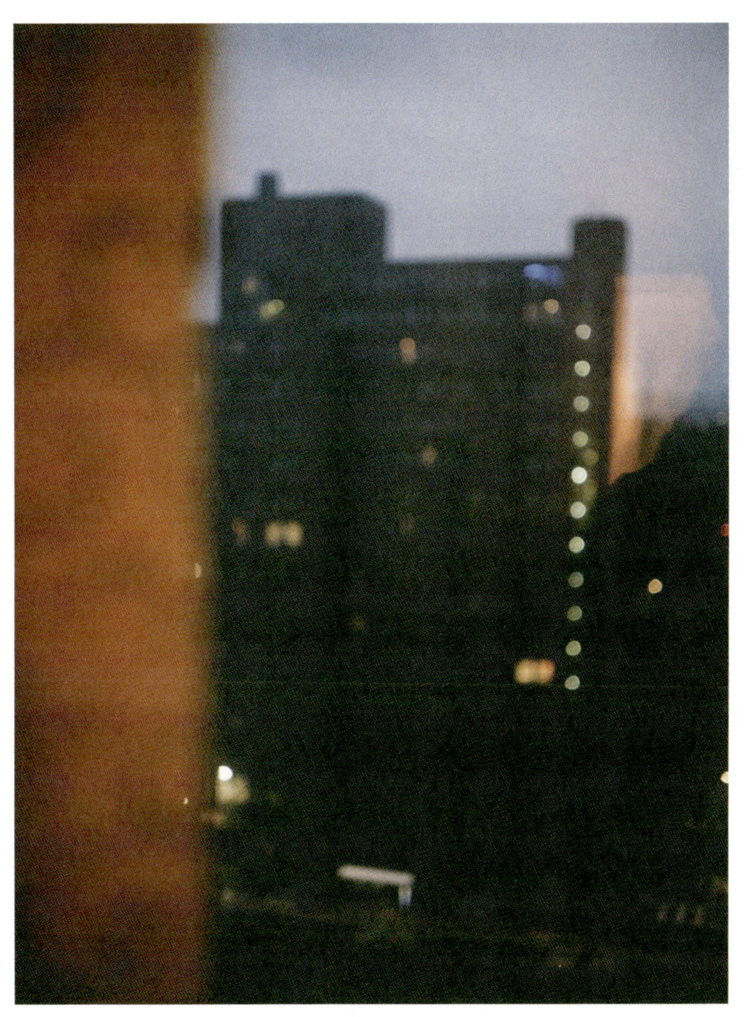

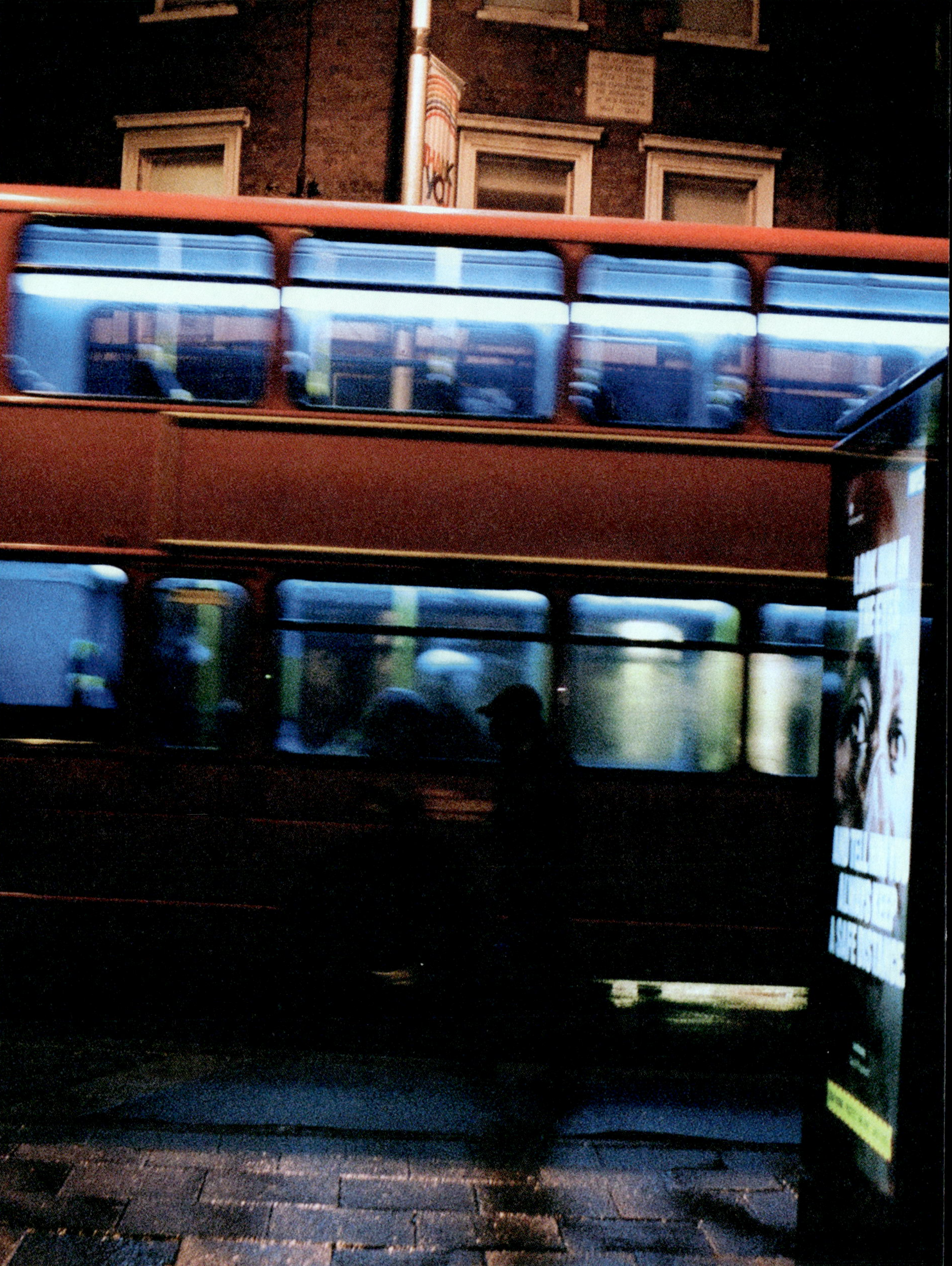

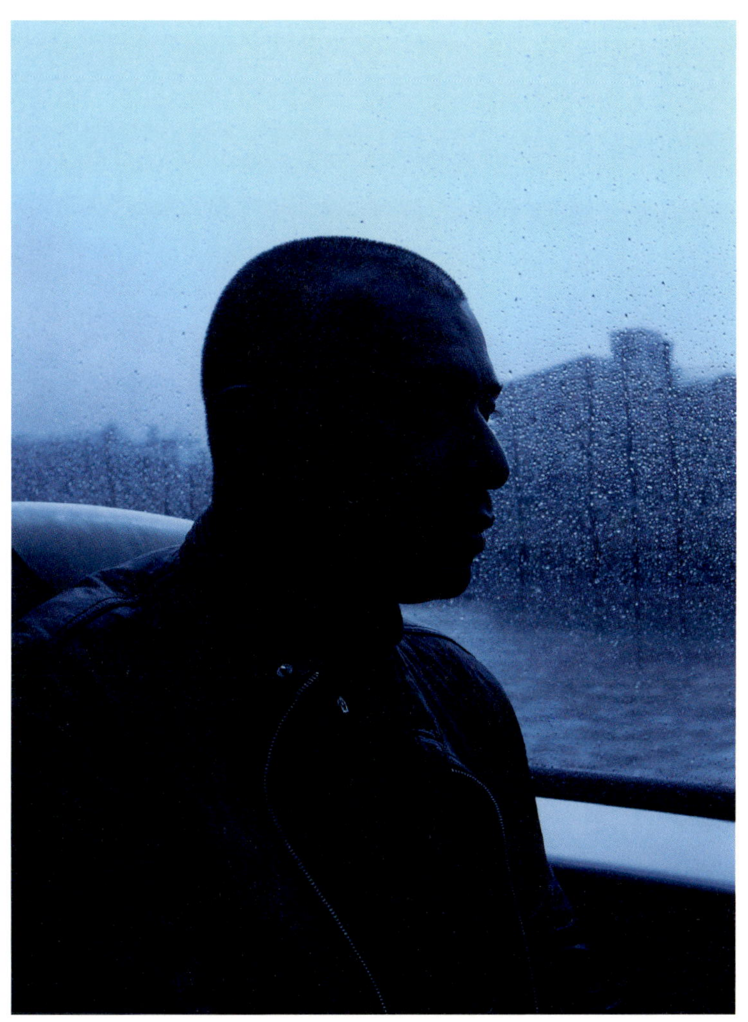

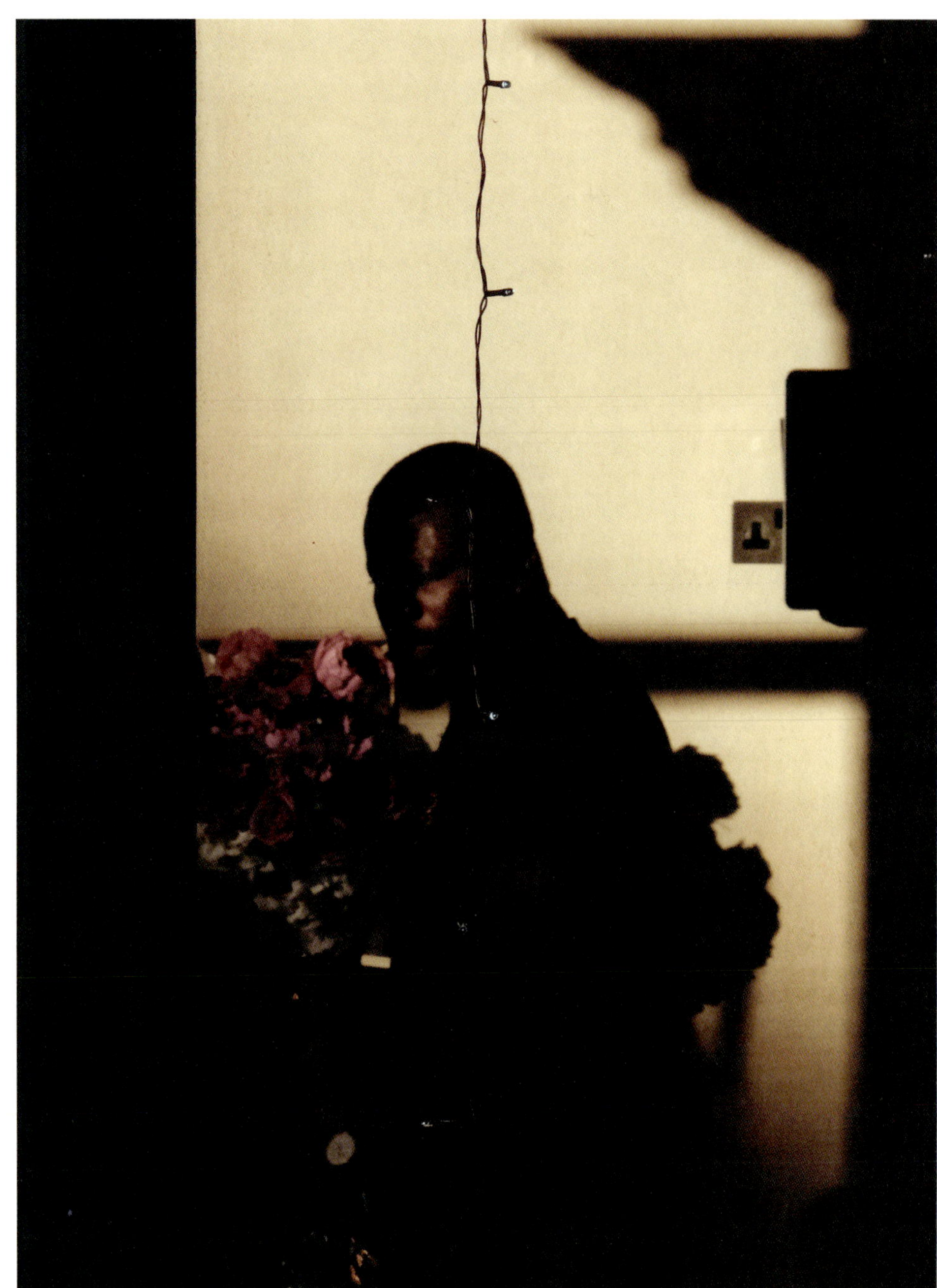

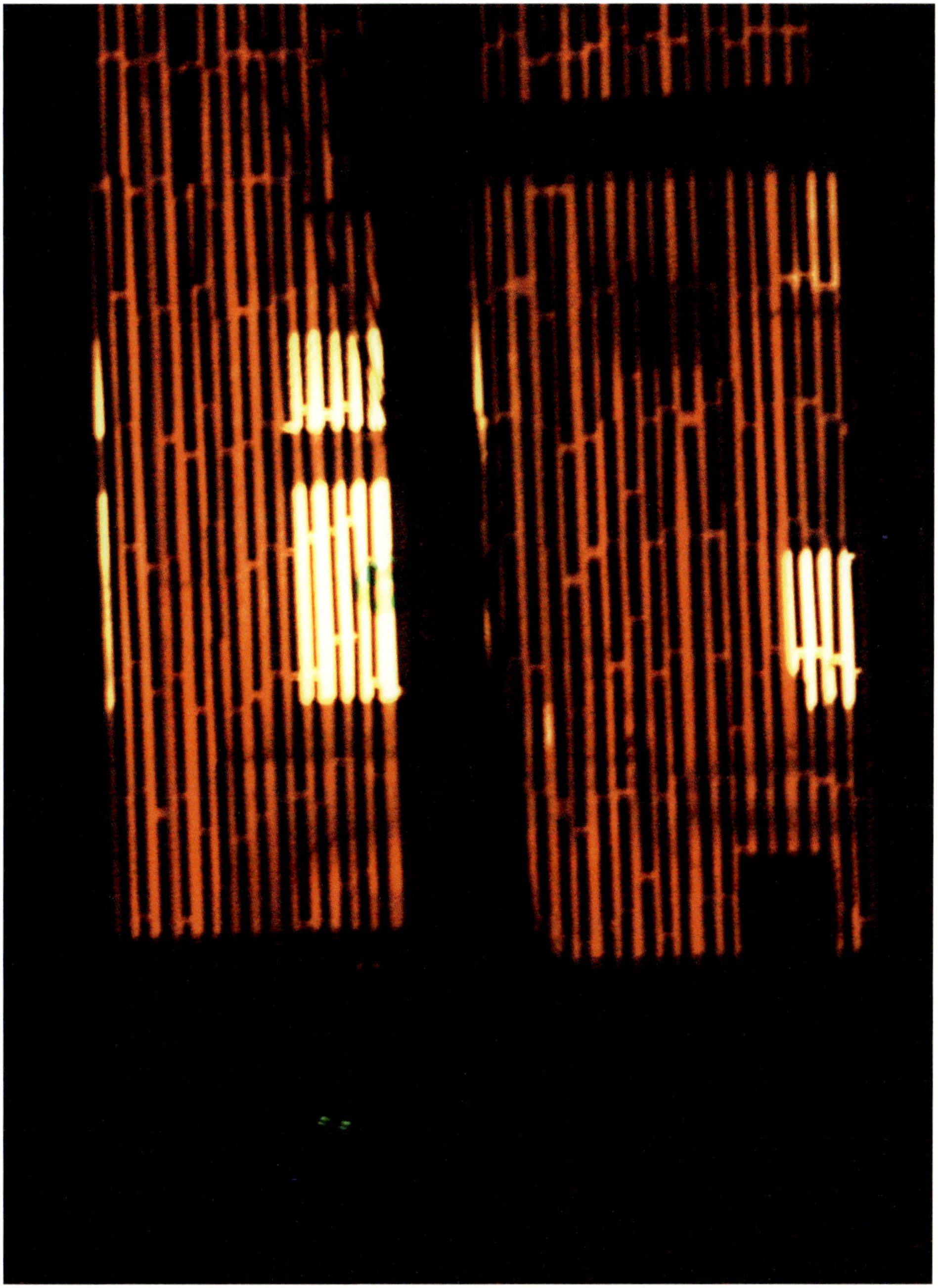

Hallway

Come in from the cold, my people. Follow me across this threshold into the hallway and remove your coats full of fog, your hats of dew, your scarf of frost. These hanging coats you see are the troubles that we've shed, wrinkled and battered, the coats that won't fit on these hooks will be laid down in a pile on an upstairs bedroom bed. But in the hallway let us now clasp our fingers and blow hot prayers of breath within them, unclench your jaw, let your bones relax, let your eyes adjust to the yellowed light of the hallway. The walls may be adorned with velveteen maps of Jamaica, of Trinidad, of Grenada, it makes no difference, clays from the same mud, fruit of the same tree.

You may pick out the traces of the DJ toasting a sermon, a slackness, a tribute, a call, a response. This is a language you know, a language you are, a language you don't switch to, a language that's in you, that's through you, a tongue in your talking. What we are building here is communion, a togetherness, a safe passage, a rite, a performance, a process, a collective choreography, a breathing in, a casting out.

The muted throb of the bass is aligning your heartbeat. Your breath slows, your neck loosens … your healing has begun, turning the volume down on the outside, so that you can soon turn up, but first, this moment between silence and sound in this hallway,

the transition between inside and out.

If you've felt like your burdens have been too heavy for too long you will soon dance it out here, soon let your frustrations seep out from your skin. Smoke and shadow projecting people in dance poses in the corridor from the main room. You've got there at 10 mins past midnight and you're still early. You can smell the garlic, thyme and pepper in the curried goat as people walk by with white paper plates and mint-green plastic forks.

You wipe your Sunday-best shoes thoroughly on the mat as a shuffle of respect to whoever owns the house, whether you know them or not. Your invitation here could be a friend's friend's friend, but you're here with a good vibration and the bottle of bronze drink in your hand that is making its own light and this is not your house, but you are surely at home here.

And soon the owner of the house pretends to know you and you pretend to know him back and he welcomes you to a swirling sea of bass, sweat and cocoa butter. Your favourite song comes on and you dive right in, your worries can no longer hold their grip while you are chanting that chorus until you're hoarse and the night is so full of bass. And no one in this row of terraced houses will get any sleep tonight so they might as well join the party.

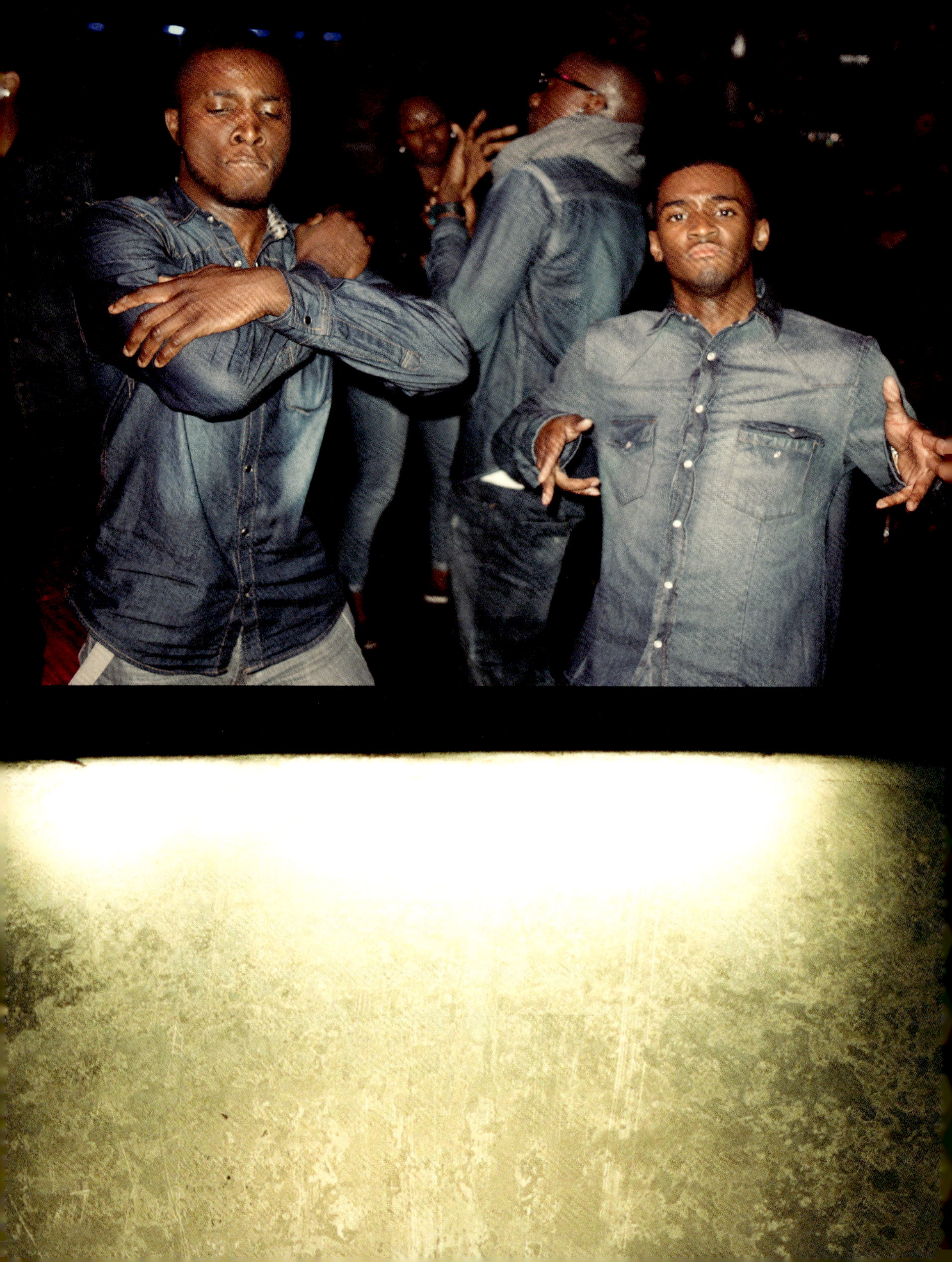

Aba Shanti-I Sound System

Aba Shanti-I Sound System could shake the trauma out of you with pure bass sound. During the hundreds of years of trauma Black people became accustomed to using particular frequencies of bass and certain rhythms of drums to relieve their generational hurt. Certain rhythms became highly valued. These healing frequencies became wailing Blues and Jazz in America, became whispering Samba in Brazil, became Soca in Trinidad and became and became and became. Now Aba Shanti-I, he has every principal healing frequency on 45 vinyl. It is said that he lives in a big house but sleeps only in one room, as every other room holds black 45s (bathroom included). As with anything else, soon white people heard of the healing and felt like they had to get some (even though they were not sure of the illness that they were suffering but rather knew that something was not right), but the frequencies spoke differently to them. It made them dance, but a dance that made them grieve the transgressions of their generations. It made them cry hysterically with a deep, deep sorrow and drop out from the system and twist their blond flowing hair into dreadlocks. Healing still, but healing different ills.

Thresholds

Holkham Beach, Wells-next-the-Sea

The view is half sea half air
when tides creep between my toes.

The gunmetal grey of the sea
meets the oyster-coloured sky

in a sacred geometry that somehow
relieves me of the ache of my burdens.

How did I get it so wrong, my feet
submerged now in sand to form a footprint.

The clouds shift just enough to allow
some slanted sunlight through

and I can feel my weight sinking
in the water now past my ankles.

This sacred conversation between
sky and sea is a stillness and solitude.

How have I missed it all, how have I been
so distracted, so dulled to the world?

Waking from my sleep to the grey static
of a TV screen to drift into a dream.

Wiping each frosted mirror with my palm,
to see a different face from the one I expected.

This passage walked from verdant trees
to wet dark sinking sand now at my shins.

This sky, this sea, this moment, this life –
    Thresholds, thresholds, all thresholds.

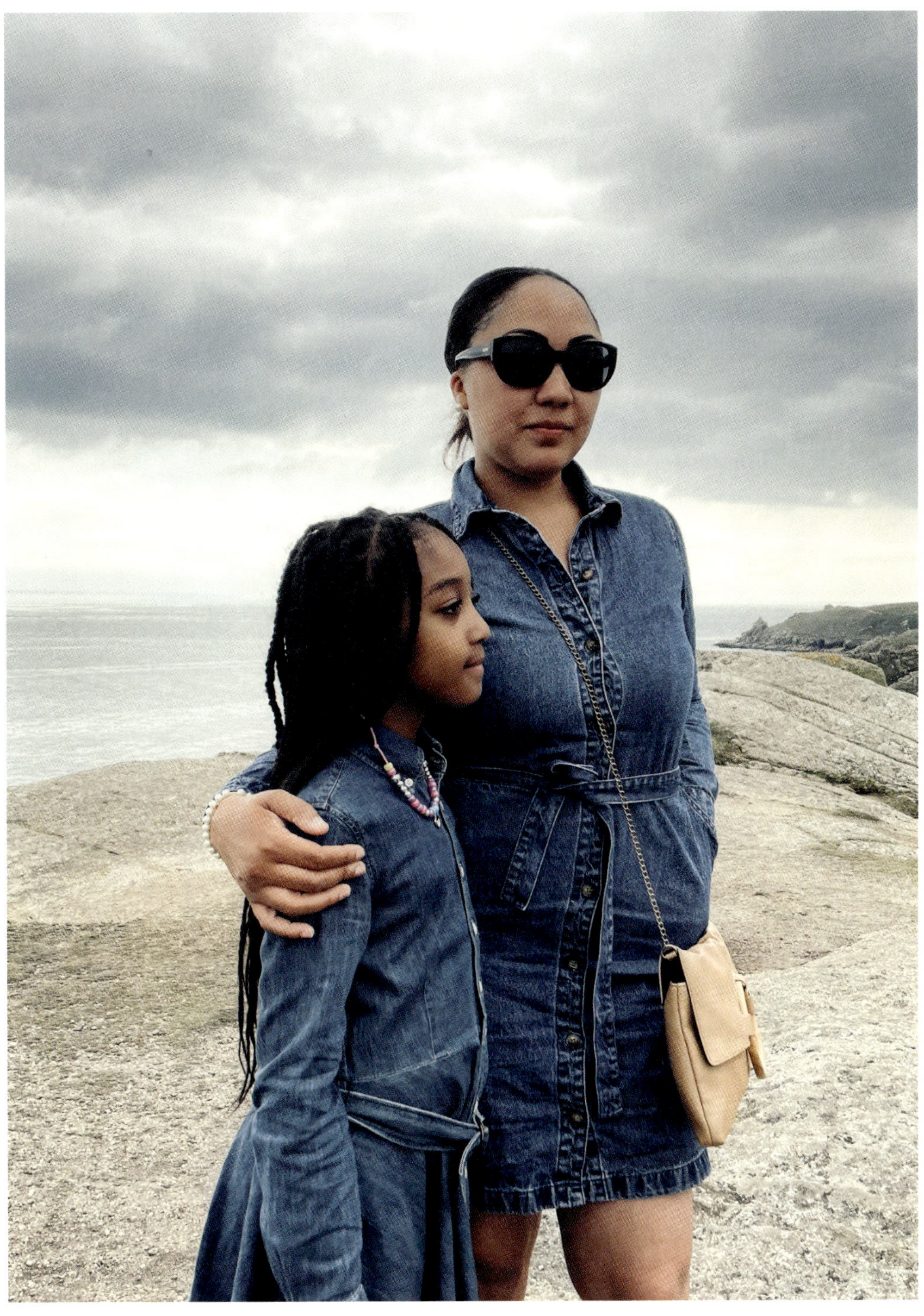

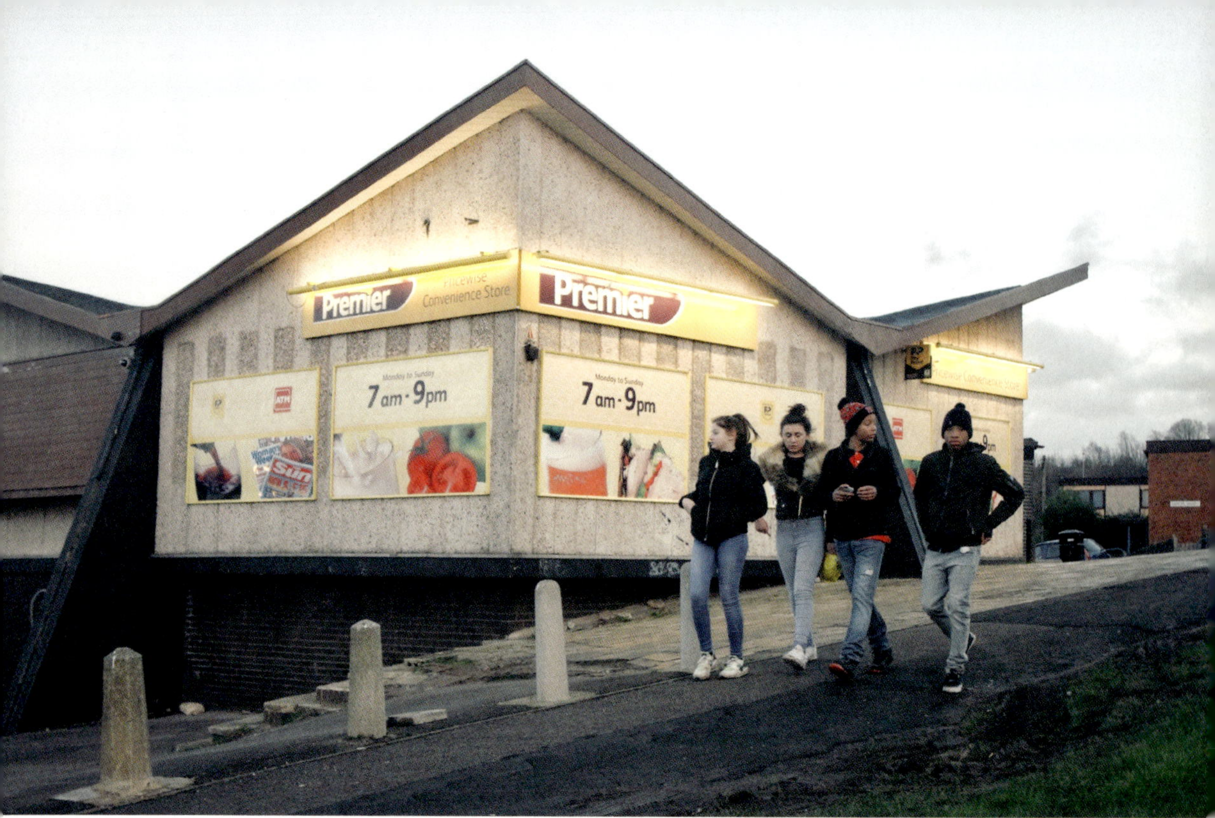

The City Kids See the Sea

For many the first time;
these kids of the tower block
and tarred playgrounds

now running towards this scene
of sea with its blended blue sky
and wave breaks of silver-tipped froth.

Most don't even bother
to take off their shoes
or roll up their trousers,

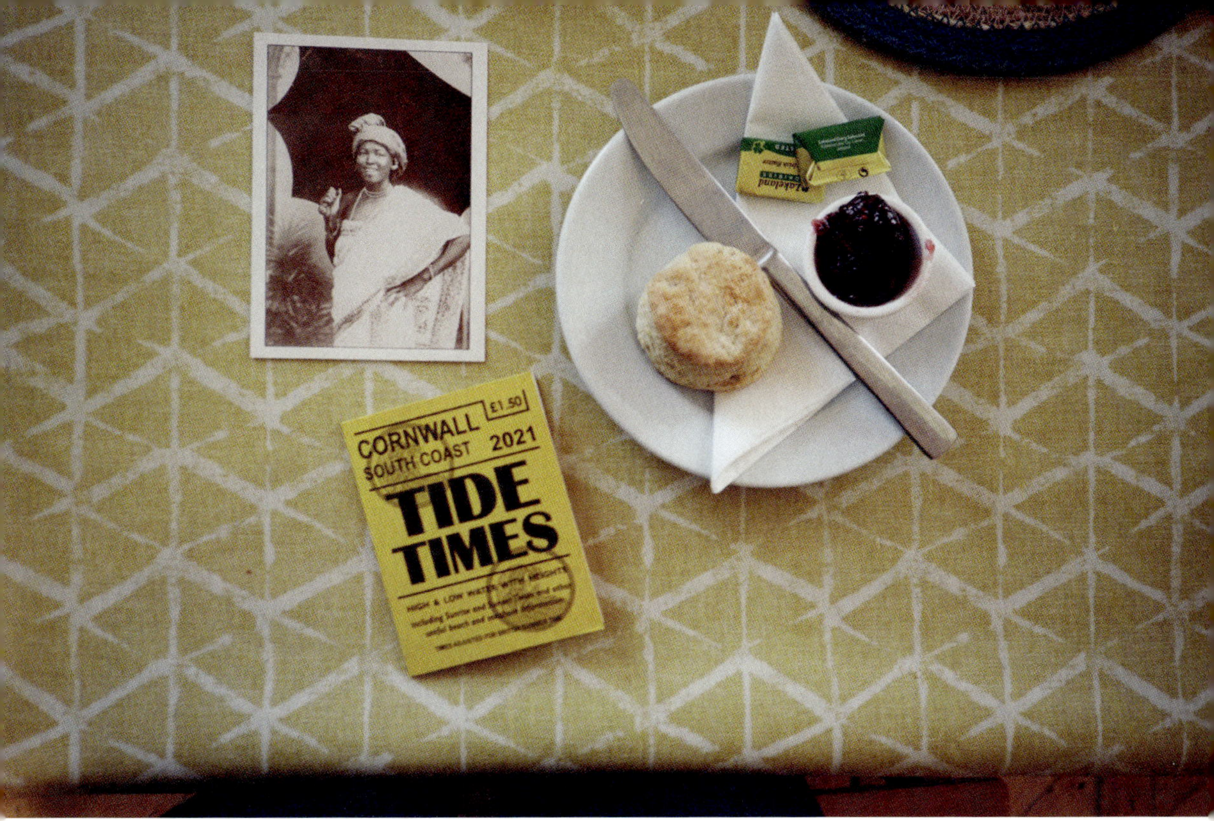

instead they run right in,
splashing each other
with arcs and sprays of delight.

Sunlight threading gold
along the sea's rippling
swells all around them

till the sea becomes the colour of smoke
and the sky lead; hijabs drip
and Nikes squelch back to the bus.

O city children you are as ancient
as water, as warm as the evening sun,
as calm as the tide slowly pulling away.

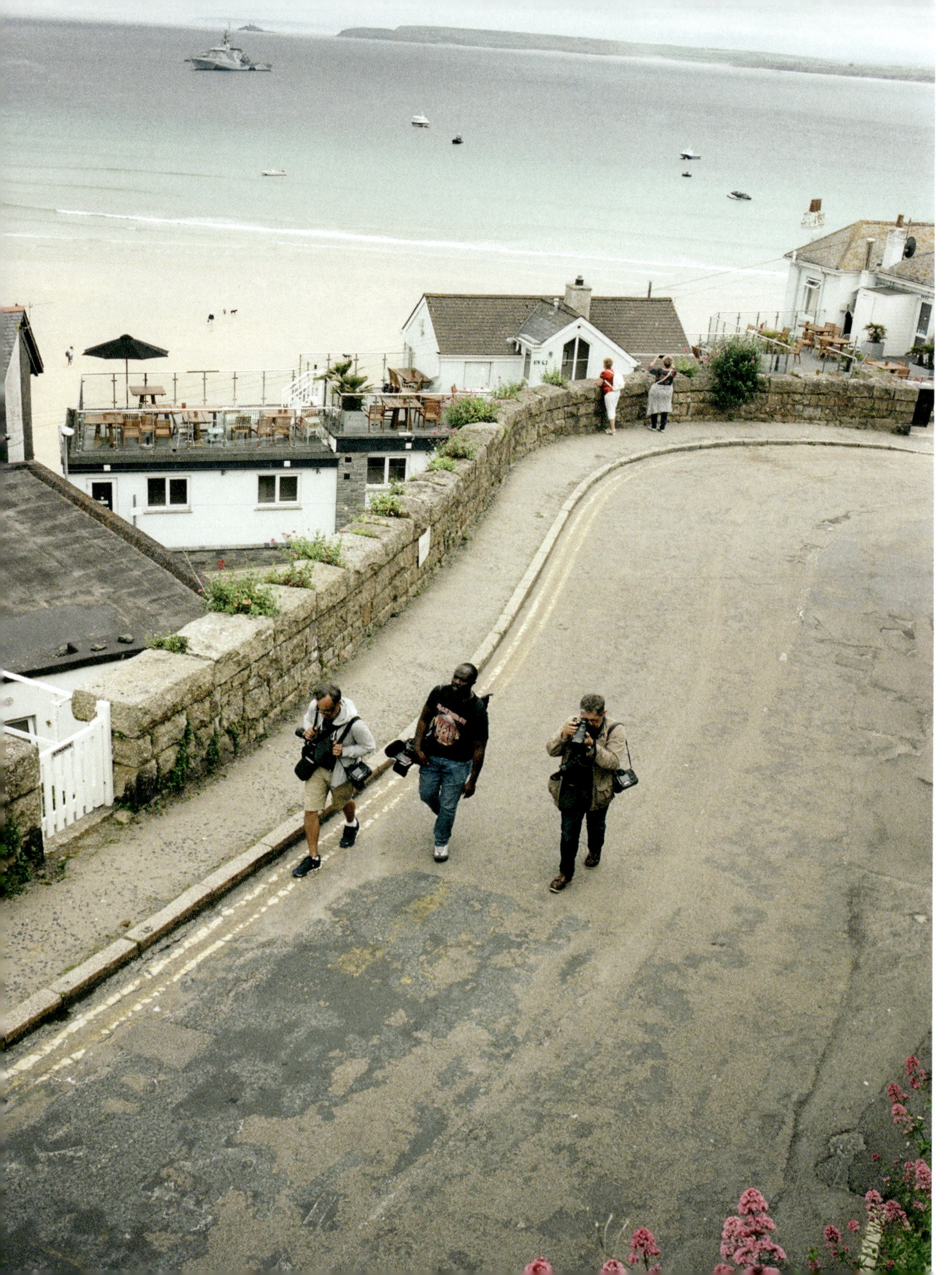

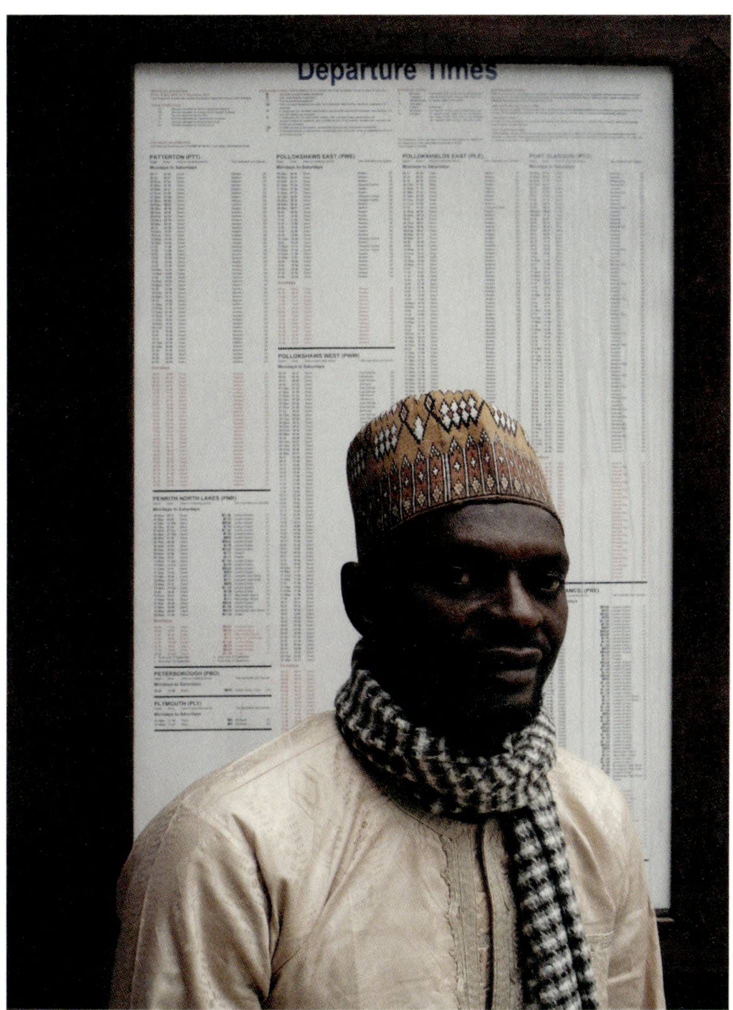
Departure Times

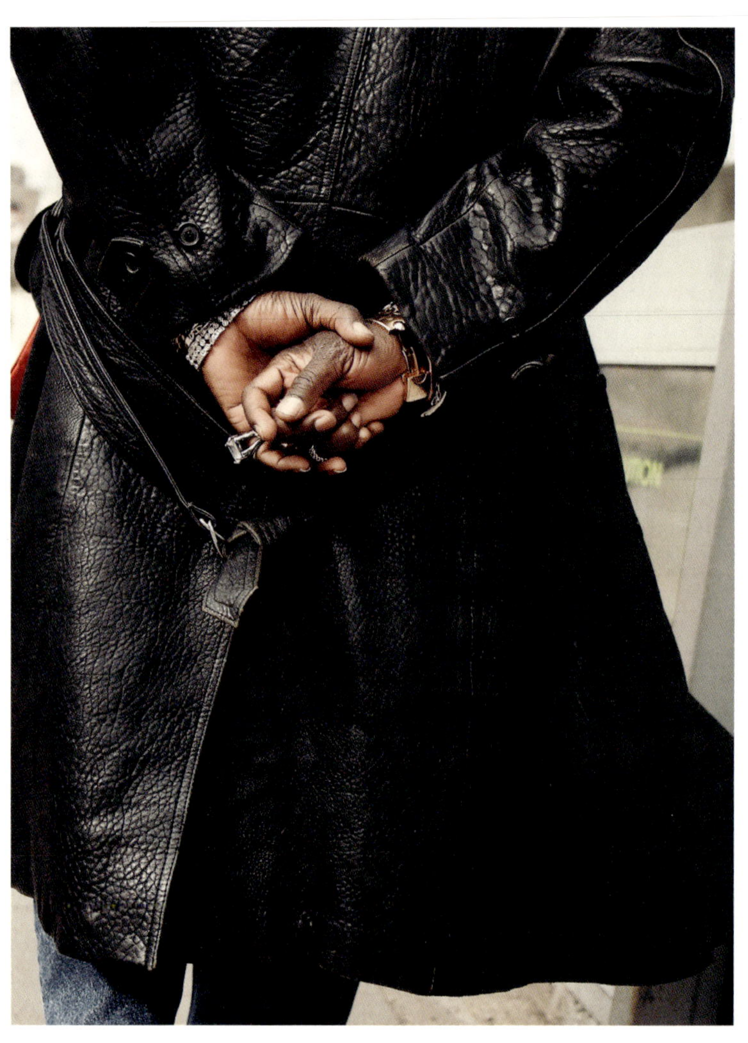

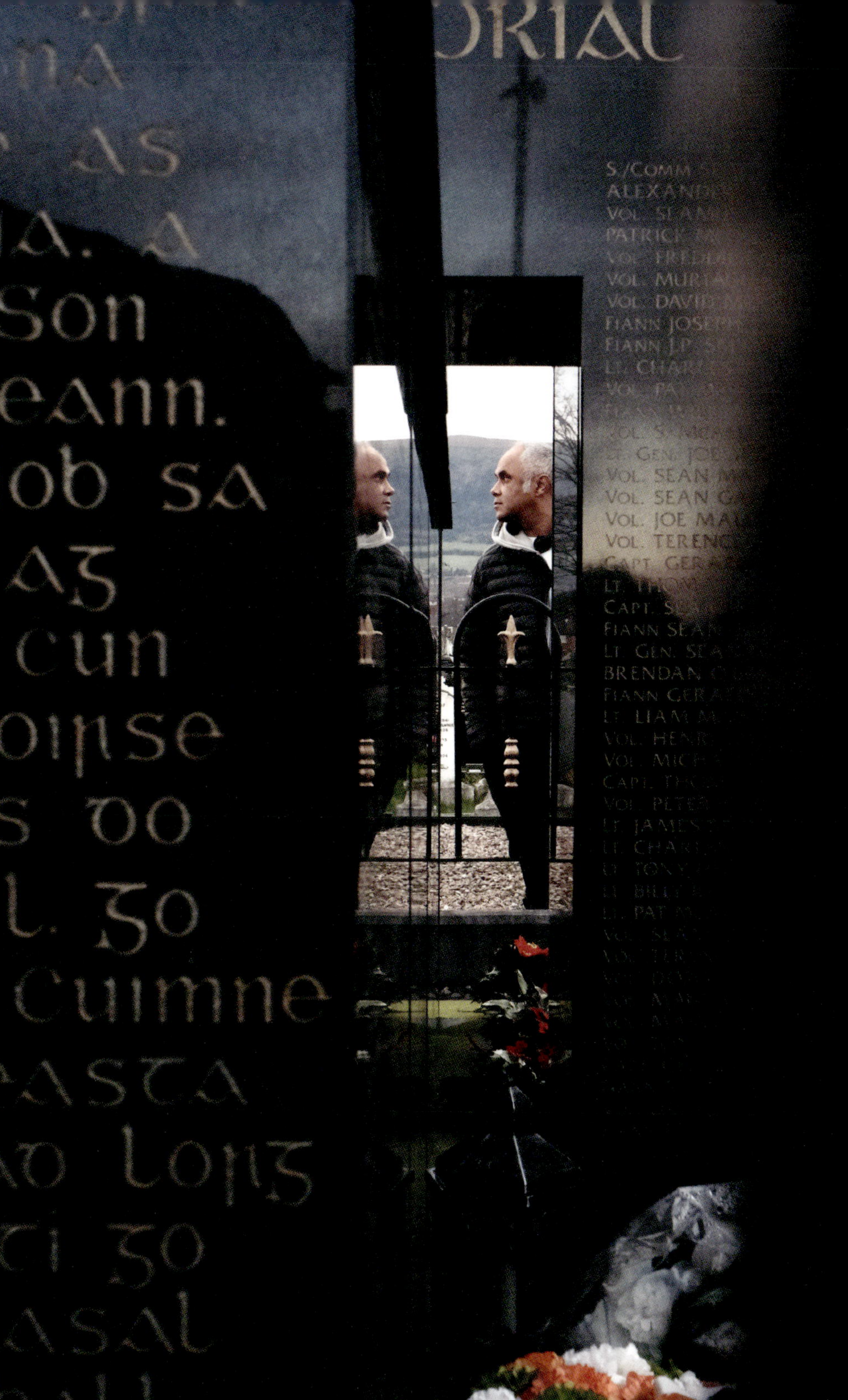
SON
eann.
iob sa
a5
cun
oinse
s oo
l. 50
Cuimne
easta
ao Lon5
ci 50
asal

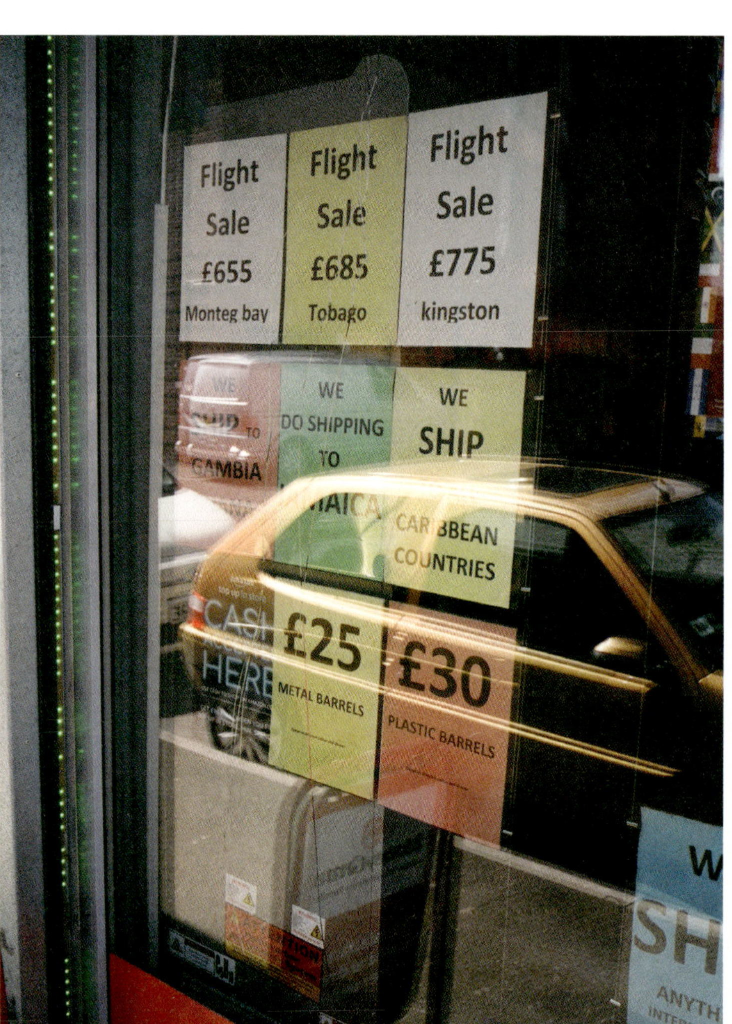

Flight Sale £655 Monteg bay
Flight Sale £685 Tobago
Flight Sale £775 kingston
WE SHIP TO GAMBIA
WE DO SHIPPING TO
WE SHIP
CARIBBEAN COUNTRIES
£25 METAL BARRELS
£30 PLASTIC BARRELS
SH
ANYTH
INTERNA

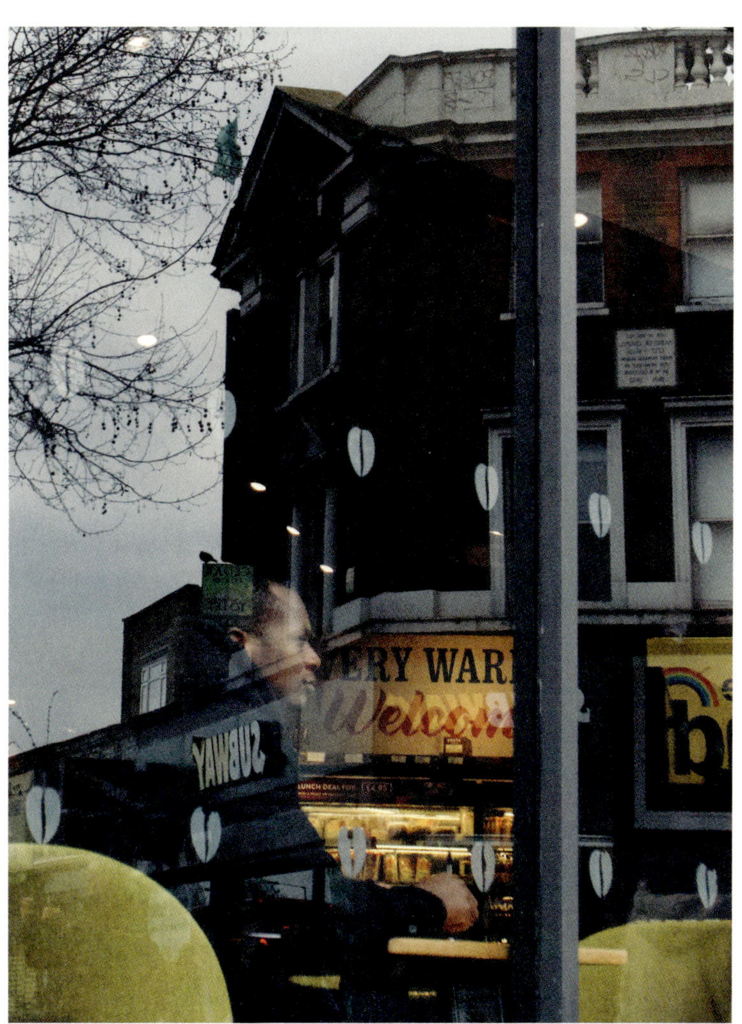

SUBWAY
VERY WARI
Welco
LUNCH DEAL FOR £4.95

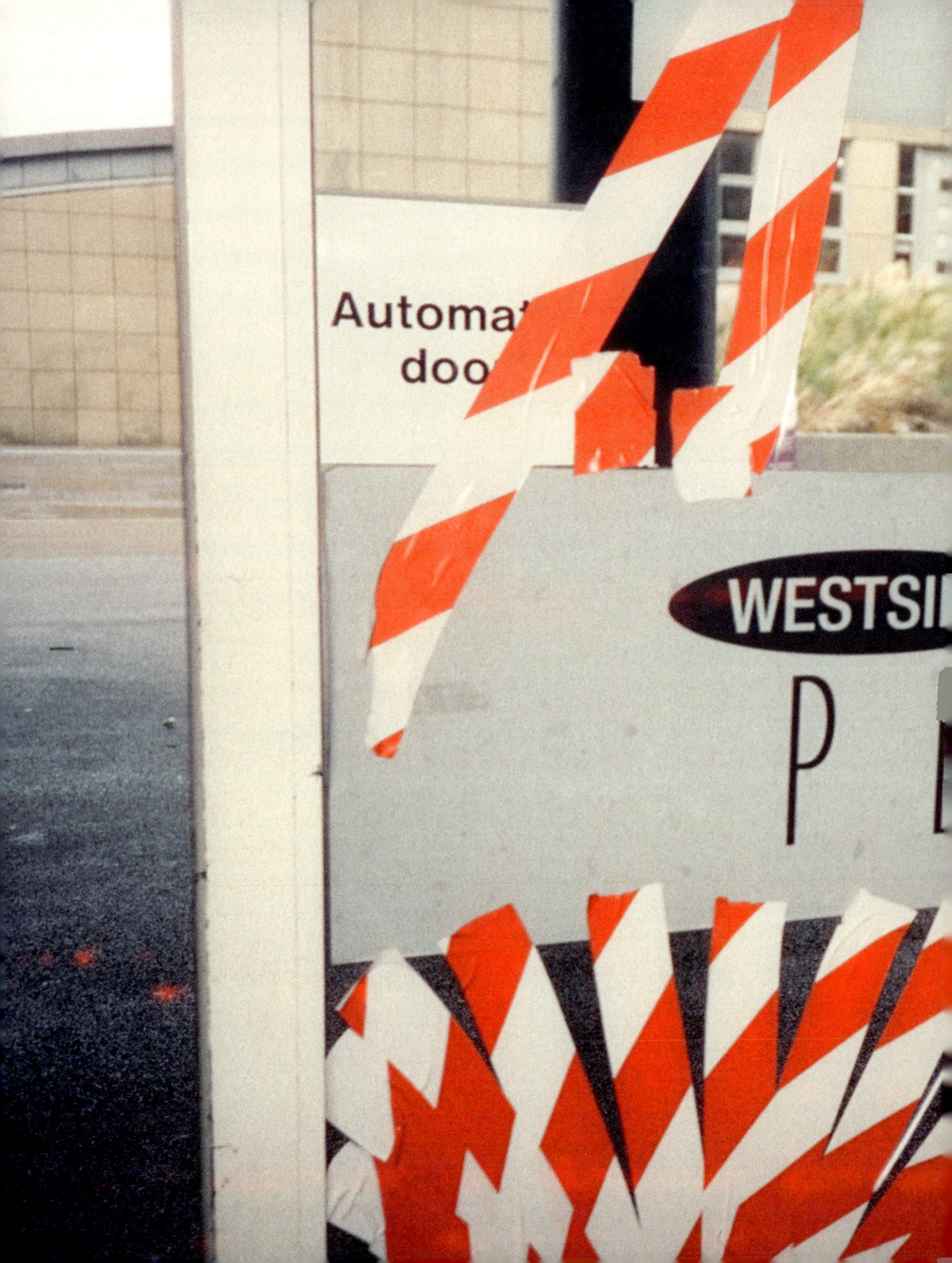
Automat
doo
WESTSI
P

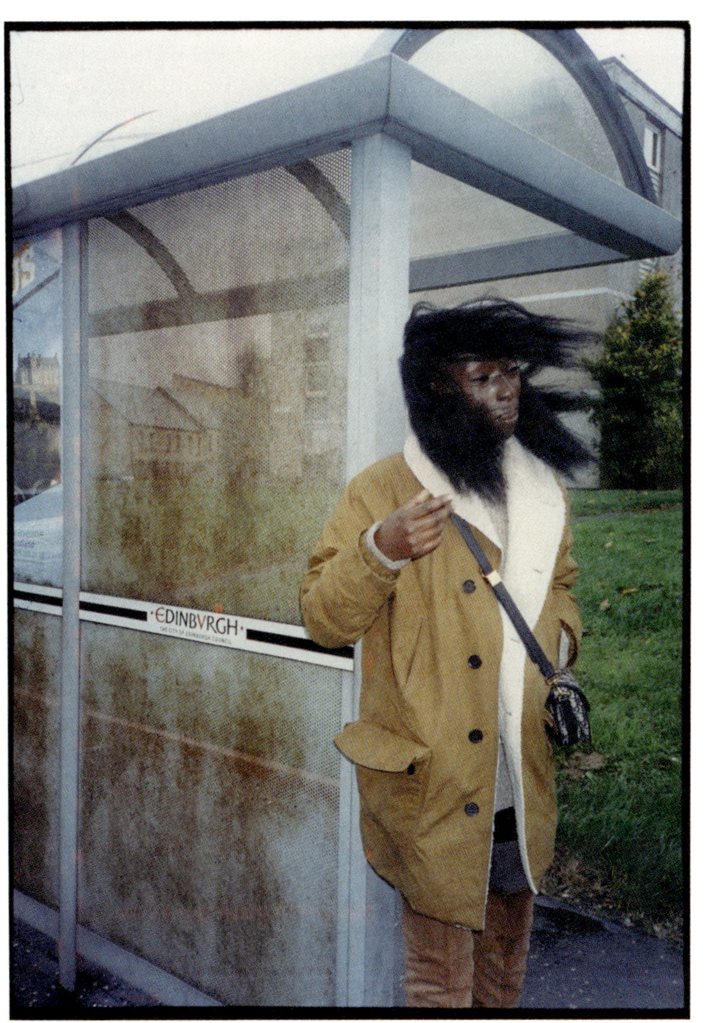
·EDINBVRGH·
THE CITY OF EDINBURGH COUNCIL

Leaving London with a B-Side Aesthetic

As soon as we get past the junction and onto the M25 Johny starts to tell me about his B-side aesthetic theory. It's already dark and the digital radio is lighting up the side of his face green neon like he was in a nightclub or a shebeen. The dub maestro scientist is pulsing through the speakers at a low enough volume that we don't have to shout.

A manifesto of sorts based on the B-side of records being made in the spirit of culture, innovation and aesthetics rather than the economic demand for hits that can corrupt the purity of art. That B-sides have led to some of the best and sometimes most underappreciated music that has stood the test of time.

Like all really good aesthetic theories it feels to me that it has always been around, and what he has said – like all good poets – has revealed something previously below the frequency to be understood. It struck me that perhaps this is Johny's superpower, to reveal hidden but experienced culture.

As the lights on the M25 begin to flash in time with the hi-hats,
Johny says that the aesthetic can be applied to any artform,
but he envisions that in photography there can be pictures
that play with the edge of failure; that bleed, that blur, that use
expired film for non-standard results and the materiality of
film warping can be photographic technologies that enhance
a picture's artistic qualities. I start talking about whether the
B-side is a combination (for Black people particularly) of a surfeit
of creativity clashing with a lack of economic opportunities.
Albums made from samples only from the one-dollar bin of the
record store. Like the sufferer-chic styling in Jamaica, where
a suit jacket (sent by a relative in the US) is worn with a string
vest and sandals, or even Lee 'Scratch' Perry's Black Ark, using
studio equipment for sounds that they weren't specifically made
for. We both agree that the B-side on vinyl and as an aesthetic
encourages taking part regardless of financial restrictions.
And as the conversation unfolds so too do the bass rhythms,
all the way to Glasgow.

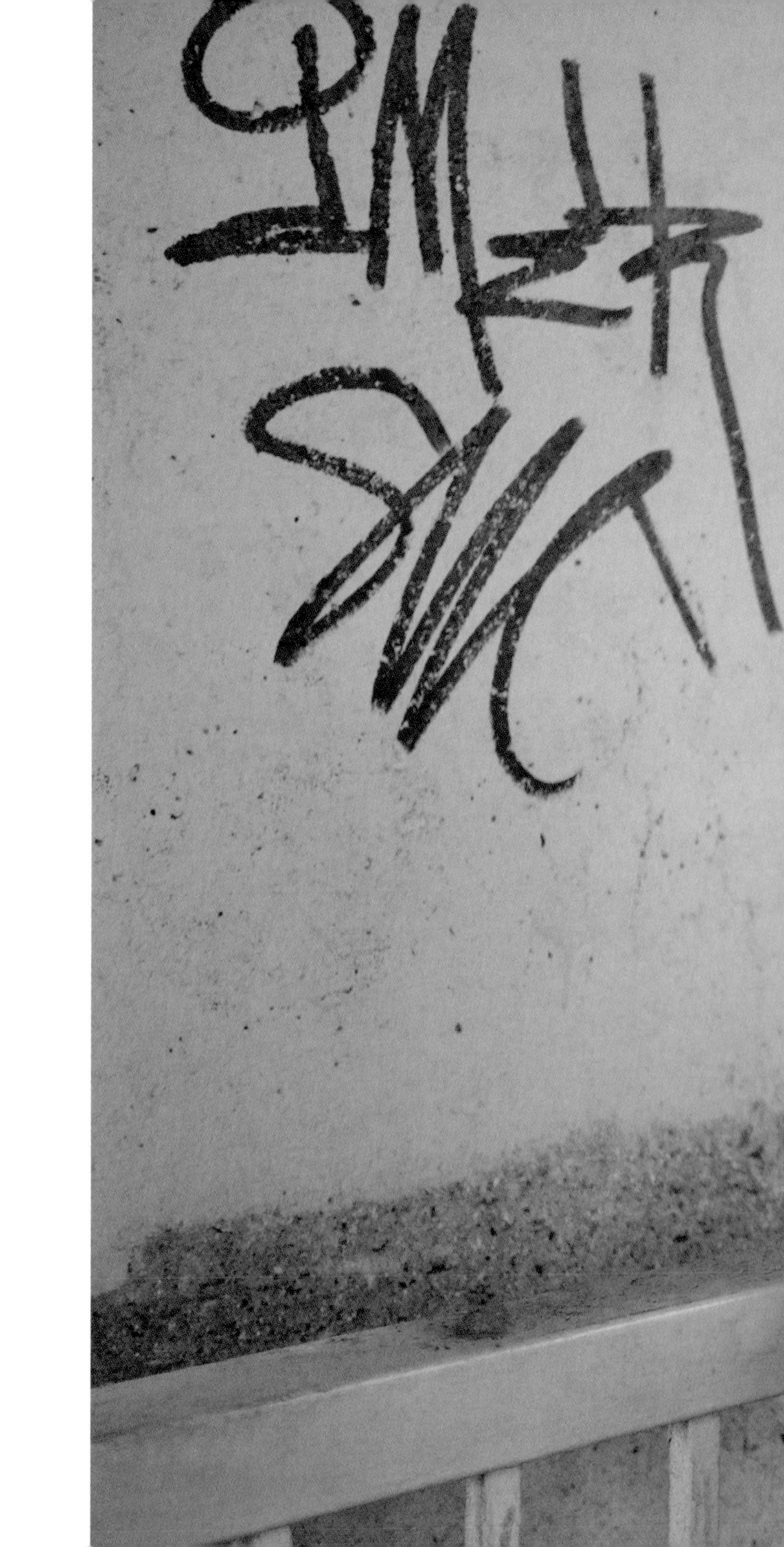

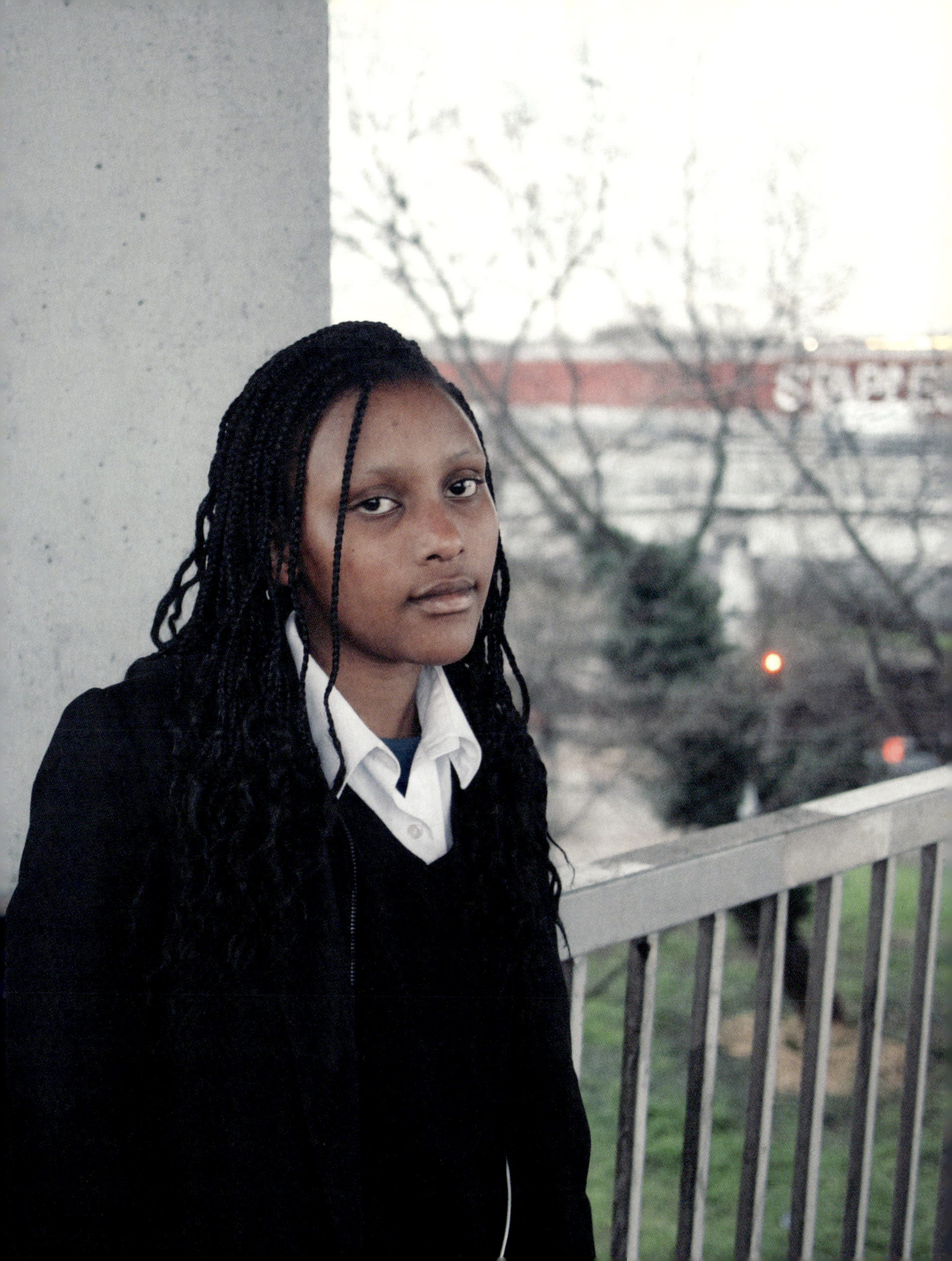

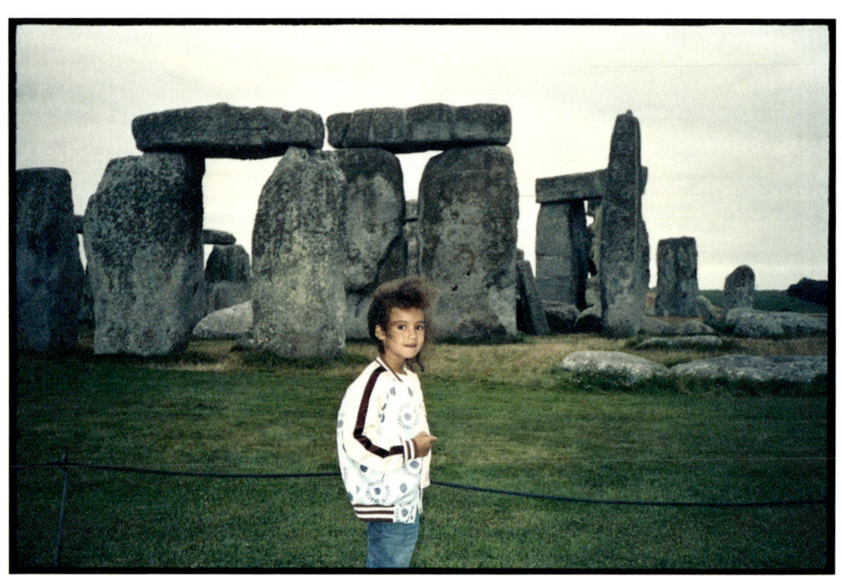

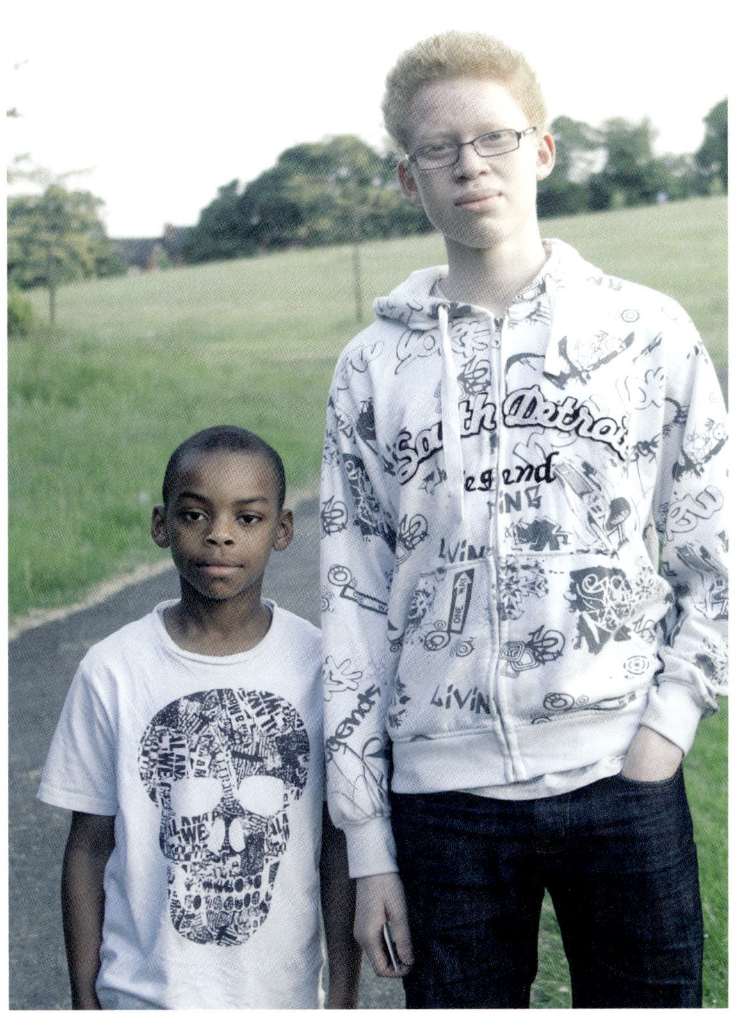

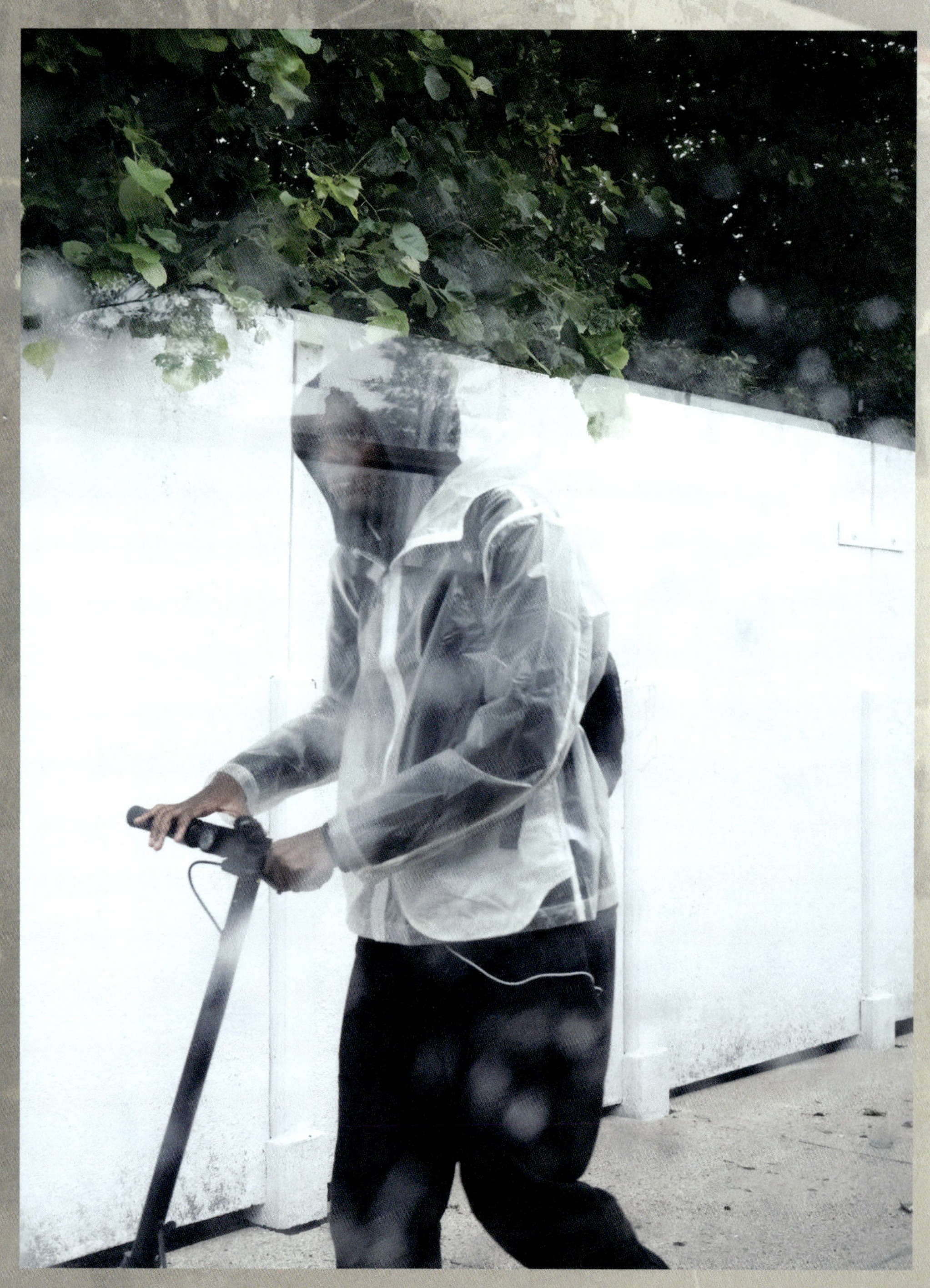

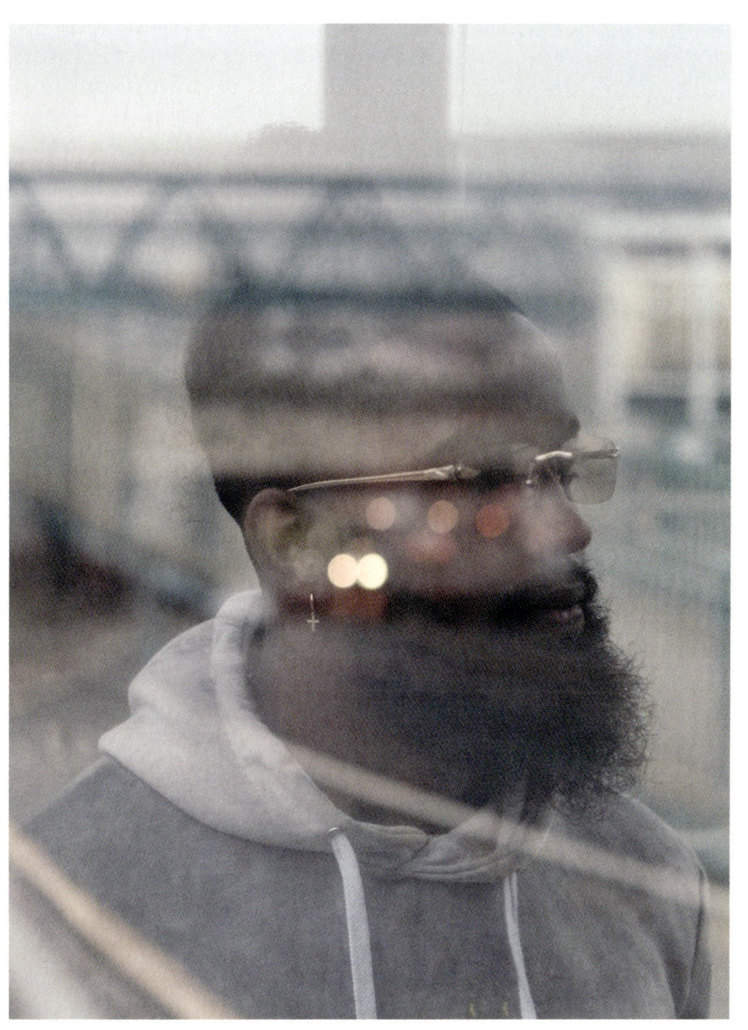

The Sea Means Something Different to Us

1. The first thing that grabs you when you look at JMW Turner's painting *The Slave Ship* is perhaps the glowing orange-marmalade sky at its heart. Somewhere in the deep crevices of your memory you think you remember that this painting was once called *The Dead and the Dying*. Your mind goes to the idea of the artist making metaphors of the dying of the day, or even the dying of the Empire.

By this stage in Turner's development he is a master craftsman, versed not just in the depiction of tragedy but also in the sympathetic weather conditions that illustrated the tragedy's depth.

You keep looking, at the cadmium-white tips of the waves that rise up like ghosts, and what looks like a suspended phantom in the centre of the canvas. The ship is tilted at a precarious angle, with a ghostly, salt-sprayed haze surrounding it, and you think (with your ceaselessly positive mind) that perhaps it's about the death of the shipping industry, or even of the slave trade itself. Then the program lets you know that the original title of the painting was *Slavers throwing Overboard the Dead and Dying – Typhon coming on* and you realise those black marks are not the waves' shadows, nor the flotsam and jetsam or fauna of the sea; you realise that these are Black people thrown overboard to die. Now you see their hands stretching out from the surf and right there in the museum you taste the salt's mist on your dry, cracked lips, the sting of salt in your eyes.

2. As the white-robed congregation at this Nigerian church baptism feels the sting of the salt in their eyes, some of them are weeping, and others are already crying from the power of

God's holy spirit reflected in the muscular breaking of the waves.

Some children turn away from their sandcastles to watch. Some sunbathing parents in bucket hats and shades with their reddened arms and necks raise up from their towels and turn their heads. One of the congregation is making a makeshift altar in the sand of giant copper crosses, flowers and crucifixion beads. Then the handheld drums start to play and something descends upon them. They begin to dance a dance distinctly Yoruba in origins but godly in focus. As the strained tones of the singing become stronger and the drummers are now breaking a sweat, the songs feel like they have turned from gospel to pure chant, sweat-drenched white robes sticking to their skin.

The sunbathing families are now gathering up their towels, buckets and spades, walking away to somewhere else, and a small crowd are looking on from a distance on the Margate steps.

3. Imagine swimming in the dark, and all you can see are the red and yellow lights of the town reflected in the water. You float on your back to catch your breath and the stars you could see so clearly back in your country are absent. It's just a void black sky. You redouble your efforts. It's hard swimming fully clothed. Your clothes are becoming heavy. The motorised dinghy that dropped you offshore has disappeared into the inky night. At a certain point you are not sure you're getting closer. You begin to panic, your breathing becomes erratic, your limbs begin to flail in desperation and just when your lungs are on fire you can feel the sea floor under your feet and you walk onto Margate beach in the night, and sit in the shadow catching your breath. You kneel to start a prayer and after that you look for a while out to the darkness of the sea where you left your life behind.

4. On 7 July over three and a half thousand people were kneeling on the steps of Margate beach in silence overlooking the sea. The occasion was in protest of the George Floyd murder; but

also to illustrate that things were equally bad in England, that something had to change, and that the change had to begin now.

I arrive in Margate to meet Kelly Abbot, one half of the duo who run People Dem Collective who were responsible for organising the march. After getting somewhat lost I find the office, and she comes out to greet me with a warm hug. She dresses like a rockstar but her demeanour is warm and incredibly welcoming.

Before we go inside she points out the arts venue that People Dem are in the process of developing to showcase Black Arts and Culture. What strikes me is that they're creating a three-hundred-year plan for the venue. I think about what Margate may have been three hundred years ago and whether Black people even had the power, opportunity or scope to have that type of vision. Margate is renowned amongst other things for being the former central residence of the right-wing UKIP Party as well as a hotbed for the far-right British Nationalist Party, so her serious long-term plans have me in awe of her positive future of a thriving Black community and arts scene flying in the face of Margate's recent history.

Inside, their headquarters remind me of an industrial New York loft. Large and open space with internal vents and roof structures architecturally exposed, and a large window that frames Margate beach like a Turner sea painting.

During the day I interview many of the members of People Dem Collective, and one thing is clear: they all have the utmost respect for Kelly Abbot. I hear again and again that the space and ideas of People Dem Collective has undoubtedly increased their quality of life in Margate. Kelly talks about how she discovered herself in Margate, that in starting People Dem Collective she found her real purpose, and that living on the seafront is much more natural to Black people than living in a tower block; she left the rat race of London in order to grow and develop socially and consciously. She tells me that every day her ancestors speak to her from the sea, that the sea holds all Black people's history from all times and if you listen and look hard enough you can feel them there.

Home Is Not A Place

for suffering. Be it house, hut or tent
turn down the volume of the outside
world and rest. Replenish.
Home a refuge, the room you return to
and if there's no return, home the dream.
Home a blessed space, a glowing hearth
from which seraphim hold in their hand
offerings of bright orange embers.
Home a space of solace
for the bones in your skin to relax.
Perhaps there'll be space to grow,
where weary minds can bloom.
And the spirit of a room? The spirit
of all rooms are degrees of warmth,
and people, and talk; so too the spirit
of a home, love.

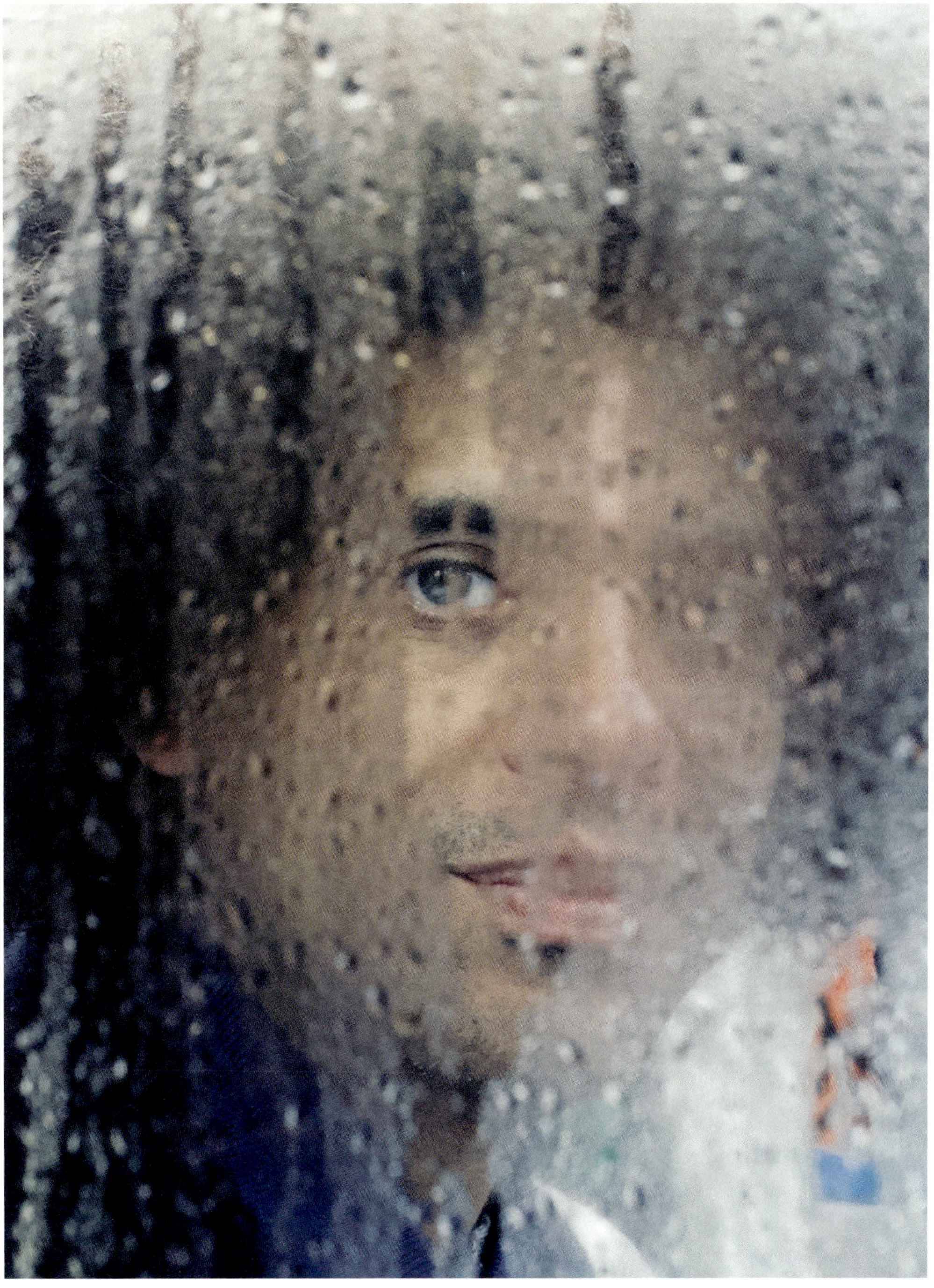

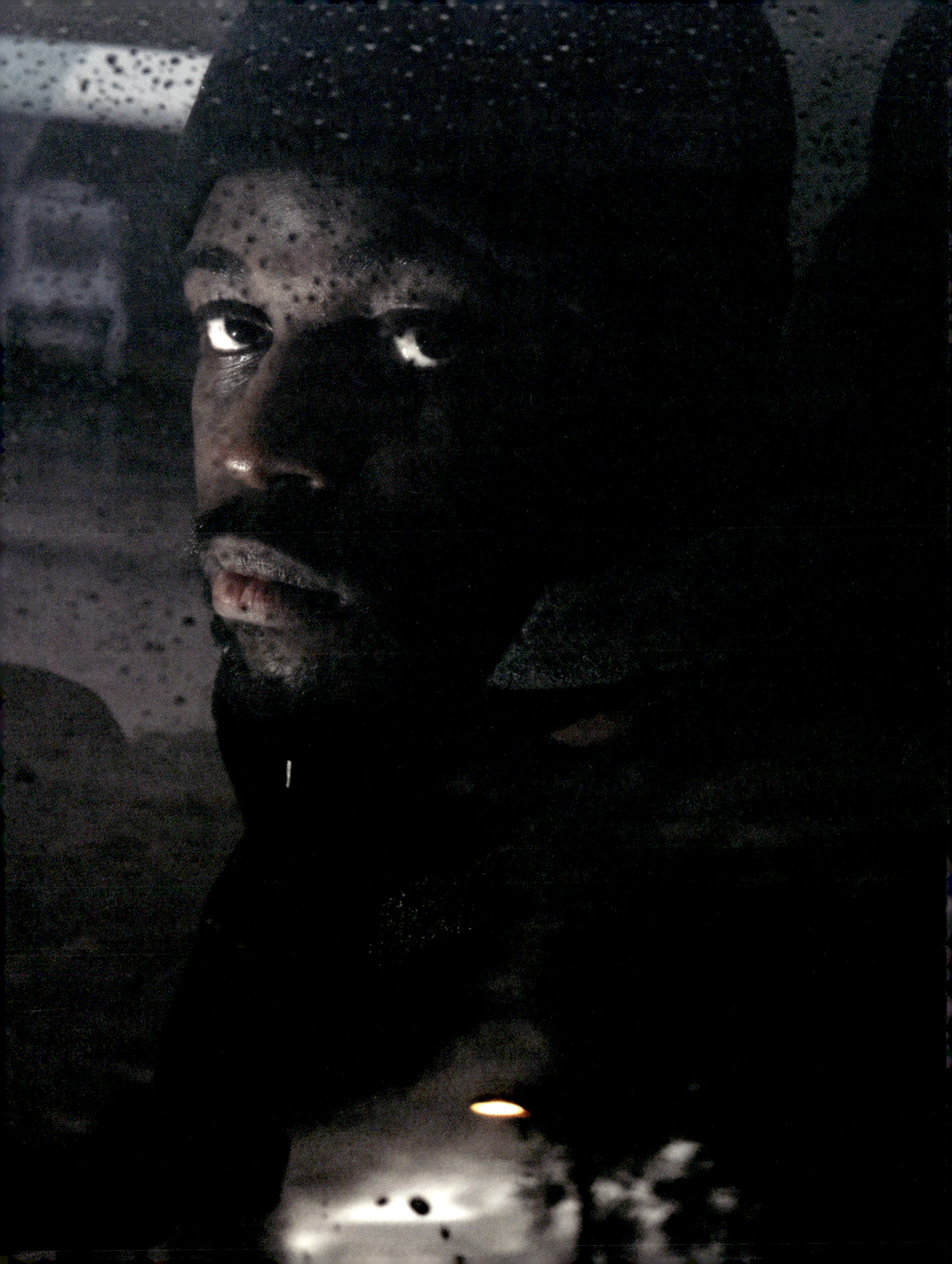

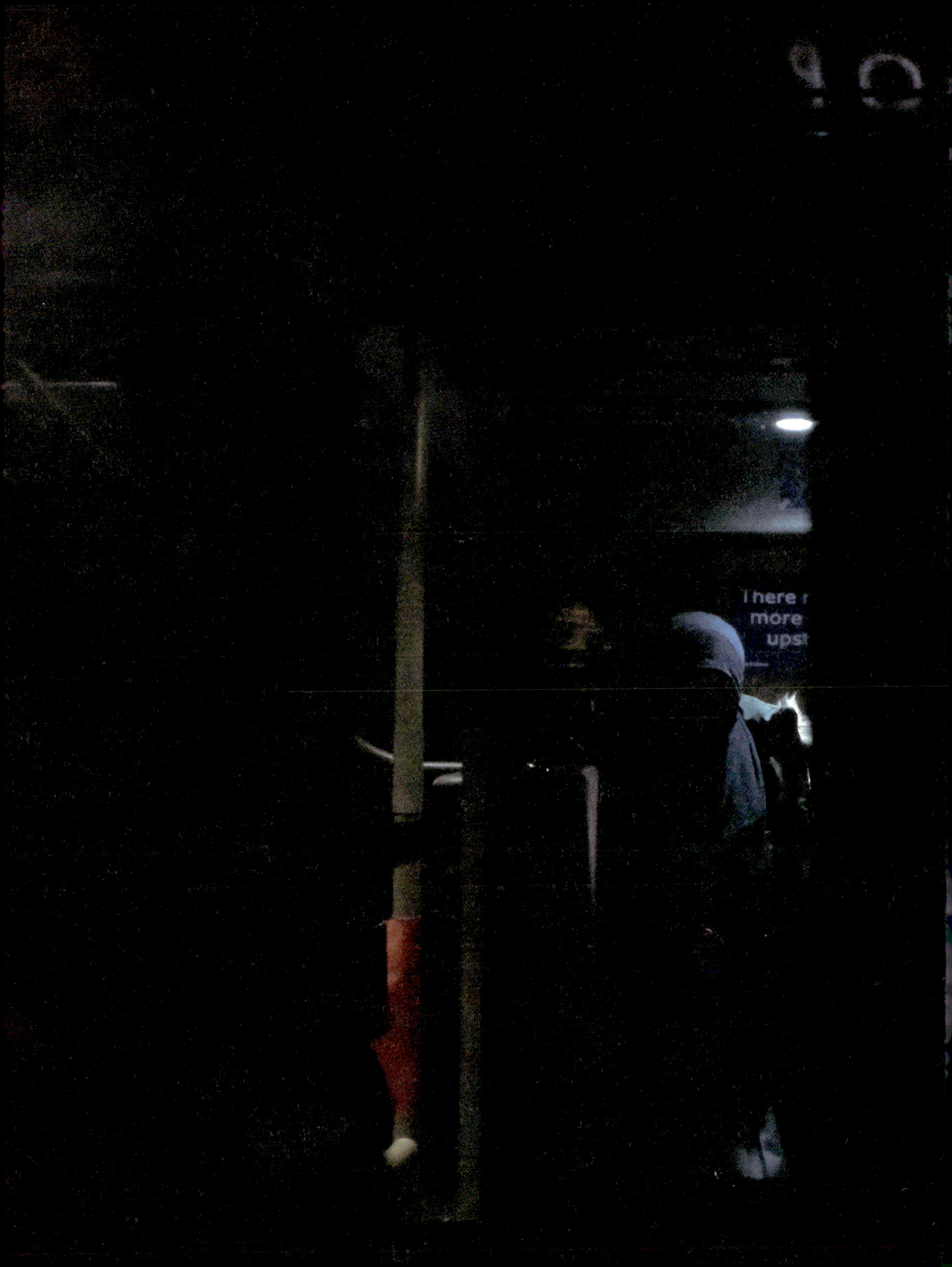
I here
more
upst

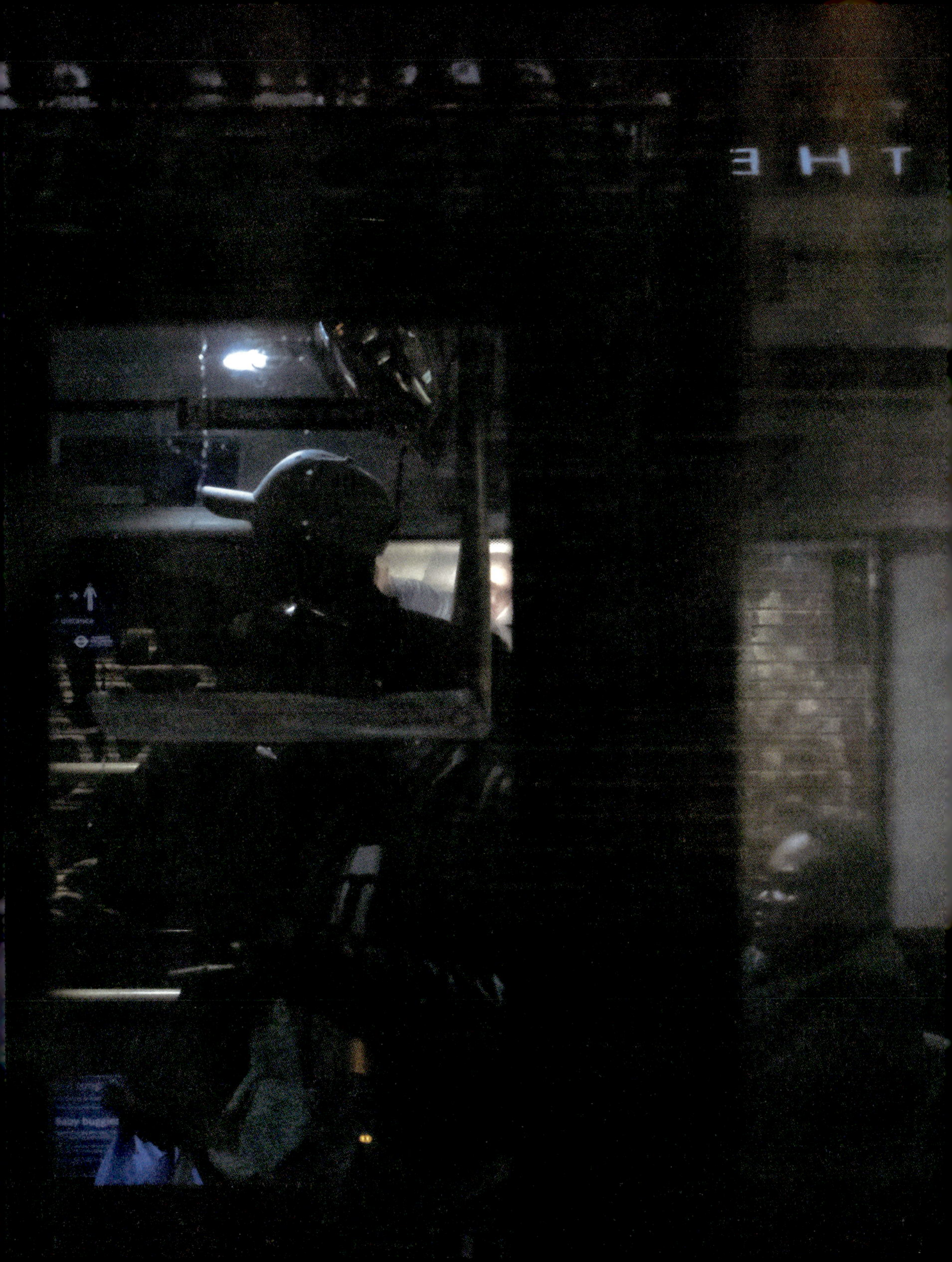

The Cliffs' Edge

These white cliffs
a screen to the churning sea;
how the salt-crested waves
are intent on washing its feet.
How the scything birds float
past trying to nest in its sheer surface.
How the green grass only goes so far
to the edge, dizzied by the distance down.
And men in boats newly arriving
project on the white cliffs letters
they must soon write home,
in their looped and crossed script
announcing their safe arrival.
But the White Cliffs of Dover
keep looking out to the sea,
with their blank expression,
with their chest pushed out.
Giving no welcome.
Giving no quarter.

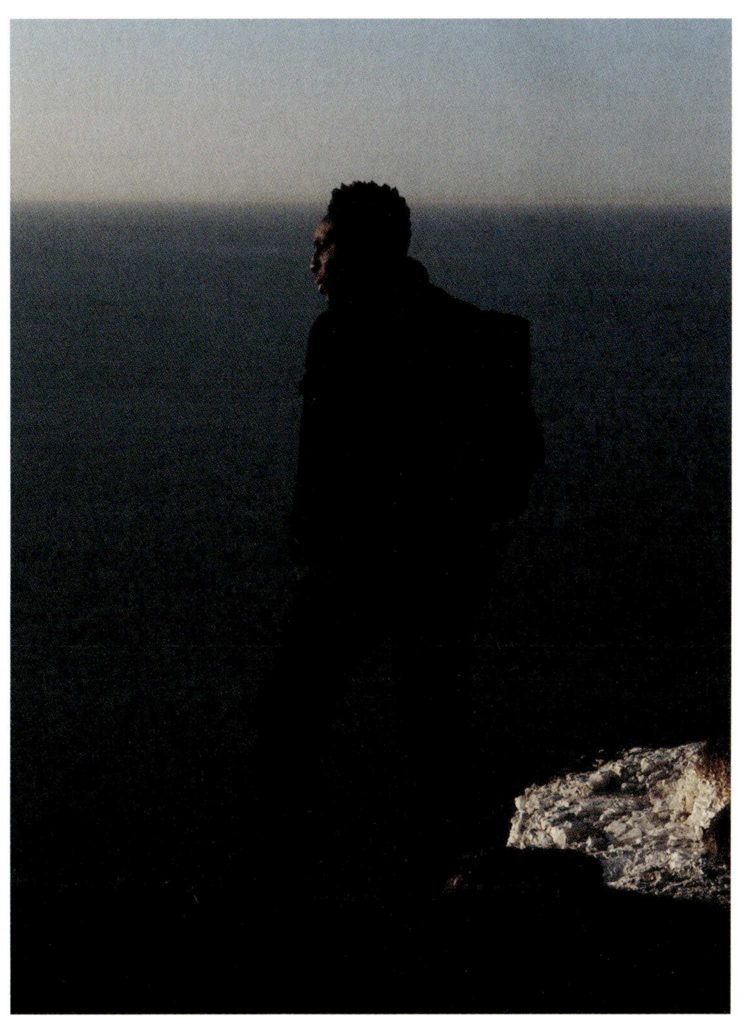

On the End of Seasons

All day the sea eagles do their work
pulling the last currents of summer
with their flat white tails.

And as the colder nights draw in
there are stacks of books my mind
will curl around in front of the fire
under our Moroccan honeymoon blankets.

And the pin-headed stars shall look
on nightly through the window
with bets that I'll be asleep
before the second chapter.

And mornings I'll rise early to stoke
the ashened fireplace as the frosts
lie quietly resting in the corners
of the windows as the house warms.

In this transition, many millennia
older than us, the end of this season
requires warmth as a change
and stillness as a response.

And, Beloved, so too do we bid goodbye
to this season of our youth, now gone.
The shock of white in your hair
and my growing-snowy beard,
my acquired distaste for rushing
and remembering now only that
something has been forgotten.

We have lived longer than we will live
but, still pleased by the slow but marked
changes of this life, we persist in this world
of wonder and quiet marvels.

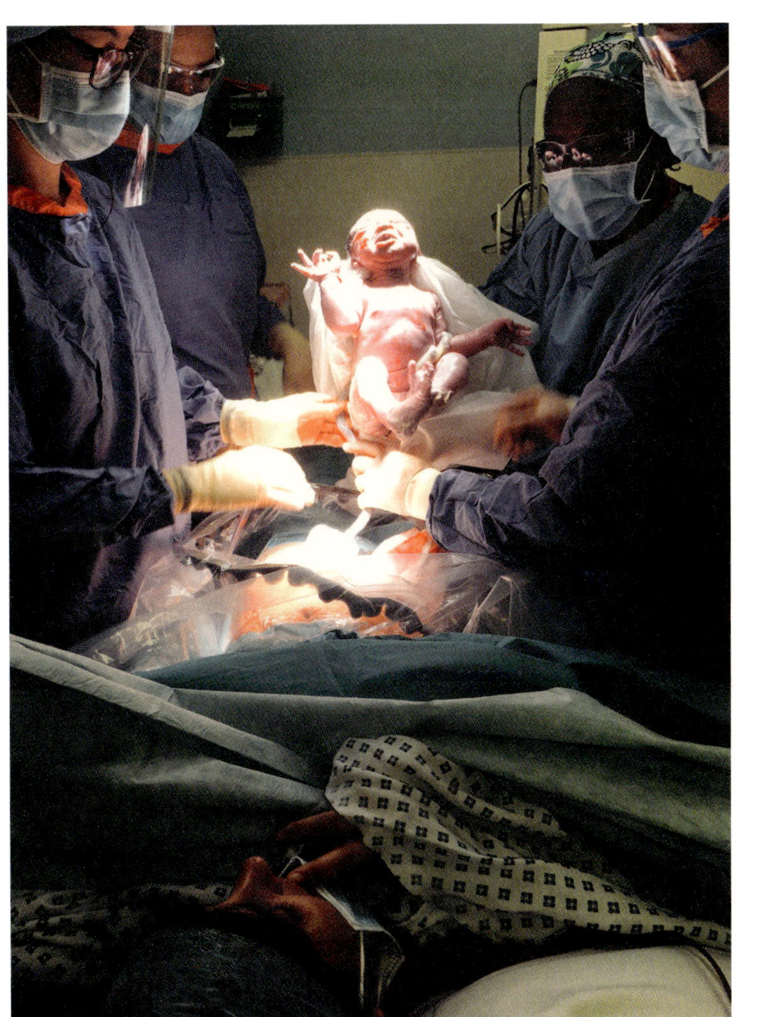

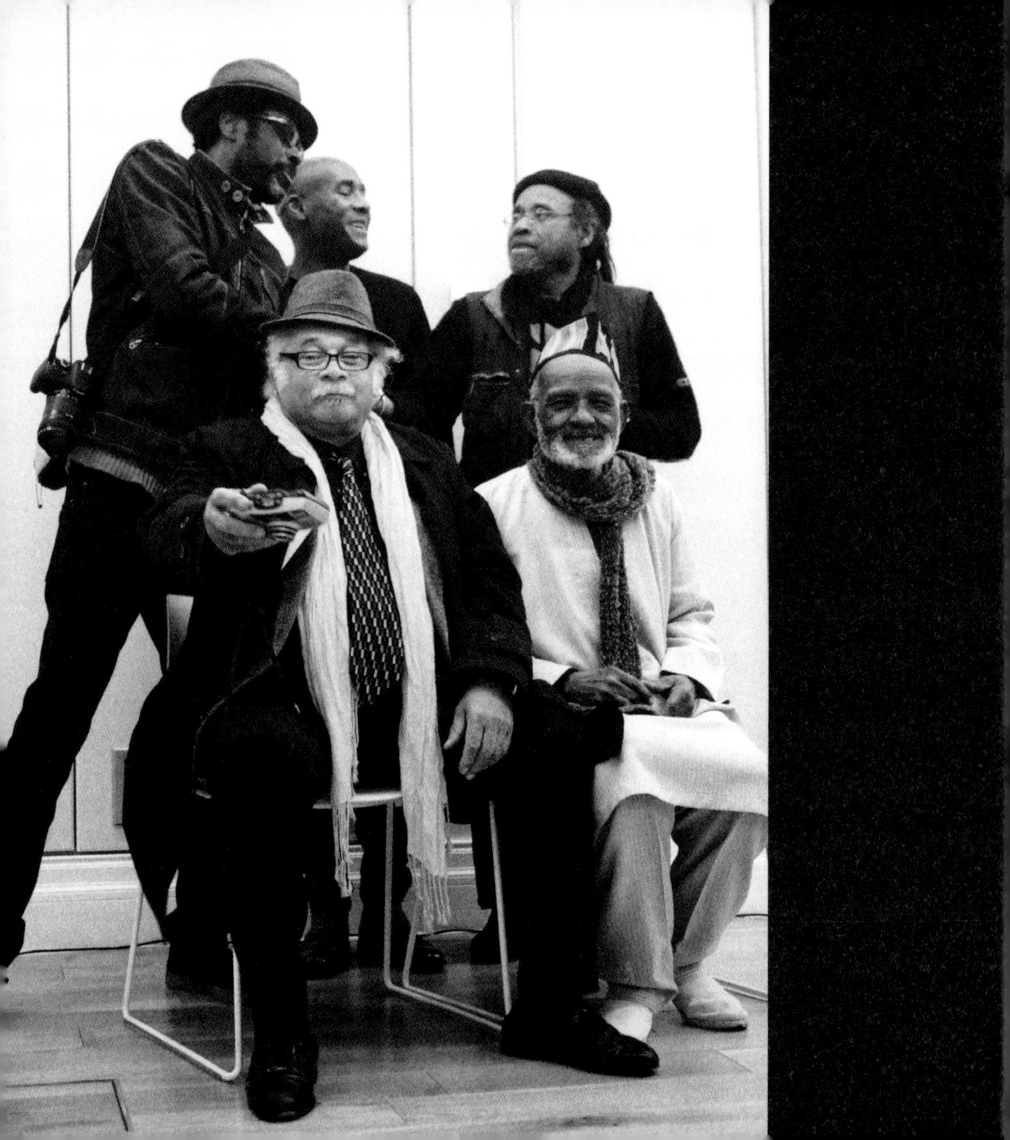

Towards a Black Psychogeography: A note on the photographs

In the first Coronavirus lockdown of 2020, having had the year's work effectively cancelled, I temporarily relocated to my childhood home in Sheffield with my young family, to await the fate of the world. During that long, liminal spring, before the rupture that was the murder of George Floyd, I spent my time searching for all the negatives my parents had kept of the family since before I was born, stretching back into the 1970s. When the negatives were scanned, I was astonished to find everyday images of my family missing from the family albums that I knew well. The albums contained the big moments of our lives, in some ways the 'official' story, for archiving can sublimate and suppress history as much as it can preserve it. In place of photos of graduations and holidays, I was now looking at images of my Dad laying on our carpet, listening to his BeBe and CeCe Winans album, my brown-skinned sister cuddling a blue-eyed doll, my brother on a pushbike in the back garden of a late seventies terrace house in Sheffield. They were, in their ordinariness, in many ways more interesting than the superlative images of my family's 'successful' moments deemed worthy of being printed and included in an album.

It made me want to organise my own vast and uneven archive of photographs from the last 15 years or so (My Mom thankfully let me keep my old childhood bedroom as an unofficial and shamefully disorganised archive of sorts, to store various fragments of my life). I found all the photos I'd ever taken seriously as negatives in old shoe boxes and shopping bags, raw files on corrupt-then-recovered hard drives and jpegs on ancient compact flash cards and forgotten 'dumb' phones.

That collection of images, most of which were taken casually, without any particular project in mind; photographs of friends, family and interesting spaces and strangers, forms the visual foundation of this book. It is a body of work taken during the in-between moments of two more considered projects that together form a loose trilogy documenting, from the periphery, the ramifications of the various crises of the first quarter of the 21st century; Afropean, a series of photographs accompanying my nonfiction book of the same name, and 'Europe; off-season', everyday images documenting my relationship with Europe during the decade – the 2010s – in which its relationship to Britain was disintegrating.

The key theme that emerged from these in-between photographs was Black life in Britain, but a Black life outside of any news cycle or on-trend hashtag – I wasn't sure that they would ever be made public. I didn't even know they were about Black Britain when I was taking them. In that way, these images aren't of a Blackness that is any way performative, but rather a document of Britain, seen through the subconscious prism of Blackness. Blackness as an internalised way of looking on the one hand, and as a record of an often all too ephemeral Black psychic map on the other; the now demolished housing estate that once served as a broadcasting tower to a pirate radio station, the community club turned into prime real estate, and so on.

Later in the year, I was approached by my friend Roger Robinson – whom I'd lent an image to for the cover of his masterful collection *A Portable Paradise* – about the possibility of a deeper, more sustained collaboration trying to capture Black life in Britain. He would craft images with his pen, I would attempt to make poetry with my camera. Thanks to a generous grant from the Ampersand Photoworks Foundation, I was able to make sense of the older images by combining them with the production of new work. These new images, though more conscious of being some sort of document of Black Britain, take the casual images from the archive as their cue.

But what is Black Britain? For me, it needed to begin with an itinerary. In the archive I already had thousands of images from all over the UK, especially London, but with the new images Roger and I came up with the idea that spaces of Black culture and memory might be found at the often overlooked coast of Britain. And so in a little rented Mini Cooper, we followed the coast clockwise through rain, sleet and snow, chasing the promise of brown skin in marine light (though in the end I would describe the colour palate of my images more as 'Kente cloth in fog'), leaving London and following the River Thames East, towards Gravesend, where Pocahontas is buried, and where, just across the river, sits Tilbury, where the *Empire Windrush* docked in 1948. Too often, that is where the history told about Black Britain begins and ends, but we continued out of London, following the coast clockwise through Margate, Dover, Brighton, Southampton, Plymouth, Land's End, Bristol, Cardiff, Liverpool, Blackpool, Belfast, Glasgow, John O'Groats, Edinburgh, Newcastle, Scarborough, Hull, Skegness, Orfordness, Southend-on-Sea. Here we not only found Black people, but the history of Empire and transatlantic slavery to which every Briton is tethered; stories of arrival, asylum and deportation, and of that inverted, imaginative unit of history and geography known as 'The Black Atlantic'.

There happens to be, among the people included in these photographs, Yale University professors, award-winning jazz musicians, high fashion models, best-selling authors, lawyers and lord mayors. They aren't named because I wanted the images to merge through time and space, to form a sort of visual dreamscape. But also because of my belief in an egalitarian process – the superlative stories are no more important to me visually than a street sweeper, nurse or mechanic, and I shot them with the same casual attention I shot everybody else.

I offer these photographs, then, as a contribution to a wider collection all too often missing from Britain's imaginary family album as constructed by white British documentary photographers; of the everyday humanity of the Black community in Britain.

Johny Pitts,
January 2022

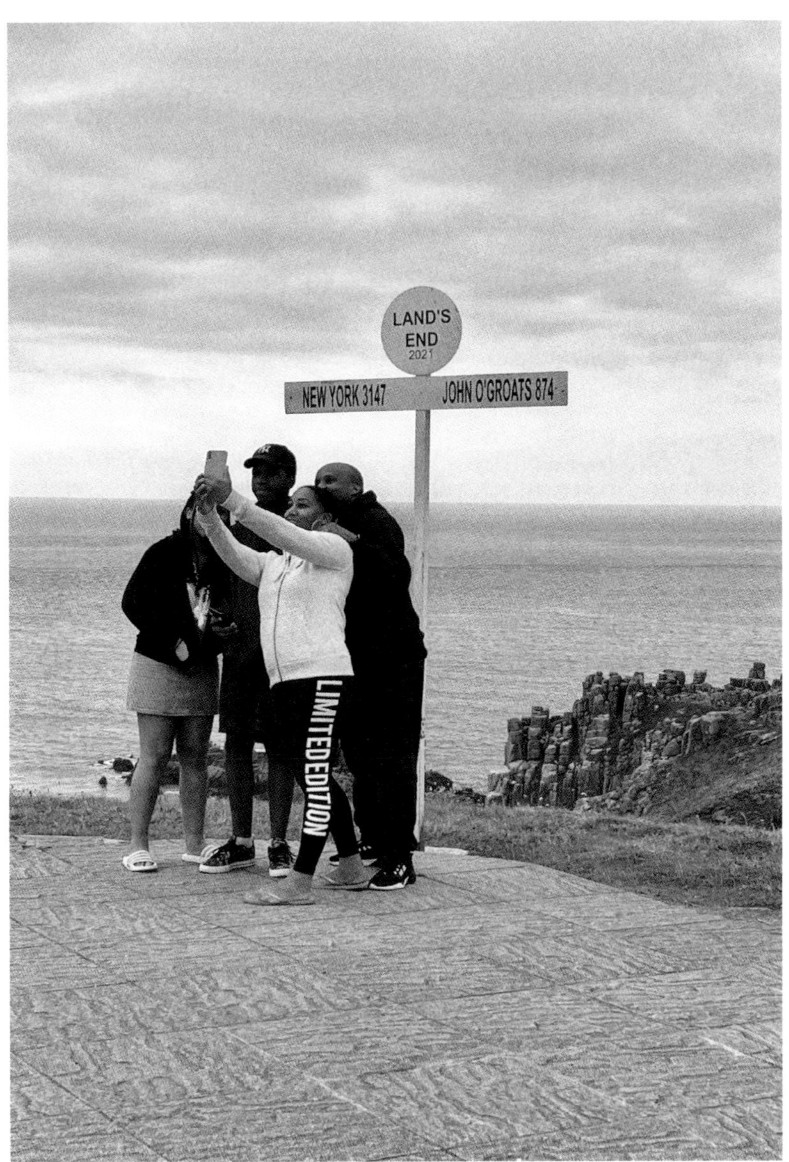
LAND'S
END
2021
NEW YORK 3147
JOHN O'GROATS 874
LIMITED EDITION

William Collins
An imprint of HarperCollins*Publishers*
1 London Bridge Street
London SE1 9GF

WilliamCollinsBooks.com

HarperCollins*Publishers*
1st Floor, Watermarque Building,
Ringsend Road
Dublin 4, Ireland

First published in Great Britain
in 2022 by William Collins

1

A catalogue record for this book is available
from the British Library

ISBN 978-0-00-846951-1

Designed by Tom Etherington

Printed in Bosnia-Herzegovina by GPS Group

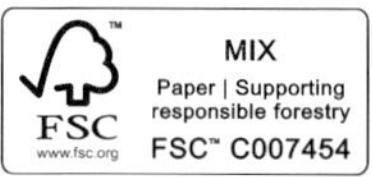

Roger Robinson dedicates this book to Nicola and Caden.

Johny Pitts dedicates this book to Natasha, Célia and Sylvie; to
the loving memory of his dad, Richie Pitts; and to Jane Murton.

Originally commissioned through the Ampersand/Photoworks
Fellowship, supported by The Ampersand Foundation and
Photoworks.

Some versions of these poems first appeared in *The Eyes*
and *Wales Bonner: A Magazine Curated by Magma.*

A small portion of these photographs were originally
commissioned by Artangel.

'Traces' was commissioned for the Anthology *Into The Light*
by The Lumiere Durham Festival 2021.
'The Quality Of Light' was commissioned by the Royal Society
Of Literature in response to 'Skinning the Lion', a dialogue
between Derek Walcott and Ben Okri.

'Twenty Parakeets' *after* Paul Muldoon.

'A World War 1 Soldier has Doubts on the Front Line' *after*
William Butler Yeats.

'Interview' and 'Benin Security Guard at the V&A' were
commissioned by the Manchester Literature Festival.

'Hallway' was commissioned for Nicholas Daley's Return
to Slygo Film by NOW Gallery.

To all the people who gave us their craft and expertise:
Thank you Shoaib Rokadiya, Tom Etherington, Shoair Mavlian,
Raquel Villar-Pérez, Eddie Otchere, Suresh Ariaratnam and
Nick Makoha for working closely with us and helping to piece
this body of work together.

Chris Ashman at Artful Dodgers, Sharmilla Beezmohun and
all at Speaking Volumes, Anthony Cairns, Taous Dahmani,
all at Graves Gallery Sheffield, Rachel Long, Robin Maddock,
Chris Morris, Caryl Phillips, all at Photoworks, Chantal Pitts,
Linda Pitts, Mica Pitts, Vincent and Veronique Prugnaud and
all at The Eyes, Joe Shakespeare, all at Spectrum, all at Stills
Edinburgh, Donovan Wylie.

To all the people who took time to give us their coastal experience:
Kelly Abbott, Dr Hakim Adi, Ayo Akinwolere, Ibrahim Alfa. Jr,
Matt Bickley, Tim Brannigan, Marcus Brown, Paul Camo, Shona
Carmen, Geoffrey Chambers, Melissa Chemam, Coco, Naomi
Cooper Davis, Cult of The Damned, Colin Grant, Trevor Gunn,
David Holden, Adrian Kilanga, Cleo Lake, Karone Pak Lum, Dr
Ullah Mackenzie, Randolph Matthews, Eunice Olumide, The
Mad Professor, Samenua Sesher OBE, Rider Shafique, Ray
Shell, Kirk St. Lewis, Eni Timi-Biu and all the amazing crew at
People Dem Collective, and all those who stopped to chat and
whose names we never got.

The photograph '"B", Thamesmead' on page 40-41 was
originally commissioned by Artangel as part of 'A Bend in the
River', for 'A Room For London' (Southbank Centre, 2012).

BLACK BRITAIN BY THE
COAST

B-side of Britain —
is the atmosphere of Bl[ack]
life? Black British [is]
British life? There [is a]
north-south divide
for the Black au[dience]
proximity to the ma[p]
place. So much of [the]
side London to Par[is]
and betting shops a[nd]
[...] and charity s[hops]
a carcass of a country[side]
I ke[pt]
by Bl[ack]

use you
[authentic...] in
[...] of [...]. a
Neo-liberal apt[...]
in: Black Britain
[...] but in [...]
ardo-
[...] are
[...] with
who